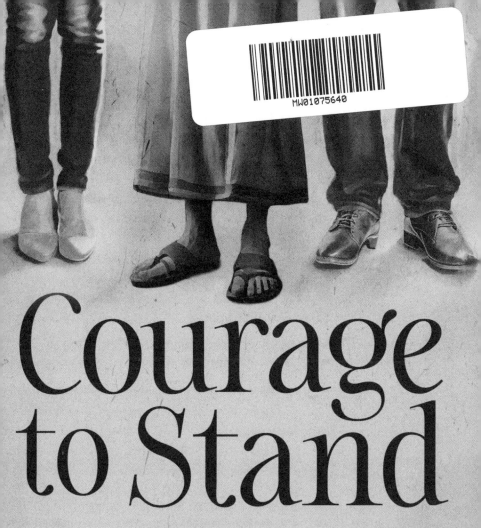

Courage to Stand

Profiles of Enduring Faith

JOHN STAMPER

First printing: September 2024

New Leaf Press, P.O. Box 726, Green Forest, AR 72638
New Leaf Press is a division of the New Leaf Publishing Group, LLC.

ISBN: 978-1-68344-377-3
ISBN: 978-1-61458-894-8 (digital)

Library of Congress Control Number: 2024943932

Cover and interior design: Diana Bogardus

Scripture taken from the New King James Version®. Copyright © 1982 by Thomas Nelson. Used by permission. All rights reserved.

All other Scripture is taken from the King James Version and is noted as such. Public domain.

Printed in the United States of America

Please visit our website for other great titles:
www.masterbooks.com

For information regarding promotional opportunities, please contact the publicity department at pr@nlpg.com.

New Leaf Press
A Division of New Leaf Publishing Group
www.newleafpress.com

Endorsements

I always say, "Speak truth, and speak it boldly," because that is
part of the Great Commission. John Stamper's *Courage to Stand* is a
reminder that Christianity requires action, and
action often requires courage. It's high time for
Christians to act boldly, take uncompromising
stands on God's Word, and conquer the fears of
the world.

— Sam Sorbo
author, filmmaker, education freedom fighter

Have you ever wondered where real courage comes from, the
kind of courage that stands in the face of absolute, don't-stand-a-
chance adversity? Well, you are about to find out! *Courage to Stand*
is packed with powerful stories that reveal the character of people,
from ancient times to today, who stood firm on God's Word despite
incredible challenges. This book isn't just inspiring—it's a guide
to help you find that same courage in your own life. With practical
application sections throughout every story, you'll gain powerful
insights on how to apply these lessons to your own journey. You'll
see how trusting God can give you the strength to face any conflict
with confidence. If you're looking to deepen your faith and live
boldly for Christ, *Courage to Stand* delivers
exactly what you need.

I have no doubt you will enjoy this book; my
prayer is that you apply these principles so that
you too can experience the *Courage to Stand!*

— Eric Hovind
president of Creation Today Ministries

Courage to Stand is a vital call for conviction and boldness in an age that demands everyone to bend the knee to the idols of political correctness. Drawing from Scripture and history, John Stamper has given us excellent examples of those who have stood for truth and righteousness in the past. These heroes provide a template for us to follow. I was stirred and challenged by this vital and timely book.

— Israel Wayne
author and conference speaker, founder of Family Renewal, LLC

Courage to Stand by John Stamper is a desperately needed work in this age of cowardice. It is masterfully written and should be considered essential reading. There are powerful lessons and examples going back to ancient biblical history all the way up to the modern era that will inspire and encourage all who read it. I can't recommend this book highly enough.

— Alex Newman
Award-winning international journalist, educator, author, and speaker

Dedication

This book is dedicated to my son Teddy who, by God's grace, will be strengthened daily with stories of God's goodness, wonder, and might. Also, to my nieces and nephews who will certainly face Nebuchadnezzars and fiery furnaces in their lives. May you always be willing and obedient to stand courageously on God's Word, knowing that He is with you in the fire. And finally, to Christians of all ages, both at present and those who will accept Christ in the future, who will positively need encouragement at times to live for God in our present Babylon. I hope these stories inspire you to be courageous for God.

Acknowledgements

My first and deepest thanks belongs to Randy Pratt. Without Randy's guidance and inspiration, I would not have written this book. Thank you, Randy! Thank you to Jerrod Vaughan for giving me the opportunity to publish this book. This amazing opportunity is not lost on me. Thank you to the wonderful teams at New Leaf Press and New Leaf Publishing Group for their constant support.

To my beautiful and brilliant wife, Jenna, for reminding me to always add depth. Thank you, Jenna.

Thank you to Jeri Stupar, my mother-in-law, for steady encouragement and practical insights.

Thank you to Jessica Tapia for graciously allowing me to interview her for this book. Keep up the good work, Jessica!

I also want to thank those who've gone out of their way to help me with this book, whose work has taught me so much, and whose dedication I greatly admire: Jennifer White, Israel Wayne, Alex Newman, Eric Hovind, Sam Sorbo, Dr. Max Lyons, Richard Hawkins, Dan Smithwick, E. Ray Moore, Dr. Marlene McMillan,

Dr. Nick Ellis, Dr. Lisa Dunne, Yvette Hampton, Alex McFarland, Frank Harber, Chuck Crismier, Bill Bunkley, Doug Truax, and Roberta Foster.

And finally, to those who've been a major source of encouragement in my life — teachers, coaches, pastors, principals, bosses, colleagues, family, and friends — thank you all!

Table of Contents

Introduction

The major theme of this book is having *courage to stand on God's Word in the face of spiritual conflict*. As Christians, we all go through spiritual conflict and trials, but hopefully, after reading the true stories in this book, you'll be inspired to live out your faith which, at times, requires great courage.

Why are stories of courage so gripping and inspiring? Perhaps, it's because courage is so rare that we are captivated whenever we see it. And when we hear such captivating stories of boldness and godly courage, we're compelled to evaluate our own spiritual condition and ask ourselves: Would I be able to take such a courageous stand? Have I been obedient to God's Word? Am I willing to forsake all else, to take up my cross, and follow Jesus? How do I bridge the gap from fear and unbelief to obedience and faith?

Every Christian holds biblical convictions, but sometimes we fail to act on them. Every true Christian wants to obey God, but sometimes we don't know what that looks like; we just aren't sure which way to go. Why is that? Why do some Christians know exactly what God wants them to do while others don't have a clue? Why do some have the courage to stand on God's Word while others crumble under the pressure? How is it that one minute we can be courageous, and the next minute we're cowardly? Maybe it's because we compromise, we get scared, or we feel insignificant.

Maybe sometimes we're flat out selfish and follow our own will instead of God's will; after all, we are still living in this sinful flesh.

The idea of "having courage to stand" isn't meant to imply that we have some sort of hidden strength inside of us, or that it's up to us to tap into it. Truth is, it's not even about us. The idea of "having courage to stand" is meant to remind us just how good, powerful, loving, and faithful God is — it's all about Him. And when we know who God is, we can act courageously despite our fears; we can have complete confidence in His Word, and trust that whatever He calls us to do, He will be with us.

Where Does Courage Come From?

When David faced Goliath, David was a just a young shepherd and Goliath was a giant, a battle-tested warrior, and a champion. All the men of Israel, including David's brothers and even King Saul, were terrified of Goliath and his threats; but David's stunning response to Goliath was, "Who is this uncircumcised Philistine?!" David's immediate, gut-reaction was to fight the giant, but Saul refused to allow it; after all, who would've believed that David could defeat Goliath? If King Saul sent the young shepherd David out to fight the brutal warrior Goliath, and David was massacred, it would've brought shame on all of Israel. David could've walked away from the conflict and saved himself the hassle, but to David the thought of walking away was inconceivable. And when Goliath stood to fight David, the Bible says David got up and ran straight toward Goliath, flung his rock, and killed the giant!

David's courage was undeniable and unmatched. But why didn't David back down when everyone else around him was backing down? How was it that David, a young shepherd boy, had the courage to stand up to an intimidating enemy like Goliath? Where did David's courage come from? And what inspired Saul to change his mind and send David to face Goliath? To answer those questions, let's look at God's Word and retrace David's steps.

1 Samuel 17:32–37

When David first approached Saul and sought permission to fight
Goliath, Saul couldn't even take David seriously. Saul basically
said to David, "Are you crazy? You're just a kid. Goliath has been a
trained and feared warrior since before you were born!" And to be
fair, Saul wasn't wrong. After all, David was just a shepherd and, as
far as anybody knew, he was completely unequipped and incapable
of being a warrior. But then David shared a story with Saul of how
one day, out in the field, as he was tending his sheep, he killed a
lion and a bear with his own two hands. Because of that miraculous
experience, David was convinced he could also defeat Goliath.
David's boldness must've inspired Saul to change his mind, because
as soon as David left the conversation, he suited David up for battle.
But let's not gloss over the fact that David killed two ferocious
beasts with his bare hands. How could anyone do that? It seems
impossible. To answer that question, let's go back another chapter
and retrace David's steps.

1 Samuel 16:13

Before he defeated the lion, the bear, and the giant, David was
anointed by Samuel. The Bible says when David was anointed,
"The Spirit of the L*ORD* came upon David from that day forward"
(1 Samuel 16:13). So, before David ran out to meet Goliath, before
he approached Saul, before he approached his brothers, before he
killed the lion and the bear, before David did *anything*, the Spirit
of the Lord was upon him. *This* is the critical point! "Where did
David's courage come from?" To put it plainly — David's courage
came from the Lord.

Inspirational Profiles

This is a book of profiles containing inspirational stories of biblical
figures, historical figures, and contemporaries who stood on God's
Word in the face of intense spiritual conflict; some stories may be

familiar to you, and some may be new. Each chapter features a
different story told through the lens of the three Hebrew children
(Shadrach, Meshach, and Abed-nego). I chose this approach
because, despite being over 2,500 years old, their story still
resonates with Christians everywhere today. We all live in a fallen
world (Babylon), we all have spiritual conflicts (Nebuchadnezzar),
we will all face consequences and persecution for our faith (fiery
furnace), and despite all that, God is still with us (the fourth man
in the fire). The three Hebrew children share one story and are
always mentioned together in the Bible, never separately; they will
be the focus of the first chapter. My hope is that this inspiring story
will set the tone for the rest of the book and encourage you to find
the courage to stand against whatever spiritual conflicts you face
in your life and in your world. The rest of the chapters will follow
suit, discussing what each person's Babylon looked like, what their
Nebuchadnezzar demanded, what their fiery furnace was, and how
God was with them through all of it.

As a former teacher, I began writing this book specifically for
Christians in the public school system, hoping to encourage them
as they navigate their public school "Babylon." But I soon realized
these stories apply to Christians of all ages, and all backgrounds —
not just those in public schools. So, whether you're an adult who
loves the Bible and loves history, or you're a teenager who's never
heard of Dietrich Bonhoeffer, Corrie ten Boom, William Tyndale,
or anyone in between — this book has a message for everyone.

The spiritual conflicts discussed in this book — both past and
present — parallel the spiritual conflicts we experience today,
even though separated by hundreds, or even thousands, of years.
I want you to see yourself in each chapter and profile and connect
these stories with your life. Most of all, I want you to see how God
was present in each story and in each fiery furnace, because when
we see how God brought other people through the conflicts they
faced, we can be encouraged that God will bring us through the
conflicts we face. This is a powerful message worth pondering and

sharing. It's reassuring to see how God has moved repeatedly and consistently, over long periods of time, through His children and on behalf of His children — and that's a very important concept to get a hold of. And since God is no respecter of persons, that means what He's already done for others, He will do for you as you strive to act in willingness and obedience to His Word.

"Your word is a lamp to my feet and a light to my path"
(Psalm 119:105).

God gave us His Word as a roadmap for our lives, knowing it would be just as relevant today as it was thousands of years ago. We're all unique and our lives are nuanced; the same is true for the people and stories in this book. But even though our stories are different, we can appreciate the fact that God can use our little nuances, even things that look like flaws and imperfections, to do something that matters for His kingdom. So yes, we're all different, but we also have things in common — even with people who lived thousands of years ago. God's Word is the standard and the common thread that ties us together.

A Message of Encouragement

My hope is this book will be an encouragement and a blessing to you, in a way that is scripturally sound and biblically accurate. I'm writing about courage, not because I am the model of it, but because real courage is quite rare, and I want to be encouraged. The people in this book have demonstrated great courage, and their stories inspire me. I hope they inspire you as well. In all honesty, this book is for me just as much as it is for you.

In my first book, *Conflicted: Pulling Back the Curtain on Public Education,* I discussed many of the conflicts that Christians are facing in the public schools. And whenever we face a spiritual conflict — whether as a teacher, a student, a doctor, or a plumber — it's important for each of us to seek God's guidance and hear from Him for ourselves.

"Ask, and it will be given to you; seek, and you will find; knock, and it will be opened to you. For everyone who asks receives, and he who seeks finds, and to him who knocks it will be opened" (Matthew 7:7–8).

Courage to Stand tells inspiring stories of courageous and obedient Christians who stood on God's Word and faced their conflicts despite their fears. By sharing these stories, I want to encourage you to keep going, don't quit, hold tight to the Lord, and stand courageously in the face of the conflict in front of you.

What Does the Bible Say?

Standing firm in your convictions and acting courageously, like David did, is not an easy thing to do — that's why so few people do it. The Bible teaches many lessons on courage and strength, but I want to focus on three specific lessons.

"Now David was greatly distressed, for the people spoke of stoning him, because the soul of all the people was grieved, every man for his sons and his daughters. But David strengthened himself in the LORD his God" *(1 Samuel 30:6).*

First, the Bible says that even King David, the same David who slayed Goliath, felt weak and scared at times. We too will face challenging circumstances in life, but it's in those most difficult moments that we must strengthen ourselves in the Lord our God, like David did — the point is to find strength in God! Courage is not the absence of fear, but it's the resolve to act, despite your fear. It's in the middle of overwhelming opposition that we must turn our eyes away from the problems and onto our Heavenly Father — *"our refuge and strength, a very present help in trouble" (Psalm 46:1).* The words "refuge" and "strength" can mean the same thing, but a refuge is something we run to for protection; it's outside of ourselves. The type of strength David had, which is the type of strength I'm encouraging in this book, didn't come from within himself — it came from God.

"Therefore comfort each other and edify one another, just as you also are doing" (1 Thessalonians 5:11).

Second — after strengthening ourselves in the Lord — the Bible tells us that we should encourage, or strengthen, one another. The word *edify* means "to build up," so God's Word instructs us to build up each other in our labor for the Lord. As I've already mentioned, Shadrach, Meshach, and Abed-nego were never written about separately; they were always together in Scripture — this has great significance and should be very encouraging for all of us as we walk through whatever God commissions us to do. These three men most definitely encouraged one another and built each other up throughout their entire ordeal. In the same way, we also need to be encouraged as we aim to encourage others. It's imperative that we surround ourselves with other like-minded believers who can speak into our lives and implore us to follow God, no matter the cost. The importance of having people in our lives who share our values and speak God's truth cannot be overstated — this is the sacred duty of parents.

"We will not hide them from their children, telling to the generation to come the praises of the LORD, and His strength and His wonderful works that He has done ... which He commanded our fathers, that they should make them known to their children; that the generation to come might know them, the children who would be born, that they may arise and declare them to their children, that they may set their hope in God, and not forget the works of God, but keep His commandments" (Psalm 78:4–7).

Third, God's Word instructs us to remember the wonderful works of God and to share them with the next generation. This is both a parental duty and a blessing to a child. The Bible says we should strengthen ourselves in the Lord, comfort one another, and tell the next generation about God's wonderful works. This book aims to accomplish all of that through the telling of nine true and inspiring stories.

Telling stories and knowing history, especially biblical history, are acts of preparation and defense. Dr. Marlene McMillan talks about the importance of storytelling in her book, *Mountains of Deceit.*

> "History is really a story and whomever tells the story in the most believable way will rule the future.... History helps make sense of the future. Someone who is ignorant of the past is prey to anyone who claims to understand. What you don't know about history will hurt you."[1]

So, yes, remembering the former works of God should encourage us, and we should tell those stories to encourage others. But, knowing history, especially biblical history, is also a way to defend from falsehoods, error, and twisting of Scripture.

It's imperative to understand that while you and I will be the beneficiaries of this book, this book is not about us; it's not even about the people featured in this book. This book is all about lifting up the name of Jesus and prioritizing the Word of God. The only reason I'm pointing to the people in this book is because they first pointed to Jesus (John 12:32).

Defining Terms

The terms *courage, faith, strength,* and *conviction* are closely related and are sometimes incorrectly used in place of one another. This often results in a slight disagreement between the intended meaning and the actual meaning of a phrase or thought. While courage is the focus of this book, the other terms are important and necessary as well. So, to make my delivery as clear as possible, I'll provide definitions of these key terms. And, for the sake of consistency and accuracy, Noah Webster's *1828 American Dictionary of the English Language* will be used to define each term. Definitions are not exhaustive.

---

1. McMillan, Marlene. *Mountains of Deceit.* (Forth Worth: Liberty View Media, 2011), 13.

- FAITH: belief; the assent of the mind or understanding to the truth of what God has revealed; the assent of the mind to the truth of divine revelation on the authority of God's testimony, accompanied with the cordial assent of the will or approbation of the heart; a system of revealed truths received by Christians.

- CONVICTION: the state of being convinced or convicted by conscience.

- COURAGE: bravery; that quality of mind which enables men to encounter danger and difficulties with firmness, or without fear or depression of spirits; valor; boldness; resolution.

- STRENGTH: firmness; solidity or toughness; power or vigor of any kind; support; power of mind; the quality of binding, uniting, or securing; confidence; soundness; vehemence; degree of brightness or vividness; fortification; maintenance of power.

I'll explain my view of how these terms are related, and as I use them in this book:

- FAITH comes first, everything else follows — like dominoes. You must believe in something, or someone (Christ and Him crucified), before you can have a moral or spiritual conflict; if you are not rooted in your faith, then you will go wherever the wind blows.

- CONVICTION follows faith; it's the state of being convinced of what, or in whom, you believe. You have a belief and are convinced of that belief.

- COURAGE is the next domino to fall; it's the action that follows faith and conviction. Conviction begs for an action, and courage is the action part of faith and conviction.

- STRENGTH, finally, is the level of firmness, the quality, or the measure of your conviction and/or courage. Some have a weak conviction; others have a strong conviction.

You may have a different perspective, and I realize that my understanding might not be perfect. However, to convey my point clearly, this is the way I structured the book.

chapter one

The Three Hebrew Children

When Nebuchadnezzar conquered Jerusalem, he took control of everyone and everything in that city — including the vessels in the Temple as well as God's people. Nebuchadnezzar sent officers to search through the captives and identify those who could be useful servants in Babylon. He specifically wanted to identify those who were *"of the king's seed, and of the prince's children in whom was no blemish, but well favored, and skillful in all wisdom, and cunning in knowledge, and understanding science, and such as had ability in them to stand in the king's palace, and whom they might teach the learning and the tongue of the Chaldeans" (Daniel 1:3-4 KJV)*. Shadrach, Meshach, Abed-nego, and the prophet Daniel were among this group.

Nebuchadnezzar wanted the best of the best, the cream of the crop. He wanted to take the children of the most high God and use their God-given abilities for his own gain and glory. In his arrogance and pride, it seems that Nebuchadnezzar esteemed himself higher than God's children; either that or he simply wanted to corrupt God's children — maybe both. Nebuchadnezzar would force the king's children to leave their ways and to learn of his ways, to live in his palace, to practice his religion, and to worship his idol. To accomplish this goal, he would train, groom, and re-educate God's children. The Bible says that Nebuchadnezzar *"appointed them a daily provision of the king's meat, and of the wine which he drank: so,*

*nourishing them three years, that at the end thereof they might stand
before the king" (Daniel 1:5 KJV).* During this sort of re-education
process, the king's officer even changed the names, or identities,
of God's children. Daniel was given the name Belteshazzar; the
captives Hananiah, Mishael, and Azariah were given the names
Shadrach, Meshach, and Abed-nego (Daniel 1:7). Once the Children
of Israel learned the tongue of the Chaldeans and had been given
new names, only then would Nebuchadnezzar find them to be
acceptable, according to his standards.

Application ---

We've all been given directives or instructions that are contrary
to what the Bible says. Whether on the job or in the culture
surrounding us, there is a push for us to accept an alternate
reality that contrasts with God's Word.

Take the transgender issue for example. Many schools today
are training teachers and students to "affirm" someone's chosen
gender identity by using their preferred pronouns. Some schools
have even gone so far as to give students new names behind
their parents' back, further brainwashing an entire generation
of children into thinking they were born in the wrong body. One
biblical response to this attack on God's design comes from Isaiah
45:9, "Woe to him who strives with his Maker.... Shall the clay say
to him who forms it, 'What are you making?'"

Many businesses and organizations have also implemented
policies based on "Intersecting Identities" and **Diversity, Equity,
and Inclusion (DEI),** both of which I wrote about in my first book
and experienced first-hand in my teacher trainings with Chicago
Public Schools. The doctrine of Intersecting Identities claims that
we're either privileged or marginalized based on our immutable
characteristics. For example, white, Christian men are labelled
as threatening, intimidating, and abusive simply because they're
white, Christian men. DEI policies pick winners and losers based

on skin color, sexual orientation, or income level, but the Bible has this to say on the issues of race, class, and gender: *"For as many of you as were baptized into Christ have put on Christ. There is neither Jew nor Greek, there is neither slave nor free, there is neither male nor female; for you are all one in Christ Jesus" (Galatians 3:27-28).* The only label God recognizes is whether we're baptized into Christ.

In the same way the three Hebrew children were taught a new language and forced to receive the king's provisions, the culture surrounding us seeks to invade our lives on every level and pressure us into using a new language that's contrary to God's Word and is meant to change our biblical worldview into a secular one.

The Old Testament Book of Daniel is the only place in the Bible where we are told the story of the three Hebrew children and how they became captives of Nebuchadnezzar, were taken out of their holy city, and were brought into Babylon — a city full of idolatry. We first learn of Babylon in the Book of Genesis, which tells how the people of that city wanted to make a name for themselves by building a tower that reached heaven. Building this tower was about taking authority, seeking autonomy, and gaining independence from God; to be the ultimate authority over themselves. Babylon became such a powerful city that it was known for conquering other powerful cities. Babylonians were also known for idolatry and sacrificing children on a fiery altar to satisfy their false god, Molech. Even though it was such a wicked city, God used Babylon to carry out judgement on other nations, knowing that Babylon would one day be judged as well.

Application -

Throughout this book, Babylon represents a place or a system that has rejected God and morality; it represents man's pride and fall. For the three Hebrew children, Babylon was a literal city, but for Christians today, Babylon could be work, school, extended family, or our nation.

We are living in a spiritual Babylon today. It's important to see the similarities between the world we're living in today and the world of Shadrach, Meshach, and Abed-nego, because just as God was with them then, He will be with us now if we are willing to stand with Him in the face of an entire world that's committed to rejecting Him. Very similar to how God's children were faced with idolatry in Babylon, Christians today are tempted to worship a multitude of idols such as work, money, friends, possessions, celebrities, or our own image; even our own comforts and luxuries can be idols. Anything and anyone in our life that we put before God can be an idol (Exodus 20:3–4).

Thankfully, God provides for His children, even when He allows them to experience great hardships. That was true in the Bible and it's true in our lives as well. We should ask ourselves when we are faced with a spiritual conflict, "Will I have the courage to stand against it?" As we continue through this chapter, we'll see how the three Hebrew children stood courageously against the wickedness they faced.

Nebuchadnezzar

Nebuchadnezzar was the powerful and wicked king of Babylon who worshiped golden idols. As a true idolator, Nebuchadnezzar believed that whenever something bad happened, or he had an unpleasant dream, it was because his god was angry. So, to appease his god, Molech, Nebuchadnezzar resorted to child sacrifice — offering children on an altar of fire. Thinking that these child sacrifices brought him back under Molech's good graces, Nebuchadnezzar would then summon his wise men and expect to hear their pleasant interpretations of his dreams. But, one day, when these so-called wise men could not interpret one of his dreams, Nebuchadnezzar became so angry that he demanded all the wise men in Babylon be killed; the prophet Daniel was part of this group of wise men. When Daniel learned that he was sentenced to be killed along with the other wise men, he asked for an opportunity to interpret the king's dream. If successful, Daniel could potentially save his life as well as the lives of others; no doubt, Daniel was led by the Lord in doing this.

The Bible says that immediately after Daniel offered to interpret Nebuchadnezzar's dream, Daniel held a prayer meeting with his friends Shadrach, Meshach, and Abed-nego. They didn't hash out a plan of escape. They didn't plan an uprising to overthrow Nebuchadnezzar. They didn't fall down in fear and trembling at the thought of losing their lives. They went to God in prayer. After all, this was a serious situation — their lives were on the line and Daniel had to be certain that his interpretation was correct. Daniel 2:18 says these four men joined together, *"that they might seek mercies from the God of heaven concerning this secret, so that Daniel and his companions might not perish with the rest of the wise men of Babylon."* Right after this prayer meeting, God gave Daniel the meaning and interpretation of Nebuchadnezzar's dream. Not only did God hear their prayer, but He answered it! God gave Daniel the revelation he needed exactly when he needed it, and the Bible says Daniel began to praise and thank God. We might stop there and think the story is over, that Daniel got the interpretation he needed and now he and the wise men would not be killed. But this was just the beginning of God's divine orchestration. God would use Daniel to prepare Shadrach, Meshach, and Abed-nego for their own crisis of faith.

Soon after the prayer meeting, Daniel was granted a meeting with Nebuchadnezzar to interpret his dream. Many lives hung in the balance and Daniel was the last hope. Even if Nebuchadnezzar was pleased with Daniel's interpretation, there still was no guarantee that he would change his mind and spare the wise men. The only thing that Daniel knew for sure was the message God gave him. So, Daniel's big moment had arrived, and he was brought in to stand before the wicked king, who had the power (and the desire) to kill him. Nebuchadnezzar asked Daniel if he would be able to interpret the dream, and Daniel responded that nobody was able to do such a thing — not the wise men, not the astrologers, not even the magicians or soothsayers. Given that Daniel had initiated this meeting, Nebuchadnezzar probably expected to hear good news, but instead he was given a message he did not want to hear. I could imagine that Nebuchadnezzar was angry, even shocked, to be told "no." Perhaps he thought, "If you can't help me, then why are you here? You're wasting my time!"

But Daniel wasn't done; he established a hard truth and followed with another truth. Daniel told Nebuchadnezzar, *"But there is a God in Heaven who reveals secrets, and He has made known to King Nebuchadnezzar what will be in the latter days. Your dream, and the visions of your head upon your bed" (Daniel 2:28).* Daniel didn't sugarcoat his message; he didn't change what God told him; he didn't beg the king to spare his life. Daniel told the king that the only one who could interpret his dream was God in heaven. He was showing Nebuchadnezzar that the God of heaven is above all things — above the wise men, above the idols, and above his false gods — and instead of taking the credit for himself, he gave credit to God where it belonged.

Daniel then explained the meaning of the king's dream: even though Babylon had become the most powerful kingdom, it would eventually be conquered by a more powerful kingdom which would stand forever; Daniel was ultimately referring to the Kingdom of Heaven. Daniel's message was so powerful that Nebuchadnezzar promoted Daniel to rule over Babylon, over the governors, and over the wise men. As soon as Daniel was given this title and position of power, he promoted Shadrach, Meshach, and Abed-nego to oversee certain affairs of Babylon. What a turn of events! One moment Daniel and the three Hebrew Children were on the chopping block, sentenced to be killed, and the next moment they were ruling over the city. *"And we know that all things*

work together for good to those who love God, to those who are the
called according to His purpose" (Romans 8:28).

Application —

When Daniel and the three Hebrew children were confronted
with death, the first thing they did was go straight to God in
prayer. That's the example we should follow: when we face a
conflict, the first thing we should do is go to God in prayer. Then,
once we hear from God, we must have the courage to follow
through with His direction — come what may. While you may
not be facing death like Daniel was, the stakes could feel very
high for you as well. Every conflict we face presents at least two
opportunities: one for us to be obedient, and one for God to move.

Shadrach, Meshach, and Abed-nego

We can see how God orchestrated events between Nebuchadnezzar
and Daniel, but why was it important for Shadrach, Meshach,
and Abed-nego to be given higher offices? We will see that it was
more than just Daniel taking care of his buddies. God placed these
men in higher office at a specific time and for a specific purpose.

Overall, the Bible doesn't tell us much about Shadrach, Meshach,
and Abed-nego. In the first two chapters of Daniel, we learn that
these three men were living in Jerusalem when it was captured
by Nebuchadnezzar, and we know they were led as captives into
Babylon. We know that Daniel trusted them as friends and as men of
God because they all prayed together concerning the interpretation
of Nebuchadnezzar's dream. We know they were faithful because
even though their home had been destroyed and they had been
taken to live in a wicked city under a wicked king, they still believed
God was able to deliver. We also know that Daniel promoted them
to a high office in Babylon, which means they were knowledgeable,
experienced, and wise men. And as previously mentioned, we know
that Shadrach, Meshach, and Abed-nego are always mentioned

together in the Bible — never separately. So, as far as the Bible is concerned, their lives tell the same story.

Many years after Daniel's interpretation and promotion of the three Hebrew children, Nebuchadnezzar built a large, golden idol in Babylon. Unfortunately, it seems that Daniel's divine interpretation did not have a lasting effect on Nebuchadnezzar, and the king once again followed his own ideals. Nebuchadnezzar made a big show of his golden idol in front of the Babylonians, including a policy that required everyone in Babylon to bow down and worship the golden idol whenever music was played; otherwise they would be thrown into the fiery furnace and burned alive. So, the very first time the music was played in Babylon, everyone obeyed Nebuchadnezzar's policy and bowed down to worship the golden idol — everyone except Shadrach, Meshach, and Abed-nego. It's important to remember that these three Hebrew children held positions of power in Babylon, which means they stood out among the people. Because of their position, it was a big deal when they disobeyed Nebuchadnezzar; they weren't just privately defying the king (their boss) — they were publicly defying him. Now, we begin to see why it was important for Daniel to promote these men — because if they had not been promoted, then perhaps nobody would have noticed their stance against Nebuchadnezzar's policy. God wanted these men to be seen standing, not bowing!

Daniel 3:8 says, *"at that time certain Chaldeans came near and accused the Jews."* Everyone in Babylon saw their act of disobedience, and the three men were immediately reported to Nebuchadnezzar. Upon hearing the news of this rebellion, Nebuchadnezzar was thrown into a fit of rage and demanded that the offenders be brought to him at once. Nebuchadnezzar thought this meeting would allow him to demonstrate his power, to make a show of these three Hebrew children, to save face in front of the people, and to make an example of them for anyone who might consider rebelling in the future.

The three Hebrew children were brought to Nebuchadnezzar who restated his terms: the men must bow the knee to the golden idol, or they would be cast into the fiery furnace. Nebuchadnezzar was not used to anyone standing up to him in his own city; in a way, he positioned himself as a god who must be obeyed. So, with great hubris Nebuchadnezzar scoffed, *"Who is the god who will deliver you from my hands" (Daniel 3:15)*? If there was ever a time for Shadrach, Meshach, and Abed-nego to step down and take the easy way out — this was it! This was the perfect opportunity for them to compromise, to give in, bow down to the idol, and live to fight another day.

But that's not what they did. They didn't need to take a few minutes to formulate a convincing argument; they didn't quiver or give a lukewarm response. They didn't fight to save their own lives; rather, they fought for their faith.

"Shadrach, Meshach, and Abed-nego answered and said to the king, O Nebuchadnezzar, we have no need to answer you in this matter. If that is the case, our God whom we serve is able to deliver us from the burning fiery furnace, and He will deliver us from your hand, O king" (Daniel 3:16–17).

This statement went straight to the heart of Nebuchadnezzar's pride, because these men were not impressed with the king's power, and they weren't intimidated by his threats. These men knew from experience that God — the one true God — was able to deliver them. What a powerful and encouraging stance!

Their next statement is as inspiring as it is difficult to grasp. They spoke straight to Nebuchadnezzar and said:

"But if not, let it be known to you, O king, that we do not serve your gods, nor will we worship the gold image which you have set up" (Daniel 3:18).

I wonder, would I be willing to say the same thing? These three men didn't need time to think about their response; they knew what their answer was even before being asked. They were willing to accept Nebuchadnezzar's consequence — death — because they had complete trust in God. "But if not ... we do not serve your gods, nor will we worship the gold image which you have set up." These men knew there was the possibility that God would choose to not deliver them from the fiery furnace; they accepted the fact that God might allow them to die in the fire for doing the right thing. This show of faith and resolve is similar to when Job said, *"Though he slay me, yet will I trust Him" (Job 13:15)*. These godly men and giants of faith were so persuaded in what they believed, and in the character of God, that they were willing to die for it. Whether God would deliver the three Hebrew children from the fire or whether they would die in the furnace — it wouldn't change the fact that they were still God's children. Fear of consequence had no impact on the stance they took.

Application

In this book, Nebuchadnezzar represents a spiritual conflict that results in a crisis of faith. Nebuchadnezzar's policy required all the people to bow down and worship Baal, even if it meant denying their own God. For Christians today, we might face policies, mandates, or laws that require us to do or say something that violates our biblical convictions. No matter what it is or what that conflict looks like, we are all pressured at times to do or say things that oppose our faith. Even if our jobs — or our lives — aren't hanging in the balance, most of us care about being liked and accepted; it can feel devastating to simply lose the respect and acceptance of our peers. So, whether it's in our church, at work, around our neighborhood, in school, or with family members, it takes courage to stand up against an opposing point of view.

Additionally, many times these crises of faith are accompanied by threats. It's not enough that you're living in wicked Babylon and subjected to wicked rulers, but you may also be confronted with consequences for your obedience to God. Nebuchadnezzar used the fiery furnace — a horrifying and torturous death — to deter anyone from stepping out of line; this was his scare tactic. Similarly, you might face serious backlash for taking a biblical stand; you might be threatened with embarrassment, humiliation, a suspension, termination, or even a lawsuit. These are real fears and real consequences for many Christians today. And because of that fear, no matter how radical or evil a mandate might be, there will always be people who go along with it — just like the people who reported the three Hebrew children to Nebuchadnezzar. In fact, you might be the only person in your community to take a biblical stand, so don't be surprised if you're pressured and persecuted for it; you should expect it to happen.

In the same way that God placed the three young Hebrew men in a specific position, at a specific time, and for a specific purpose, God has a specific purpose for you. In this age of social media, there's always someone watching, and that can be a good thing if it leads people to God. We may be pressured or intimidated to fall in line with ungodly policies, and we may be given an opportunity to voice our concerns about it. But before giving any response, we must first seek God; we must be rooted and established in our faith and resolved to act in accordance with that faith, no matter the consequences. We should strive for a faith that says, "My God is able to deliver me, but if not, I will not serve your gods." As we learn in the Bible, there is a cost to following Jesus, and holding on to faith isn't easy, especially in the face of intense conflict.

It's important for us to see the similarities between ourselves and the three Hebrew children: we have faith in the same God, and the courage they had to stand up in the face of death is the same courage we must have today. They told Nebuchadnezzar that his golden idol was something "which you have set up." His idol wasn't divine; it had no real power or significance. Similarly, the policies that are set up by men today are powerless against the

Word of God. Shadrach, Meshach, and Abed-nego knew who God was and they knew why they trusted in Him (faith); we must know the same. They were convinced of their beliefs (conviction); we should be too. Finally, their resolve led them to act (courage); our faith should also be accompanied with action.

FIERY FURNACE

The story didn't end when Shadrach, Meshach, and Abed-nego stood up to Nebuchadnezzar. The king didn't have a change of heart, he didn't show tolerance, and he didn't agree to disagree. The three Hebrew children said what they needed to say, and they did what they needed to do — the rest was in God's hands. After their rebuke, Nebuchadnezzar became so irate that he ordered the fiery furnace to be made seven times hotter, but the three Hebrew children continued to stand their ground. They were bound up, their hands were tied, and they were thrown into the scorching fire. The three men could have cried out as soon as they felt the searing heat and they could have begged for a second chance. If they would've agreed to bow down and worship the golden idol, they probably would have been returned to their esteemed positions.

Not only that, but God could've also intervened at any time. Up to this point, these three Hebrew children had been nothing but faithful. I mean, after all, these three men were carrying a heavy burden, and they were doing their best to help. They prayed, showed obedience, acted courageously, and they were willing to die for their convictions. By all accounts, they did everything right. Couldn't God have just put the fire out somehow? Couldn't He have sent a rainstorm to quench the flames or caused the three men to vanish into thin air, like Enoch and Elijah? Well, yes, God could have done any of those things — but that's not what happened. Shadrach, Meshach, and Abed-nego were literally thrown into a literal fiery furnace.

"And these three men, Shadrach, Meshach, and Abed-nego, fell down bound into the midst of the burning fiery furnace" (Daniel 3:23).

Shadrach, Meshach, and Abed-nego not only had the courage to stand up to Nebuchadnezzar, but they proved to be faithful to the very end, even to death.

Application

There will come a time in our own circumstances — after we've said everything we can say, and we've done everything we can do — that the only thing left to do is watch God move on our behalf; that's exactly what happened with Shadrach, Meshach, and Abed-nego. None of us want to be persecuted for our beliefs; none of us want to be disliked in our community or placed under increasing pressure. But we will not always be free from difficulty, nor are we meant to be. Sometimes the Nebuchadnezzar in our life will land a blow and it will hurt, and sometimes we will go through what seems to be the worst-case scenario. But the one constant throughout the conflict must be our unwavering, unflinching faith in God Almighty, even if it feels like He is letting us experience the pain of the fiery furnace.

In this book, the fiery furnace represents the consequences we could face because of the stand we take on God's Word. For the Hebrew children, the fiery furnace was real, and it was hot. Your fiery furnace could be anything from the fear of losing your job to the fear of being ostracized from your community — or even worse. No matter what it is or what it looks like, we all experience our own fiery furnace (or, sometimes multiple fiery furnaces). It's important for us to see the similarities between the biblical fiery furnace and our own crisis because, just as we're about to see how God protected the three Hebrew children in their fiery furnace, He's able to bring us through our crisis as well.

We cannot always trust what we see or how we feel — in most cases it's wise not to — and that's why it's so important to know the truth of God's Word, to believe it, and to stand on it. God let Shadrach, Meshach, and Abed-nego go into the furnace and it's possible they wondered where God was while they were bound and thrown into the flames. That doesn't mean God won't still come through, but it does mean we don't always see or feel Him, and we need to have faith regardless.

4TH Man in the Fire

"When you pass through the waters, I will be with you; and through the rivers, they shall not overflow you. When you walk through the fire, you shall not be burned, nor shall the flame scorch you" (Isaiah 43:2).

Nebuchadnezzar was able to save face in front of the people and preserve his reputation by punishing these three Hebrew men. He had built his golden idol, he showed it off in front of the whole city, and he required everyone to bow down and worship it — on command. And the first time anyone disobeyed his orders, he made an example out of them by throwing them into the fire; he did what he said he would do. The consequence was clear and from now on nobody would dare to stand against him again.

Though it's a seemingly tragic ending, everything up to this point is still a great story of courage. These three men did something that was extremely difficult and inspiring. They stood up to the most powerful king of the most powerful nation — not to mention their boss — and they were willing to lay down their lives to put God first. They knew the consequences going into it and if they were to die in the fiery furnace, they would go into Paradise — not because of their works, but because of their faith. Even if God let them die in the furnace, Shadrach, Meshach, and Abed-nego still would have trusted Him. If the story ended there, it would still be inspiring. But God prepared a different ending to their story.

The Bible says that after Nebuchadnezzar threw the three men into the fire, he looked into the flames and was astonished, or terrified, at what he saw. He said:

"I see four men loose, walking in the midst of the fire; and they are not hurt, and the form of the fourth is like the Son of God." (Daniel 3:25)

When Nebuchadnezzar looked into the flames, he most likely expected to see the shapes of the three Hebrew men lying dead on the ground. But instead of seeing three dead men, he saw four men walking around in the fire, and the fourth looked like the Son of God! The men were thrown into the flames bound up, tied so tight that they couldn't keep themselves from falling down. But when Nebuchadnezzar saw them, they were not bound at all; they were loose, walking around, and they were not harmed — not a scratch on them. They weren't burned, their hair wasn't singed, they didn't even smell like smoke! There is no natural explanation for what happened — it's not possible in the physical world. This divine protection, from beginning to end, was entirely prepared, designed, orchestrated, and superintended by God.

When Nebuchadnezzar was able to gather his wits, he shouted into the fire:

"Shadrach, Meshach, and Abed-Nego, servants of the Most High God, come out, and come here" (Daniel 3:26).

And all the people and officers gathered around to witness this great miracle; it was undeniable — the God of Heaven was greater than the god of the Babylonians. Even Nebuchadnezzar had to admit that the God of Shadrach, Meshach, and Abed-nego — the God they said was able to deliver them — was indeed the Most High God! No golden idol could have performed a miracle like this. This series of events had a profound impact on Nebuchadnezzar as he made a new law, saying that anyone who spoke against the God of Shadrach, Meshach, and Abed-nego shall be cut into pieces and have their house destroyed. Again, what a turn of events!

Application -

Everything changed the moment God stepped into the situation.
The three Hebrews didn't perform any miracles, they didn't
elevate themselves to a higher position, and they didn't persuade
Nebuchadnezzar to change his policy about worshiping the
golden idol — God did all of those things. But because they
were faithful, courageous, and obedient, God was able to use the
three Hebrew children and move in their lives — and the lives
of everyone in Babylon — in a miraculous way. The same is true
for us. As much as we might try to speak the truth, get ourselves
out of a conflict, or plead our case when we are persecuted — we
can't do everything on our own. There are things that only God
can do, and we must learn to trust Him and allow His plan to
unfold, even when it means going into the fiery furnace.

Had the three men compromised their convictions at any point
throughout this story, they could've escaped the heat of the fiery
furnace. That sounds pretty good in the natural, but without
the fiery furnace these men would have forfeited their great
deliverance. They would've failed to see God's power and they
would have missed an opportunity to deepen their relationship
with Him for the rest of their lives — for any future crisis they
may encounter. And what would that have meant for us? We
would have missed out on this timeless, inspirational, true story
of Godly courage.

If we take the easy way out and avoid every spiritual conflict in
life, then we too will forfeit our great deliverance. We will miss
out on seeing God's power and having a deeper relationship with
Him — which we can build on for the rest of our lives. That's why
it's so important for us seek God and allow ourselves to be used
by Him — according to His will and His purpose — even when
it means going through a fiery furnace. We can gain courage
by hearing true stories like this and, in turn, we can encourage
others as well.

The fourth man in the fire represents the presence of God
in our lives. Actually, the fourth man in the fire really isn't a
representation at all — it's quite literal! For the Hebrew children,
the fourth man was the literal presence of God. The presence
of God can be demonstrated in different ways, such as in the
way that God strengthens us, the way God encourages us, and
the way God shows up in our situation. It's important to see the
similarities in the fiery furnace and our trials today, because just
as God brought the three Hebrew men out of that fiery furnace,
He can bring us out of ours as well.

chapter two

Jessica Tapia

"What has happened to me can happen to anybody. My story is not just mine. It is the story of every teacher of morals and faith. It's also the story of every parent whose first priority is protecting their children."[1] —Jessica Tapia

From 2016–2022, Jessica Tapia was a teacher in the Jurupa Unified School District (JUSD) in southern California, but in January 2023, she was fired for refusing to allow boys into the girls' locker room during her Physical Education classes. Like the three Hebrew men, Jessica was given an ungodly command that violated her Christian convictions, and she was fired from her job for standing on her faith. Jessica's story demonstrates the level of hostility that exists in our culture toward the Bible and toward Christianity, not just in public education, but everywhere.

The first time I heard Jessica's story, I saw her as the victim of a corrupted education system. But as I learned more about her story, I saw Jessica less as a victim and more like the three Hebrew children — a willing and obedient Child of God who faced an intense spiritual conflict, and chose courage; to be clear, that's a position of great power, not weakness. My goal in this chapter is to show how God's hand was on Jessica's life, before, during, and after

---

1. https://www.foxnews.com/us/christian-ex-teacher-sues-california-district-refusing-hide-kids-gender-transitions-parents.

she was fired — and to show how He honored her willingness to take a risky and courageous stand.

Jessica's Background

Jessica grew up in southern California and had a strong sense of moral conviction from childhood. For example, when Jessica was seven years old, she lived in an unstable home with family members who struggled with drug addiction. And even though she was just a child, Jessica made the extremely difficult, yet impressive, decision to leave home and move in with her grandmother. Jessica spent most of her childhood being raised by her grandmother who sacrificed a lot to give Jessica a better life. But the greatest gift Jessica ever received from her grandmother was an introduction to Jesus and the Bible.

Jessica married her high school sweetheart, Jon, and they have three children together. Jessica and Jon were both on the swim team in high school, and Jon's mom happened to be their swim coach. One night Jon's mom invited Jessica over to their house for a women's Bible study, and Jessica observed just how loving Jon was toward his mom. Jessica was instantly smitten with Jon, and the two have been together ever since. Jon Tapia is a military veteran, having served in the United States Marine Corps. But when the Covid crisis came to America in 2020, Jon took a principled stand and was discharged from the Marines (we will discuss this near the end of the chapter). But, before we go any further into Jessica's story, I want to point out Jon's bravery, conviction, and backbone; it turns out that Jon and Jessica are equally yoked in more ways than one.

Jessica went to college to be an Occupational Therapist, but after working as a substitute teacher realized her calling was to be a teacher. Jessica said the reason she became a teacher was to be a source of hope, light, and love for students who came from a similar background as her. She always believed her difficult upbringing would somehow be a part of her ministry as a teacher.

"I thought how amazing it would be to be a light to kids possibly coming from very rough homes like I did when I was a child. And so, it was just so exciting for me to get to work in a field where it was just way beyond a paycheck, where I would be able to make a difference in a way that was priceless on young lives."[2]

Jessica was a student at JUSD before she became a teacher there. So, in one way or another, she was a part of the same school district for nearly 20 years. JUSD was Jessica's home; it's where she grew up, met her husband, met her friends, found her love for teaching and coaching, and it's where she earned a living.

In her six years of teaching for JUSD, Jessica had an impeccable work record; in fact, she had never been disciplined or reprimanded at work prior to being fired in 2023. Her supervising principal of four years wrote:

"Jessica distinguished herself among the rest by always focusing on her student's mind, body, and heart.... She is a caring, positive, kind, student-centered teacher that has motivated her students to excel in ways that are unconventional.... Her positive attitude and high expectations make her students believe in themselves and therefore strive to achieve their potential."[3]

Not only was Jessica a loving wife and mother, but by all accounts, she was a great teacher, a great coach, a great colleague, and a great role model. Jessica earned her reputation over many years, but it was nearly brought to nothing literally overnight.

Application ------------------------------

When I began writing this book, Jessica's story was the first one that came to mind. Jessica was gracious enough to sit down with

---

2. https://static1.squarespace.com/static/5460e86be4b058ea427aec94/t/64e7f44a43 766a3c10a47da6/1692922957665/1st+Amended+Complaint.pdf.
3. Tapia v. JUSD, Hansen & Brooks, 5:23-cv-00789-FMO-E. 5 (2023).

me for an interview, so you'll read several of her quotes and takeaways in this chapter. When I saw Jessica's story on the news in February 2023, it was the first time I had heard of a teacher being fired for not complying with gender policies. When I taught for Chicago Public Schools (CPS) in 2020–2021, I saw first-hand how Gender Ideology and Critical Race Theory were being snuck into classrooms, shaping school policies; and just like Jessica, my biblical convictions precluded me from adopting those policies. But when I approached my school board and warned them about the dangers of Gender Ideology and Critical Race Theory, they refused to listen; I discuss this in my first book.

Jessica's story contains powerful themes and lessons that are universal, extending beyond public education. Jessica was, in many ways, a "normal" Christian: she loved her job, worked hard, and was well-liked. Then she made national headlines for taking a strong biblical stance; this could happen to any of us. But just as spiritual persecution can happen to any of us, God's protection can happen to any of us, too. The good news is that if we are obedient to God, we have every reason to trust that He will protect us even in our persecution.

The Bible teaches us that God uses people like Jessica who seek His will and are obedient to His call. But Jessica's story proves there is a cost that comes with choosing God's way in a spiritual conflict; there are consequences for not bowing the knee to Nebuchadnezzar's golden idol. This uncomfortable truth causes a lot of Christians to cower in fear; it's why so many Christians are afraid to publicly share their faith. After all, nobody wants to be falsely accused and persecuted. Jessica was very afraid at times during her spiritual conflict, but that's why her courage to stand is so inspiring.

 **BABYLON**

In the Bible, and in this book, Babylon represents an ungodly place that's hostile toward Christianity and God's Word. In Jessica's story, Babylon is the modern public education system (or much of it). The Bible was once the principal text in America's schools, but since the mid-1800s, America's education system has become increasingly ungodly and hostile toward the Bible and Christianity. Horace Mann and John Dewey pushed for the Utopian concept of "religious neutrality" in American education, and since the implementation of their ideas, our education system has "morphed into a fully secularized system that breeds all sorts of immorality."[4] That doesn't mean every teacher or administrator in a public school is secular or immoral — Jessica certainly wasn't — but they are in a type of Babylon; and everyone in Babylon will either bow to the "golden idol" or face the consequences. So, even though there are many Christians involved in the public education system, it's still a system that's completely secular by design. Jessica's school district is a prime example and that's why JUSD represents Babylon in her story.

The Social Media Post That Started It All

After school one day in May 2022, Jessica went to a well-known department store to buy some clothes for her three kids. When she arrived in the children's clothing section, she noticed the store was selling PRIDE clothes specifically designed for toddlers and babies. As a Christian mother, Jessica was saddened that young children were being sexualized so openly, and that homosexuality was being promoted to children so casually. Jessica decided to post a video to her personal social media account about it, sharing these sentiments.

---

4.   https://teachdiligently.com/articles/horace-mann-utopian-vision-for-public-education.

Soon after, Jessica noticed students from her school had somehow seen the video and were leaving comments, accusing her of homophobia or transphobia. Jessica had a personal rule that she never followed students on social media, and she never allowed students to follow her on social media either; so, she decided to delete the comments instead of interacting with students online. However, after noticing their comments were deleted, the students commented again saying that Jessica was too late, they had already sent screenshots of her social media to school administrators.

The very next day, Jessica was removed from her 4th period class, suspended, and placed under investigation. She didn't realize it then, but her teaching career had just ended.

Application -------------------------------

Have you ever had to defend yourself to a group of people who are convinced of your guilt? That was the case for Jessica. She was persecuted in her own community, by her own community, and then removed from her community; she didn't go looking for a conflict, the conflict came looking for her. And if standing up to Gender Ideology was difficult for her as an adult (which it was), just imagine how difficult it is for children to resist indoctrination in school; it's almost impossible. Jessica was about to step into a heated conflict where she would have to make very difficult decisions. What have you faced that made you stand up for what is right?

Nebuchadnezzar

If Jessica's school district represents her Babylon, then her administrators represent Nebuchadnezzar; they were the ones enforcing the district's gender policies. In this section we will see how JUSD administrators gave their decree that Jessica must bow to Gender Ideology or be fired. But Jessica's Christian faith precluded her from bowing to Gender Ideology, and that's why she faced the fiery furnace.

Gender Ideology has a vague definition, but it's easy to recognize when you see it. For example, Gender Ideology claims that there are more than two genders, that humans can be born in the wrong body, and that boys can become girls and girls can become boys. It's based on the sexually perverted theories of Alfred Kinsey and John Money, and it's more aptly defined as "Gender Confusion," because that's what it creates. Sadly, school districts across the country, including administrators and teachers, have bowed the knee to the idolatry of transgenderism, often celebrating and promoting it higher than anything else. In fact, the celebration of transgenderism in public schools has had such a profound impact on children that in just the last five years the number of children identifying as trans has doubled, and young people (ages 13–17) are approximately five times more likely than adults (age 65+) to identify as trans.[5] I discuss this movement much more in my first book.

Meeting 1: Jessica's Suspension and Investigation (May 2022)

When Jessica was pulled from her 4th period class (the day after her social media post) she was taken to an unscheduled meeting with school administrators and told there had been several complaints about her personal social media account. Jessica was told these allegations were so serious that she was being suspended and placed under investigation. Then she was told that for her own safety, she needed to leave school grounds immediately. So, Jessica went straight to her office, gathered all her personal items, and went home.

"The Holy Spirit made it clear that I was stepping into spiritual warfare."[6]

Jessica remembered that while she was being suspended in this surprise meeting, her administrators kept apologizing to her,

---

5.   https://williamsinstitute.law.ucla.edu/publications/trans-adults-united-states/.
6.   https://youtu.be/Y4lT-fpaXgQ.

because they knew she was an outstanding teacher with a spotless work record. They apologized because they knew they were wrong, but they lacked the conviction and the courage to stand up for the truth. Jessica knew she was in trouble, not because she did anything wrong, but because she refused to bow the knee to their sacred idol. Jessica didn't create this problem, she exposed it.

Meeting 2: Accusations and Directives (Fall 2022)

Jessica spent the summer of 2022 waiting to hear back on the results of her investigation, but word never came. So, as the new school year was approaching, Jessica reached out to her administrators and asked if she was allowed to return to work. To her surprise, Jessica was told she could not return to work until they had another meeting.

The moment Jessica stepped into the meeting, the conflict heated up. JUSD administrators presented Jessica with a packet of "exhibits" (screenshots) of her personal social media posts, most of which contained Bible verses and quotes about God; these images were supposed to be some sort of proof of Jessica's hate speech. Jessica was accused of proselytizing during class, and district officials said her social media posts were racist, offensive, disrespectful, and mocking toward individuals based upon their sexual orientation.[7] They suggested that Jessica had discriminated against her students and that her behavior was motivated by hate. Certainly, Jessica wasn't the only teacher in the district with political or religious posts on their personal social media accounts — many teachers in the district did the same sort of thing — but none of them were given a list of directives to follow. None of them were pulled from class, questioned, removed from campus, put on leave, investigated, or accused — only Jessica.[8] Why the double standard?

---

7. https://www.foxnews.com/us/christian-ex-teacher-sues-california-district-refusing-hide-kids-gender-transitions-parents.

8. https://www.foxnews.com/us/christian-ex-teacher-sues-california-district-refusing-hide-kids-gender-transitions-parents.

But it didn't stop there. In addition to being falsely accused and slandered, Jessica was given a list of district directives, or behavior modifications, and was told she needed to comply with these directives or be fired.

- DIRECTIVE ONE required Jessica to use preferred pronouns with students. No student had ever made a request for Jessica to use a preferred pronoun, so this directive was pre-emptive and unfounded. But it was presented, nonetheless. Lying to children and encouraging gender confusion is not loving or compassionate, and directly conflicted with Jessica's Christian beliefs. Jessica could not comply with this directive.

- DIRECTIVE TWO required Jessica to withhold information from parents about their child's gender identity. Jessica read this directive and asked her administrators, "Are you asking me to lie to parents?" They responded with a clear and unapologetic, "Yes, for the student's safety and privacy." So, not only was Jessica required to lie to students about their identity, but she was required to lie to parents as well. This directive was also in direct conflict with her Christian beliefs as it undermined parental authority and placed the state in the position of authority instead; this is not what it looks like to honor parents.

- DIRECTIVE THREE required Jessica to refrain from discussing her personal beliefs with students. Proselytizing means trying to convert someone; it does not mean answering a question, giving an opinion, or having a discussion about religion.[9] Jessica never proselytized her students (and had never been accused of doing so before this meeting), but students did sometimes ask innocent questions like, "Mrs. Tapia, where do you go to church?" In these instances, Jessica would answer the question. It was important to Jessica to be a biblical example to her students, and to not be ashamed of the gospel when asked about it. Again, this directive violated Jessica's beliefs.

---

9.   https://www.merriam-webster.com/dictionary/proselytizing.

"I essentially had to pick one. Am I going to obey the district ... or am I going to stay true ... to the way the Lord has called me to live. And so, it was crazy to be in the position where I realized that I couldn't be a Christian and a teacher."[10]

Jessica came into this meeting expecting to be reinstated; she expected to be back in the classroom. Instead, she was accused of racism, hatred, disrespect, and mocking others. Her personal life and her Christian beliefs were used against her, and she was forced to comply with a list of behavior modifications, all of which violated God's Word. This was spiritual warfare and Nebuchadnezzar had given his decree: bow to the golden idol or be cast into the fiery furnace. Jessica had to remind herself, "Your fear is in the Lord, not in man."

Application

This meeting rocked Jessica's world, and understandably so. Jessica knew her accusers, and she knew the administrators who were trying to validate these accusations against her; but everything Jessica thought she knew was turned upside down. Her reputation, job, and livelihood were hanging in the balance, and she was confronted with a "compromise": follow the directives and keep everything you've worked for, or say no and lose it all. That placed an extreme amount of pressure on her to take the compromise; that's the common and relatable response. Jessica's initial reaction was what anyone else's reaction would've been — she was confused, scared, and hurt. But her next reaction was the one that mattered most — she took time to seek the Lord.

Jessica understood right away this was a spiritual battle that required a spiritual answer. Her employer was requiring her to violate God's Word and she needed to know what God thought

---

10.   https://www.foxnews.com/media/christian-teacher-loses-job-refusing-deceive-parents-kids-gender-transitions-devil.

about it all. What would you have done to stay faithful to God's call on your life?

Jessica's Divine Phone Call

Jessica left her second meeting in shock. By the time she got back home she was trembling and sobbing; she was absolutely wrecked by what just happened, and her head was spinning with questions: Is my career over? Should I ignore the Bible? Doesn't God want me to be a teacher? What am I going to do? What can I do?

Jessica knew that teaching and coaching was part of her ministry as a Christian. She remembered her difficult upbringing and how she so greatly desired to be a source of light, hope, and love for her students and athletes. She didn't want to leave her students, but at the same time she couldn't, in good conscience, go along with her district's directives. Plus, she had a family to consider. Losing her job wouldn't just impact her own life, it would impact her husband and children, too. But, if she bowed down to her school's gender policies, what kind of example would she be setting for her own children? Jessica understood that being a wife and a mother meant she could no longer make selfish decisions; this is the challenge and the beauty of marriage and parenthood.

Jessica struggled with her next steps and felt like she was getting pulled in every direction, but she didn't know exactly which way to go. She saw three paths forward:

- She could bow to her district's gender policies and keep her job.

- She could quit her job and lose her salary.

- She could stand firm on her convictions and tell the truth, despite the consequences.

Jessica was under a great amount of stress and personal anguish. She said that during this time she suffered constant spiritual attacks and that, in her own mind, she could not see beyond the fear of losing her salary. Family and friends, many of whom were Christians, were urging her to either quit or just go along with her directives if it meant getting back to her students. With the new school year quickly approaching, Jessica was running out of time to make her decision.

In the middle of her whirlwind of conflicting opinions, there was one opinion Jessica hadn't heard yet — God's. Jessica needed time to seek God and to hear from Him for herself, so she took a medical stress leave from work and spent three months fasting and praying.

During this period (September–December 2022), Jessica's prayer was, "Lord, please just make it clear what I'm to do." She was leaning toward quitting her job, and she had even started writing a resignation letter, but she was never able to finish it — it was as if God was putting a roadblock in front of her. When Jessica thought she knew what to do, God stepped in and changed everything.

Near the end of her medical leave, Jessica was contacted on social media by a husband and wife from the state of Washington. The two were Christians and somehow heard about Jessica's situation. They reached out to Jessica through social media and asked if she would be willing to accept a phone call; Jessica accepted the invitation. The couple simply wanted to pray for Jessica and support her in any way they could. Jessica mentioned to the couple that she was leaning toward quitting, and that she had already started writing her resignation letter. The husband on the call happened to have a background in law and cautioned Jessica that if she quit, she would have no case against the school district if she ever wanted to file a wrongful termination lawsuit; if she stayed and they fired her, then she would have a case. Jessica had never considered a lawsuit, but once she heard it, she felt the presence of the Holy Spirit and knew this was her turning point. Immediately after this divine phone call ended, Jessica felt at peace and on fire for God! Knowing she had just received the answer to her prayer, she threw away her resignation letter and set up another meeting with her school district.

Application -

This is one of the most important sections in Jessica's story and in this entire book, because it's about the need for Christians to make time to seek the Lord — and to continue to seek Him even when it feels like we're not getting answers (yet). Jessica never could've predicted how things would play out. She didn't know this Washington couple; she'd never seen or talked to them in her life. But God was moving in their hearts just as much as He was moving in Jessica's. This shows that our stories aren't just about us. God has a way of using His people to encourage, strengthen, and edify one another. But if Jessica had never taken the time to seek God, this conversation most likely never would've happened, and she never would've heard from God in this powerful way. Instead, she would have quit — and her story would look very different.

Jessica was waiting to hear from God while it seemed like her life was falling apart all around her. How many of us can relate to that?! This period of waiting is excruciating at times and can cause us to compromise and make unwise decisions. The difference maker in Jessica's story was seeking God's will over her own, and hearing from Him for herself. We see here how God often moves unexpectedly, and sometimes discreetly without our knowledge. So, if you're in a period of waiting on the Lord, which we all find ourselves in at times, you can be encouraged by Jessica's story to know that God can move at any moment and in the most unexpected ways.

Meeting 3: Jessica's Response (January 2023)

Jessica said she was "on fire" after her phone call with the Washington couple, having finally received instructions from God;

she was ready to respond to her district's directives with a sound biblical defense. Her responses are outlined below.

Jessica's Response to DIRECTIVE ONE (using preferred pronouns):

> Staying true to my faith and beliefs, I can and will only refer to students by the name and gender/pronouns provided by their parents/legal guardians...."[11]

"So, God created man in His own image; in the image of God He created him; male and female He created them" (Genesis 1:27).

Jessica's Response to DIRECTIVE TWO (withholding information from parents):

> "I cannot purposely lie and withhold information from parents about their child."

"Honor your father and your mother, that your days may be long upon the land which the Lord your God is giving you" (Exodus 20:12).

Jessica's Response to DIRECTIVE THREE (refraining from discussing her personal beliefs):

> "I must be prepared with an answer for the hope I have, for anyone who comes asking."

"But sanctify the Lord God in your hearts, and always be ready to give a defense to everyone who asks you a reason for the hope that is in you, with meekness and fear" (1 Peter 3:15).

While Jessica explained why she could not obey the district's directives, she also provided alternate solutions that she hoped would be mutually agreeable. For example, she offered to refer to students by the name listed on the school roster; she suggested the school require students to use the facility that aligns with their biological sex as opposed to their gender identity; she even suggested that she be transferred to another position within the

11. https://static1.squarespace.com/static/5460e86be4b058ea427aec94/t/64e7f44a43
    766a3c10a47da6/1692922957665/1st+Amended+Complaint.pdf.

district, which would remove her interactions with students. JUSD administrators rejected Jessica's proposals and set up a Religious Accommodations Meeting instead.

Application ------------------------------

This section is about obedience to God's Word and activating your faith. Jessica didn't respond with her own opinions she responded with God's Word. She didn't have to come up with some new argument to outsmart her administrators, because God's Word is eternally true and could take care of that; there's comfort in knowing that you're shielded by the power of God's Word. All Jessica had to do was obey and act. It's a simple formula, but it's very difficult for us to do. While Jessica did the inspiring thing and took the courageous stand, the situation would get worse before it got better. Nebuchadnezzar made the fire seven times hotter, remember?

Meeting 4: Religious Accommodations Meeting (mid-January 2023)

"Tear down every lie, set the wrong thing right.
'Cause when You have Your way, something has to break."[12]

By now, half a year had gone by since Jessica was pulled from her 4th period class and placed on suspension. After six months of meetings, questions, accusations, threats, and demands — Jessica felt that something had to break.

It turned out the only reason JUSD administrators asked for this meeting was to grill Jessica about her Christianity with their lawyers present; essentially, she had asked for a "religious accommodation" to the secular directives, and the school did not want to give her one. So, instead, they were focused on trying to undermine her claims of being a Christian. Jessica was asked what

---

12. J. Drew Sheard II, Jonathan Smith, Kierra Sheard & Mia Fieldes, "Something Has to Break" by Red Rocks Worship & Essential Worship.

church she attended, how often she attended church, how often she read the Bible, and where in the Bible it says she can't obey the district's gender policies. She was forced to defend her biblical convictions to a group of people who, most likely, put zero stock in what the Bible says; but JUSD never had to defend its radical and ungodly beliefs (i.e., Gender Ideology).

But that which was intended to break Jessica turned into a Gospel presentation. Jessica's interrogation became a wide-open door for her to share with these administrators and lawyers the truth of God's Word.

As the meeting started to wrap up, Jessica was asked if there were any other religious accommodations she might possibly need. Jessica explained that as a Physical Education teacher, she was in the unique position of overseeing locker rooms. She added that not only would she not lie to students and their parents, but she would not allow boys into the girls' locker room. JUSD administrators said, "Well then we have a whole other problem."

> "According to my school district ... if a student shares information regarding a pronoun preference or thinking there may be the opposite gender ... we are supposed to keep that info from parents in case the parent doesn't know.... I don't believe kids should have this "privacy" to where their parents are being left in the dark about some very pertinent information about their well-being.... I don't believe in my faith that that's how God's calling us to love by affirming those lies and confusion. I believe firmly that God created man and woman, and you are who He made you to be. And when someone has confusion about that, I believe that's lies and confusion from the devil."[13]

Jessica recalled looking around the room and seeing several men with their heads down; these men had daughters and Jessica suspected they knew what was happening to her was wrong, but

13. https://static1.squarespace.com/static/5460e86be4b058ea427aec94/t/64e7f44a43
766a3c10a47da6/1692922957665/1st+Amended+Complaint.pdf.

they lacked the courage to resist. And that's how the meeting ended: Jessica stood on God's Word, and her school district stood on Gender Ideology. As we already know, Jessica's story didn't end there. She didn't walk out of this meeting to applause or praise; she walked into the fiery furnace.

Application

The transgender craze has dominated America culture since the mid-2010s; it's everywhere. From the White House to the schoolhouse, and even to some church houses, God's creation and design is under attack from the lies of Gender Ideology. It's literal fulfillment of Isaiah 45:9 which says, *"Woe to him who strives with his Maker.... Shall the clay say to him who forms it, 'What are you making?'"* Jessica stood against this giant, like David stood against Goliath, and she landed a major blow — all by simply speaking God's Word.

At first glance, this may seem like a loss for Jessica. But God was using Jessica in these meetings to be His mouthpiece, not because Jessica was the best speaker, but because she sought Him, she was obedient, and she was willing to act on her faith. How difficult is this to do?

FIERY FURNACE

A few days after her religious accommodations meeting, Jessica received her official termination letter which said, "We cannot accommodate your religious beliefs."[14] Jessica refused to bow to Nebuchadnezzar's idol, so she was tossed into the proverbial fiery furnace.

Stop and remember how this whole thing started: Jessica was shopping for clothes for her children and saw a bunch of PRIDE clothes for toddlers. She posted a video to her personal social

14. https://static1.squarespace.com/static/5460e86be4b058ea427aec94/t/64e7f44a43
766a3c10a47da6/1692922957665/1st+Amended+Complaint.pdf.

media account stating her belief that this was sexualizing children. Teenagers from Jessica's high school went out of their way to harass and report Jessica's social media posts to her school district; they were offended by her Christian beliefs. Jessica was suspended the very next day and six months later she was fired — not for anything she did, but for what she believed. This could happen to any of us.

Jessica did a lot of things right. She never caved to the pressure and intimidation from her school district, she didn't take the easy way out by compromising her beliefs, she spoke the truth, she sought the Lord, she heard from the Lord, she acted in obedience, and she took a courageous stand to defend children, their parents, and the truth. But Jessica lost her job anyway and was "cast into the fire," despite all the good things she did. As inspiring as her story is, inspiration doesn't pay the bills; Jessica's obedience cost her salary. She and her husband still had a mortgage to pay and three children to feed.

Jessica knew there were consequences for refusing to bow to her school's directives, and she could've changed her mind at any time — and who would've blamed her? Jessica could still be teaching Physical Education in the Jurupa Unified School District right now, if she had just chosen to compromise, to put her comfort and livelihood and reputation above God's Word. If she chose that path, we wouldn't even know her name. We would've never heard there was a Christian teacher in California standing on God's Word in the face of evil. Thankfully, Jessica's story didn't go that way and it doesn't stop here. In the next section, we'll look at all the ways God moved, and is still moving, in Jessica's life.

Application

There comes a time when we cannot obey both God and man. Many Christians are afraid to share their thoughts, opinions, and beliefs publicly because they don't want what happened to Jessica to happen to them — or even something less significant to happen to them, like having to deal with an uncomfortable conversation. Saying nothing and doing nothing is easy; going against the grain and placing yourself at risk is hard. But Jessica didn't initiate this conflict; it came to her.

The point is you can't stop the enemy from attacking you and you can't always avoid fearful situations — sometimes we have to walk into the fiery furnace, knowing that it's not the end of our story. The best we can do is to walk with the Lord, seek His guidance daily, obey His commands, and live out our faith. Jessica's story presents a complicated situation I think most people can relate to, because what's common among all of us is that life is hard, it's messy, things don't always go our way, and we are treated unfairly at times. But Jessica's story shows us, yet again, that we have every reason to trust in God and have courage to stand in the face of conflict.

4TH Man in the Fire

"You prepare a table before me in the presence of my enemies" (Psalm 23:5).

Even though God's Word is at the center of Jessica's story, it can be hard to see God's presence during her meetings, accusations, directives, and eventual termination. But this section will show how God was moving on Jessica's behalf and preparing her table, even years before her suspension.

An Open Door

In Acts 19, the Apostle Paul went to Jerusalem knowing that he would be persecuted; sure enough, as soon as he arrived in Jerusalem he was arrested and sent to the captain, then he was sent to the Sanhedrin, then to Felix, then to Festus, and eventually he stood before Caesar. But every time Paul was questioned and asked to defend his beliefs, he was actually given an open door to preach the Gospel. This was God's divine method of evangelism and shining His light in the darkness.

"You will be brought before governors and kings for my sake, as a testimony to them and to the Gentiles. But when they deliver you up, do not worry about how or what you should speak. For it will be given to you in that hour what you should speak; for it is not you who speak, but the Spirit of your Father who speaks in you" (Matthew 10:18–20).

Jessica's experience was like Paul's in that God turned her persecution into an open door for her to preach the Gospel. When Jessica was suspended and placed under investigation, district administrators demanded that she defend her Christian beliefs. This gave Jessica an opportunity to lay out, point by point, exactly what the Bible said about their gender policies. If Jessica hadn't been accused and summoned to these meetings in the first place, then the truth of God's Word wouldn't have been able to shine on these spiritually dark policies. That which was intended to harm Jessica, God turned around and used for good. This is one way God was with Jessica in her conflict.

Jessica's Lawsuit

During her six-month suspension Jessica wondered what God wanted from her, but she never thought God would lead her to file a lawsuit. It wasn't until her divine phone call with the couple from Washington that the idea first entered her mind, but once she heard it, she knew it was God speaking to her through this married couple. It turned out to be sound advice, because in May 2023, Advocates for Faith and Freedom (a pro bono law firm) filed a lawsuit over the wrongful termination of Jessica for her religious beliefs,[15] alleging that JUSD violated Jessica's First Amendment and civil rights.

In January of 2024, one year after Jessica was fired, JUSD offered to settle the lawsuit and Jessica was left to choose between two paths forward: 1) she could take the settlement, set a precedent for teachers and school districts across the country, and receive financial restitution; or 2) she could reject the settlement, go to trial,

---

15. https://faith-freedom.com/cases-all/teacher-fired-christian-beliefs-tapia.

and hope that her case makes it to the Supreme Court. By settling, Jessica could be awarded a much smaller sum of money compared to if she were to go to trial and win. But, choosing to go to trial meant Jessica would likely spend years waiting for a decision to be reached. Jessica was faced with yet another decision that carried heavy consequences, so Jessica took time to pray and seek God's guidance on how to proceed—as she had done time and time before. Ultimately, Jessica felt that God was urging her to settle the lawsuit because it was important for a message to be sent NOW— the time to stand is now! Jessica's decision inspires a sense of urgency for other Christians to act and address the spiritual battle that's raging across the country, in our schools, and over the hearts and minds of our children. Jessica was awarded $360,000 in the settlement, sending a clear message to school districts across the country that Christians have the right to live according to their faith and that denying that right would be a costly mistake.

Promise of Blessing

"And all these blessings shall come upon you and overtake you, because you obey the voice of the Lord your God: blessed shall you be in the city, and blessed shall you be in the country" (Deuteronomy 28:2–3).

The Word of God is clear that for those who will obey God's voice, His blessings will overtake them; that could mean financial blessings, spiritual blessings, or many other types of blessings. Throughout her conflict, Jessica remained obedient to God's Word, and just like the Bible says, God's blessings came and overtook Jessica and her family. Below are two examples of how God financially blessed Jessica and her family.

First, while Jessica was on leave during the fall of 2022 and seeking God for guidance, she was burdened by the stress of losing her salary. In fact, Jessica could not get her mind off her salary. But then one day Jessica and her husband received a $1,500 check in the mail from a friend; this wasn't borrowed money and it wasn't asked for, it was a blessing.

Then, after Jessica's story made national headlines in early 2023, people all over the country wanted to offer their support. So, a friend of Jessica's set up a GiveSendGo fundraiser page, a Christian crowdfunding site, and 267 people donated over $26,000 to Jessica and her family. Jessica said, before receiving this humongous gift, she prayed and asked God to provide their family with just one month's mortgage; a week later they had enough to pay their mortgage for seven months. These two financial blessings were confirmation to Jessica that God's Word is true and that He would take care of her and her family.

The Latter Days of Job

The important part of this section is showing how God not only meets our financial needs, but He causes our cup to overflow; He expands our borders. God is good and faithful, and Jessica's story captures the common Christian experience, which consists of both walking through the valley and standing on the mountaintop.

"Now the Lord blessed the latter days of Job more than his beginning" (Job 42:12).

As a teacher and a coach, Jessica interacted with hundreds of students, colleagues, and parents every day. Sadly, those interactions were taken away when she was fired. But just as God blessed the latter days of Job more than his beginning, God has brought more like-minded Christians into Jessica's life. God has been restoring what Jessica lost and is now bringing things into her life that never would've been if she hadn't gone through the fiery furnace.

> "Politics matter because policy matters because people matter!" — Allie Beth Stuckey[16]

---

16. https://www.instagram.com/alliebstuckey/reel/C3anazBLUGX/.

The previous quote is one of Jessica's favorites and it has inspired her to not only share her story, but to advocate for local and state policies; and God has given Jessica a larger platform to do this. In 2023, Jessica appeared on *Tucker Carlson Tonight* to share her story with millions across the country.[17] Locally, Jessica has become a correspondent with *Our Watch,* and the host of her of her own show called *The Jessica Tapia Show.* She was also featured in Robby Starbuck's documentary *The War on Our Children.*[18] Jessica is especially grateful for the overwhelming support of one group in particular — veterans. She is regularly approached by veterans who are upset that she was fired over her religious beliefs, something they fought to protect. And since her husband Jon is a Marine Corps veteran, Jessica is especially proud to be associated with this new support group.

In the months following her lawsuit settlement, not only was Jessica awarded $360,000—an amount more than three times what she was owed in salary—but her story of courage and faith inspired the launch of a new initiative called "Teachers Don't Lie," which works with teachers of faith across the country to provide them with legal support and guidance on their Constitutional rights. Through this movement, Jessica is now able to use her experience to help other teachers, equipping and encouraging them to take courageous stands in the face of their own Nebuchadnezzars. Jessica said this about the "Teachers Don't Lie" initiative:

> "Across the country, we are seeing teachers' freedom of speech and religious liberty violated through policies that require them to forsake their morals. I want teachers to be confident in the fact that the best thing we can do for students is educate in truth, not deception."[19]

There are many more examples of how God has blessed Jessica, but I'll finish with this one. Back in December of 2022, when Jessica had

---

17. https://www.foxnews.com/video/6321594866112.
18. https://thewaronchildren.com/.
19. https://faith-freedom.com/cases-all/teacher-fired-christian-beliefs-tapia.

her divine phone call with the married couple in Washington, she was given a message from the husband (the man who first mentioned a lawsuit to Jessica). Before the call ended, this man said:

> "Right now, I see a woman on a stage sharing this story with thousands of people. This is your story, stand firm and do what's right."

Since that phone call, Jessica has stood on more than one stage. As a teacher, Jessica stood before dozens of students every class period and she would have been fortunate to reach just one. Now she's stood before millions, and her story is reaching more and more people every day. This part of Jessica's story is still developing, and there may be many more blessings to add to the list in the years to come.

Preparations

I just pointed out a few ways that God has blessed Jessica's obedience since she was fired. But I also want to talk about the ways God prepared Jessica to take her courageous stand because that's inspiring and applicable to our lives, too. We rarely understand what God is doing while we are going through a situation, and we can't predict the future; but when we look back over our lives, it's much easier to see that, all along, God was right there preparing us for what lay ahead. This is as true for Jessica as it is for any of us.

"For precept must be upon precept, precept upon precept, line upon line, line upon line, here a little, there a little" (Isaiah 28:10).

STORY ONE: During her suspension in 2022, Jessica wondered what God's plan was for her and if she would be bold enough to take a stand. Then God reminded Jessica of the stand she took as a child by choosing to move in with her grandmother, and these words started rolling through her mind: "You started standing for what was good, right, and true when you were seven.... Now, you're standing for other kids." God brought this memory back to Jessica, and it became a source of encouragement for her in her conflict with her school district. Since childhood, Jessica has been standing up for herself and for others; now she's standing up for her own children and children across the country. God knew Jessica would go through this trial and He's been preparing her since childhood.

STORY TWO: Near the end of 2020, Jessica and her husband were invited to visit Pastor Jack Hibbs' church because, unlike most churches in California in 2020–2021, his church refused to close its doors during Covid. So, on their first visit, Jack Hibbs preached from the Book of Revelation, that it's a sin to be a coward.

"But the cowardly, unbelieving, abominable, murderers, sexually immoral, sorcerers, idolaters, and all liars shall have their part in the lake which burns with fire and brimstone, which is the second death" *(Revelation 21:8).*

In this verse, cowardice is listed alongside sins such as murder, sexual immorality, sorcery, and even idolatry. Jessica was captivated by this sermon because she never heard this kind of preaching before, and she was reminded of this sermon during her spiritual conflict. Jessica never could've guessed that, years later, this sermon would be a major source of encouragement for her during her suspension from work, her investigation, and her termination. Jessica didn't know it would happen that way, but God did.

STORY THREE: In the fall of 2021, Jessica's husband Jon was serving in the Marine Corps when he, and every Marine, received an ultimatum to take the Covid vaccine or leave the Marines. For his own reasons, Jon decided not to take the vaccine and he was discharged from the Marine Corps. Like Jessica, Jon also took a courageous and principled stand. Jon's backbone and conviction would certainly factor into Jessica's response to her own conflict just a few months later.

STORY FOUR: Jon's situation with the Marines set the stage for the couple's next godly preparation. In December 2021, shortly after Jon left the Marines, he and Jessica decided to move to Alabama.

Jessica happened to be on maternity leave with their third child and the family saw this as an opportunity to leave California. The plan was that Jessica would resign from her position at JUSD once they found a house. They found a house they wanted to buy and for once, everything seemed to be going according to plan. But as they were preparing to buy the house and finalize their move, Jessica said that God intervened and changed their course in a big way.

"God grabbed me and shook me and told me to go home!"

Jessica felt so strongly that God told her not to move to Alabama, and that California was where He wanted them to be. Despite Jessica's strong feelings on returning to California, it wasn't an easy decision for the couple. For starters, Jessica and Jon had already fully committed to moving to Alabama and they didn't have a home to go back to. But after much deliberation and prayer, they decided to trust the Lord and they returned to California. It's important not to miss the point of this little story. God told Jessica to go back to California, knowing that she would be suspended just five months later. Looking back on everything, it's hard to come to any conclusion other than God was orchestrating the situation and preparing both Jessica and Jon for the trial with Jessica's school district.

Jessica's Advice

In my interview with Jessica, she explained that, through all her trials and conflicts, it's as if her and her husband's faith had quadrupled! Whenever we go through a conflict or challenge in life, there are always lessons we can take away from the experience. Here are some of the things Jessica learned from her experience.

* There were times when Jessica didn't know what to do and she couldn't see a clear path forward. But time and again, God provided an answer and made a way when there seemed to be no way. These experiences reaffirmed just how trustworthy, reliable, and faithful God is. Jessica learned to activate her faith because she knew, through experience, that God cannot fail; she

began to see God in new ways, and her eyes were opened to how He could move in any situation.

♦ After Jessica's second meeting, when she was given her list of directives, God didn't give Jessica an immediate answer as to what she should do; Jessica wanted to hear from God, but she kept coming up empty. She could've made her own decision, which probably would've led to her quitting her job, but she needed God's guidance first. Through this experience, Jessica learned that we must be intentional about taking time to seek God. His instructions don't just fall into our lap; we must ask, seek, and knock. "Ask, and it will be given to you; seek, and you will find; knock, and it will be opened to you" (Matthew 7:7).

♦ During this time, Jessica also received advice from friends and family. It's natural and normal for friends and loved ones to care about your situation and to want to help you through a difficult time; that's understandable. But Jessica learned that instructions and advice, even advice from fellow Christians, must be measured against the Word of God. If what we're hearing from friends, family, even from preachers behind the pulpit, doesn't agree with the Word of God, then we shouldn't accept it. Christians are not exempt from giving bad advice, even though it's well-meaning and sincere. It's imperative that we hear from God for ourselves and that we only accept advice that lines up with the Bible; we must trust God's Word and not man's word.

♦ Jessica has faced many difficulties in her life: a rough childhood, a move to Alabama that didn't work out, and of course her work conflict. And as is often the case, when we go through a trial we tend to focus on our problems and our eyes are drawn away from the Lord; Jessica was not immune to this tendency. But she's learned throughout her life, especially in the last few years, that we must focus on eternal things, and not earthly things; and we must be obedient to God's Word and allow Him to move in our lives. Jessica said, "If you will just follow God and allow

Him to move, He will use you. What looks like suffering and
sacrificing, can become a mountaintop!"

Jessica was a teacher and a coach, but her story is universal; it
applies to every believer. We're all living in a sinful world, we
all experience difficult and confusing situations, we all face
persecution and consequences for our faith, and we all have the
assurance that God will never leave us or forsake us. To take a bit
of advice from Jessica: if we will take time to seek God and allow
Him to move in our life, He will use us. My hope is that you find
inspiration in Jessica's story and that you're encouraged to take your
own stand on God's Word, as He leads you.

Application

Jessica's perspective as a parent really hits home for me, because
as I explain in my first book, I never forgot the reasons why my
parents decided to homeschool my siblings and me — to give us
an education rooted in God's Word. Jessica knew the example she
would set for her children would impact the rest of their lives,
and it certainly will. It's no small thing. This is another universal
element of Jessica's story.

These are real problems everyone can relate to, especially
parents. Simply being a Christian doesn't exempt you from the
real world. But the beauty of being a Christian is that we have
a relationship with God Almighty, the Creator. We have access
to Him through the Holy Spirit, and we can go to Him with
our every need and request. This was the difference maker for
Jessica, as it has been the difference maker for untold multitudes
throughout time.

Even though Jessica was fired, her courage to stand on God's
Word was greater than the fear of persecution. She didn't shrivel
up and hide or compromise her morals; she faced the fire and
came through the other side. And because of her obedience to

God's Word, Jessica's story has become an inspiration and source of strength for teachers and parents around the country.

I'm inspired to know that there are people like Jessica out there — hard-working, family-oriented, courageous Christians who are completely sold out to serving God. I'm also encouraged to know that God was with Jessica and her family every step of the way; He was never caught off-guard, He was never surprised by anything, He was always in control. And if we place ourselves in His hands as willing vessels, He can protect us the whole way through. And that inspires me to be ready and willing to take my own stand.

chapter three

Dietrich Bonhoeffer

In the 1920s, Germans were reeling from WWI, the country lacked stability, and the German church had grown weak. Adolf Hitler was a young politician who projected the strength most Germans were looking for, and in 1933 he became Germany's chancellor. But as the dark cloud of Nazism began to settle over Germany, a prominent German theologian named Dietrich Bonhoeffer began preaching on the evils of Nazism and the Church's need for revival. The paths of these two men — Hitler and Bonhoeffer — were bound to cross in the crucible of spiritual warfare: Hitler was determined to eradicate the Jews, while Bonhoeffer was pointing the nation back to God. Little did Bonhoeffer know that his devotion to God would lead him to become a spy in a plot to assassinate Hitler, a role that ultimately cost Bonhoeffer his life.

Bonhoeffer's story emphasizes two very important biblical truths:

♦ We must seek God's will for our own life.

♦ We must be obedient to God's Word and live out our faith.

Those messages, or themes, are not only present in Bonhoeffer's story, but in every story in this book.

Bonhoeffer's Parents

Dietrich Bonhoeffer was born on February 4, 1906, in Breslau, Germany. His father, Karl, was a physician, and his mother, Paula, was a teacher. Bonhoeffer was born in the middle of his seven siblings, but he was always known as the strong and chivalrous protector of the bunch. He had quite an impressive family heritage. On either side could be found doctors, lawyers, pastors, judges, professors, council members, mayors, musicians, artists, and even another famous theologian — Bonhoeffer's great-grandfather Karl August von Hase.[1]

The Bonhoeffer children were raised in a beautiful home, which consisted of three floors, multiple fireplaces and chimneys, a large balcony, a screened porch, and a garden; it was such a large home that it required a full-time staff to maintain it. The Bonhoeffer children experienced a typical childhood full of climbing trees, digging holes, and playing outside. One particularly unique feature of the Bonhoeffer home was their family schoolhouse on the second floor, where their mother was the teacher. The Bonhoeffer children benefitted greatly from the wisdom of their mother, who placed no trust in the German public schools and their Prussian educational methods. She was of the mindset that her children were the most vulnerable and impressionable in their earliest years and that she, as their mother, was best suited not only to be their caregiver and nurturer, but to be their educator as well. To that I say, amen!

The Bonhoeffer children received an education that was rooted in God's Word, though, to be fair, their father was not a professing Christian. As the chair of psychiatry and neurology in Berlin, Karl Bonhoeffer relied on a more scientific approach to life and is better described as agnostic. The Bonhoeffer children's biblical foundation came from Paula, whose brother, father, and

---

1. Eric Metaxas, *Bonhoeffer: Pastor, Prophet, Martyr, Spy* (Nashville, TN: Thomas Nelson, 2010).

grandfather were all theologians.[2] In addition to learning the Bible at their home school, the Bonhoeffer children held daily devotionals and sang hymns throughout the day, and Paula preferred to read Bible stories to the children straight from the Bible, as opposed to using illustrated children's books.

The Bonhoeffers were not very traditional in their Christian faith. For example, they rarely attended church because they found most churches to be lifeless, which is to say the pastors and their congregants were paying lip service to God but were not living out God's Word. So, instead of practicing a dry and lifeless religion, the Bonhoeffer children were taught to have a living faith, or a faith that impacted the way they acted and lived. The idea of "living faith" came from a man named Count Zinzendorf, whose teachings were foundational for the Bonhoeffers. He emphasized reading the Bible and doing devotions at home, both of which were instrumental in Dietrich's life; but to Zinzendorf, faith was more about a personal, transformational relationship with God, as opposed to just a mental assent to doctrine.[3]

Without a doubt, Bonhoeffer's parents had a great impact on his life. His father taught him to use logic and to respect others, while his mother taught him to be selfless and to help those in need. Bonhoeffer's career would be defined by his ability to apply his father's logical mind to his mother's love of theology. He balanced these two approaches masterfully as a theologian and a preacher.[4]

Bonhoeffer's Siblings

The eight Bonhoeffer children formed a brilliant and formidable group. One of Dietrich's brothers, Klaus, became a top lawyer at the German airline Lufthansa and another brother, Karl-Friedrich, was a distinguished scientist who worked with Alfred Einstein and was partly responsible for splitting the atom.[5] The Bonhoeffer siblings

2. Ibid., p. 14.
3. Ibid., p. 12.
4. Ibid., p. 15.
5. Ibid., p. 38.

inherited their father's critical and scientific mind, meaning everything was met with a challenge, a question, or a critique. They were expected to give much thought to ideas before forming opinions, and only after logic was applied could their opinions be justified. There was a benefit to this gauntlet of critique, because if your ideas could withstand the fortifying wave of questioning from the Bonhoeffers, then you really had something special. It was a type of refining process that had been perfected and honed by the Bonhoeffer children through their upbringing and education at home.[6] It would prove to be an impeccable preparation for Dietrich's future as a theologian and preacher.

Application -

Paula Bonhoeffer was ahead of her time as a homeschooling advocate. She did not trust the public schools or their Prussian methods (which were foundational for our American public education system), and she felt very strongly that homeschooling was the only option for her young children, especially when it came to their biblical worldview. I can't help but love her.

The big idea, though, is that the values parents decide to teach their children are extremely important; it's a truth that cannot be overstated. There was quite a large gap between Karl and Paula Bonhoeffer's religious beliefs, but in a way, it's similar to many families today; who among us has a perfect family? Through God's grace, Dietrich was able to balance the lessons and values he learned from both parents and apply them to his ministry; he was unique in this regard. This goes to show that only God can use our unique characteristics, upbringing, and experiences, and weave them into something of use — including in our own lives.

The benefit of this type of upbringing was, at least in part, that the Bonhoeffers learned to think deeply and to challenge not only the opinions and conclusions of others, but also their own. How many of us can explain why we believe what we believe?

6. Ibid., p. 37.

How many of us can intelligently discuss the reasons why we take stands against ungodliness? Before we stand up with courage against something, it's important that we've first taken time, not only to seek God, but to think deeply about the issue to the point we can offer an opposing view that makes sense.

You may not have siblings, but even so you probably have friends and family to contend with. And contending doesn't have to be a bad thing if it's contending for the Faith (Jude 1:3). The Bonhoeffers challenged each other constantly, but it never resulted in bitterness, distrust, or resentment; their process was always one of refinement, where the individual being challenged only came out stronger. It's important to relate to Bonhoeffer and his family, though each person will relate in different ways. And like most people, Bonhoeffer's early life was all a preparation for his later life.

Bonhoeffer Becomes a Theologian (1920s)

Bonhoeffer's love of theology came from his mother, and when he was just 13 years old, he knew he wanted to study theology. His family, however, was not entirely supportive of his decision. His siblings tried to convince him that theology denied scientific facts, that the Church was lifeless, and that pursuing theology would be futile. His parents thought that, since he was a gifted pianist, perhaps he should stay in Berlin to pursue his musical talent. Their fear was Bonhoeffer would become just another lifeless Christian who could quote the Bible up and down, but whose heart was unchanged. They wanted Dietrich to live his Christian faith, not just read and write about it. But, despite the wishes of his own family, Bonhoeffer continued with his pursuit of theology. This would become a recurring theme throughout his life: no matter what others said or did to discourage him, Bonhoeffer remained committed to the path God had laid out for him.

In 1923, at the age of 17, Bonhoeffer left his home in Berlin to study in Tubingen, Germany. During this time, it was normal to leave home to

study for a few years, and then to switch schools every few years after
that; so, while Bonhoeffer did leave home, it was understood that he
would eventually return.[7] Tubingen was a bit of a family school for
the Bonhoeffers. Karl Bonhoeffer went there, along with several of
the Bonhoeffer siblings. While at Tubingen, Bonhoeffer joined the
same fraternity as his father, the Igel fraternity, which was known for
wearing hats made from hedgehog pelts ("Igel" means hedgehog).
Bonhoeffer found the fraternity's patriotism appealing but he had
no tolerance for being pressured to drink alcohol; he was much too
confident to succumb to peer pressure. But Bonhoeffer was not a
stiff and unrelatable person; he had thick skin, but he also liked to
joke around. For example, one of his fellow fraternity members later
wrote about Bonhoeffer and described him as extremely secure,
self-confident, not vain, a tough young man with a "sharp nose for
essentials and a determination to get to the bottom of things ...
capable of subtly testing people and who had a great deal of humor."[8]
By this description, we can understand that Bonhoeffer was a serious,
measured, and controlled man, well-suited to be a theologian; but at
the same time, he was humble and light-hearted — impressive,
yet regular.

The summer after Tubingen, 1924, Bonhoeffer visited Rome to
learn the culture. His great-grandfather, the famous theologian,
had visited Rome many times and Bonhoeffer wanted to follow
in his footsteps. While in Rome, Bonhoeffer took special notice
of the artwork and architecture, such as the Sistine Chapel and
Michelangelo's *Jonah*, which was his favorite artwork. This trip
proved to be pivotal in Bonhoeffer's life as his view of the Church
came into focus while attending a mass at St. Peter's in Rome.

At this mass, Bonhoeffer saw people of all colors and backgrounds
participating as members of the clergy, dressed in robes, and
involved in the service. He heard the beautiful songs ring out
from the choir and suddenly he realized this is what the Church

---

7. Ibid., p. 42.
8. Ibid., p. 43.

should look like! His father's logic met his mother's theology and he thought, "If there are Christians all over the world (which there are) and each one is a member of the Body of Christ (which they are) then the Church, in that sense, is universal; Germany and Rome did not hold exclusive rights to Christianity." To Bonhoeffer, this was a revelation! This fresh view of the Church was so radically different from traditional German churches and the increasingly popular push for the Nazi German national church.[9]

> "Ideas had consequences, and this idea, now just budding, would flower in his opposition to the National Socialists and bear fruit in his involvement in the conspiracy to kill a human being."[10]

Bonhoeffer's new understanding of the Church harkened back to what he learned from his parents. His father taught him to use a scientist's mind, which does not rely on feelings or emotions; and his mother taught him to serve others, as Christ did, and to put faith into action. Balancing these two approaches, Bonhoeffer seemed to conclude that since the Church consisted of believers from around the globe, then the tribalism or national church organization didn't make sense; it didn't align with the Bible. And since Bonhoeffer was convinced of this belief, he was obligated to live it out. This shows how Bonhoeffer's parents played a huge role in his spiritual formation and that the values he learned as a child did not depart in adulthood. In fact, they drove his life's work.

Bonhoeffer left Rome and returned to his theological studies at Berlin University, bringing with him a well-formed theology and a new passion to live it out. He chose Berlin in part because it was his home, but mostly because the theological faculty at Berlin was world-renown. There, Bonhoeffer had the opportunity to study under legendary theologians and even debate them. But remember, Dietrich grew up in the Bonhoeffer home where every thought and word that proceeded from one's mouth was scrutinized — in that

---

9. Ibid., p. 53.
10. Ibid., p. 54.

sense, he was born for this. Soon, Bonhoeffer gained the reputation of being an independent thinker with a remarkable talent for analyzing Scripture. But to Bonhoeffer, as was impressed upon him from childhood, a well-formed theology was useless if it couldn't be communicated effectively to others.

> "If one couldn't communicate the most profound ideas about God and the Bible to children, something was amiss."[11]

Bonhoeffer was an intellectual genius, but he was also a gifted communicator — two skills that usually don't mix. He was able to take the most complicated biblical subjects and explain them in such a way that a child could understand. Bonhoeffer put his gifts and talents to use by accepting an invitation to teach a Sunday school class for youth.

> "This offer seemed to bring to fruition a wish that had grown stronger and stronger over the past few years and months, namely, to stand on my own feet for a longer period completely outside my previous circle of acquaintances."[12]

Application

Before he became a preacher, Bonhoeffer had to know what he believed, and he had to be absolutely convinced of it — his trip to Rome and his studies at Berlin helped to solidify his convictions, and the experiences prepared him for his coming role as a preacher.

We also need to know what we believe and why we believe it. Do we take advantage of the many opportunities we have all around us to learn and grow in faith and knowledge? We are commanded to *"Love the Lord your God with all your heart, with all your soul, and with all your mind" (Matthew 22:37).*

---

11. Ibid., p. 64.
12. Ibid., p. 68.

Bonhoeffer was described as brilliant, a genius, and remarkable, but he was never so full of himself that he didn't have time to teach Sunday school to children. It's important that we don't take lightly the opportunities God gives us to grow in our faith, no matter how small or insignificant they may seem.

Bonhoeffer Becomes a Pastor (late 1920s)

Occasionally, Bonhoeffer was given the opportunity to preach from behind the pulpit and he began to wonder if preaching was his path forward, instead of theology. His parents urged him to stay in academia, but Bonhoeffer felt himself being pulled to the pulpit. So, after earning his doctorate in 1927, Bonhoeffer moved to Spain and became the assistant pastor at a church in Barcelona. Once again, he chose the unpopular path, not out of rebellion to his parents, but out of obedience to God.

Bonhoeffer's first impression of Barcelona was not good. His living quarters were old and rickety, hardly anyone spoke German, his lead pastor was unambitious, and the youth were materialistic and lazy from having not lived through the first world war. Everyone seemed to waste their days sitting at cafes, eating oysters, and talking about menial things. But Bonhoeffer didn't insult the people or look down on them, he didn't mock or chide them, and he didn't complain. He refused to be a gloomy Christian and was resolved to be an effective leader in the church. So, to improve his interactions with the people in Barcelona, Bonhoeffer decided to join a German club, a tennis club, and he even played the piano in the Chorale Society. His plan was to learn how to relate to different people from different backgrounds; he was willing to get his hands dirty and his feet wet, and it paid off. Bonhoeffer grew to appreciate Barcelona and found that it was, at least, a lively place.

At church, Bonhoeffer was responsible for overseeing the children's services, sharing pastoral duties, and occasionally filling in to preach. On his first Sunday, he had only one student in Sunday school, but he kept a good attitude, and he kept communicating with the congregants. The next Sunday he had 15 students and the Sunday after that he had 30 students. From that time on, he had at least 30 students every week. The children had almost no knowledge of the Scriptures, but Bonhoeffer saw this as a positive because, as he said, "They have not yet been tainted in any respect by the church."[13] Then, when the lead pastor went on vacation, Bonhoeffer preached his first sermon, which was on "salvation by grace through faith." Then he preached another sermon, then an Easter sermon, then another Sunday sermon, then another, and another, and every time Bonhoeffer preached, church attendance grew. Bonhoeffer put great effort into being able to communicate with the people, and his preaching especially resonated with youth who had been neglected by the church. He knew how to reach young people and connect with them, and before the year ended, Bonhoeffer had effectively become the church's lead pastor.

Despite the success of his ministry, one of the most impactful experiences for Bonhoeffer was his work with a local charity. Through this work, he was exposed to people from different backgrounds, mostly those who lived outside the prestigious university walls and away from the warmth of a loving mother and father. Every morning, Bonhoeffer would speak with the homeless, the victimized, the impoverished, and even outright criminals. For the first time in his life, his heart was pricked by the sufferings of the poor and the outcasts. He realized this is what a living faith looked like. Bonhoeffer explained this experience below:

> "All in all, they are people who feel homeless in both senses, and who begin to thaw when one speaks to them with kindness — real people; I can only say that I have gained the impression that it is just these people who are much more under grace than under wrath, and that it is the Christian world which is more under wrath than grace."[14]

---

13. Ibid., p. 77.
14. Ibid., p. 79.

Moved with compassion for the lost, Bonhoeffer decided to offer more lectures on the Bible, sharing his new burden for those in need and those who had been forgotten. He realized that, for the most part, the church wasn't reaching the youth or the poor, so he was determined to do all he could, while he could. To address this issue, Bonhoeffer decided to conduct one lecture per month, for three months, all on the concept of biblical Christianity.

> "The religion of Christ is not a tidbit after one's bread; on the contrary, it is the bread or it is nothing. People should at least understand and concede this if they call themselves Christian."[15]

Bonhoeffer encouraged listeners to give their all to Christ, to let His light shine, and not to hide His light in a box in their heart. Bonhoeffer felt that the Church was limiting Christ and keeping Him from congregations by not inviting them to be transformed by His Spirit. As Bonhoeffer's year in Barcelona came to an end, he had reached many souls with the good news of Jesus Christ, and he felt his pastoral feet had been firmly planted beneath him.

In 1930, Bonhoeffer traveled to America to visit the seminaries and churches in New York City, and to learn of the theological condition of the Americans. Much like Barcelona, Bonhoeffer was not impressed with the state of Christianity in America. He noted that the seminary students knew nothing of theology, and that preachers preached on everything under the sun except what really mattered. He wrote:

> "In New York, they preach about virtually everything; only one thing is not addressed, or is addressed so rarely that I have as yet been unable to hear it, namely, the gospel of Jesus Christ, the cross, sin and forgiveness, death and life."[16]

Bonhoeffer did, however, find life in the Black churches. He discovered how the Black population in America had been

---

15. Ibid., p. 69.
16. Ibid., p. 106.

ravaged by the terrible sin of racism. He was shocked to learn that Black people were required to ride on separate railcars, use separate bathrooms, and were often refused service at restaurants and businesses — and that was just the beginning of the issue. Bonhoeffer attended a Baptist church in Harlem where the pastor was a Black man — the son of slaves — and most of the congregation was black. Bonhoeffer was moved by the power of the praise and worship service and noted how the pastor preached like a revival preacher, full of the Holy Ghost and fire.[17] Bonhoeffer concluded that the only churches in America that had any power were the ones with a history of suffering. He saw a truer form of Christianity in those Christians, just as he did with the poor and outcasts in Barcelona.

Bonhoeffer's trip to America had a lasting impact on his life and ministry. He saw a church that was full of life, full of people who had been touched by God, and he gained a better understanding of how to reach the downtrodden. Plus, he witnessed racial discrimination for the first time, which would help prepare him to teach and preach against the coming persecution of the Jews in Germany.

Bonhoeffer's Spiritual Awakening (early 1930s)

Bonhoeffer left America a changed man. It's as if his upbringing, studies, travels, preaching, and teaching had finally culminated in a spiritual awakening. He later wrote how radically his faith had changed during this time.

"Something happened, something that has changed and transformed my life to the present day. For the first time I discovered the Bible.... Since then, everything has changed.... The revival of the Church and of the ministry became my supreme

---

17. Ibid. ,p. 108.

concern.... My calling is quite clear to me. What God will make of it I do not know.... I must follow the path."[18]

Bonhoeffer was talking about the ability of God's Word to not only change the way you think, but to change the way you live. It's more than just knowing something in your head, it's about having something in your heart. Bonhoeffer had experienced a revival within his own heart, and now his calling was to help bring a revival to the Church. He was totally sold out to God, and he was willing to go wherever God wanted him to go. So, he went home to Germany.

Application -------------------------------

Dietrich Bonhoeffer came from an educated and accomplished family, he had a love for the things of God, and he was a gifted preacher and theologian. By all accounts, he was smack dab in the middle of the straight and narrow path. As God moved on Bonhoeffer's heart, he often found himself standing alone on the most important issues. But once Bonhoeffer settled an issue in his mind and in his heart, he was determined to see the matter through to the end, even if it meant going alone.

Similarly, you may feel accomplished in your life and ministry; you've worked hard to get where you are, and you're doing good work. But maybe God has recently grabbed your attention, and He's caused you to look in a new direction. But you've become so established in your current position that this new thing may seem like anything but God.

God's path isn't all sunshine and rainbows. When Bonhoeffer's first impression of Barcelona wasn't great, he didn't quit. He refocused and remembered why he was there in the first place — to serve God. Even though things weren't perfect, or even comfortable, Bonhoeffer was ready to learn from God everywhere he went. In Rome he saw the true Church; in Barcelona he

18. Ibid., p. 123.

developed a burden for the lost and neglected; in America he learned to speak out against injustices.

Similarly, your environment may be cold and unpleasant, but it's important to see things through God's eyes and to keep a good attitude. That cold and unpleasant place may be the very reason you're there. Maybe, just maybe, God intends to use you as salt and light in a lifeless and dark place; it's not always about you.

 **BABYLON** The German church of the 1920s and 1930s was full of patriotic Germans who were eager to support their new leader. My use of "German church" refers to the mainstream Protestant Christian churches in Germany at that time. Unfortunately, the German church's eagerness to support Hitler blinded them to the wickedness of his initiatives. It's not that the Nazis and the German church leaders held the same beliefs, but the German church seemed to be more concerned with pleasing man than with pleasing God.

Germany, believe it or not, had been a strong Christian nation leading up to Hitler's reign of terror. The impact of Martin Luther's German Bible and the Protestant movement were beyond enormous there, immeasurable even. With his Ninety-five Theses, Martin Luther nailed a claim against the corrupt Church of his day and in doing so he inspired a return to obedience to God's Word. Luther's leadership gave life to the Protestant Reformation and Lutheranism, which was once dominant in Germany. But the German church of Bonhoeffer's day had become complacent and comfortable, which is to say it had become lazy and backslidden. Many of the professing Christians in Germany were Christian in name only and not in practice, which is exactly what Bonhoeffer's mother, Paula, had warned against.

Bonhoeffer's Warning to the Church

In 1932, while living in Berlin, Bonhoeffer was asked to preach a special sermon on Reformation Sunday, commemorating Martin Luther's contributions to the Reformation. What most Germans expected to be a celebration turned out to be a rebuke and a call to repentance. Bonhoeffer began the sermon with a chilling passage from Revelation 2:4–5, which says:

"Nevertheless, I have this against you, that you have left your first love. Remember therefore from where you have fallen; repent and do the first works, or else I will come to you quickly and remove your lampstand from its place — unless you repent."

Bonhoeffer warned the congregation that the German church was either dying or dead already. He minced no words when he told them, "We do not see that this Church is no longer the Church of Luther."[19] He spoke directly to the people sitting in front of him and told them they were spiritually blind. Bonhoeffer knew, as did Jeremiah in the Old Testament, that his message would most likely be rejected. He also knew it was his role, as a servant of Jesus Christ and as a minister of the gospel, to preach the entirety of God's Word. His primary job was to be obedient to God, not to control the outcomes; what happened after that was out of his hands.

Then in January of 1933, Adolf Hitler became Germany's chancellor. Germans hoped Hitler would stabilize the country and church leaders hoped he would strengthen the church. Neither of those things happened.

Bonhoeffer hit his stride as a preacher just as Hitler came to power — the timing of these two events is significant. Bonhoeffer was able to clearly identify both the dangers of Nazism and the dangers of the German church aligning with Nazism; he also had the theological understanding and the communication skills to effectively address each issue. Bonhoeffer was the right man, with

---

19. Ibid. p. 122.

the right message, at the right time. The only problem was he lived under Hitler's Third Reich, which meant he was muzzled. This is why Hitler's Nazi regime represents Bonhoeffer's Babylon.

Application -------------------------------

You may live and work in an environment where you're trying to help, trying to speak out, or just trying to be heard, but nothing is getting through; you may as well be talking to a wall. You might also feel totally alone, insignificant, discouraged, and demoralized. But we will see in the next section how God created avenues for Bonhoeffer to deliver his message despite restrictions from the Nazi propaganda machine. And if God made a way for Bonhoeffer, He can make a way for you as well.

Bonhoeffer preached a hard message to the church in Berlin, knowing it wouldn't be popular or well received, but his duty was to be obedient to God, not to be popular. Bonhoeffer shows us in this section that even while we need help ourselves, we can still be used by God to bless others. But we can't just wait for the perfect conditions to come along before we act; if we do that then nothing will ever get done.

It's important to remember that we are engaged in spiritual warfare and warfare is never easy, it's never comfortable, but what we are fighting for is worth so much more than ease and comfort. Life is very hard and messy, and we need lots of help; and sometimes God asks us to go through an uncomfortable situation just to help someone else — this is our place on the "battlefield." There is a cost that comes with surrendering to the Lord, but the cost is worth it. If we don't speak up, then the truth cannot be heard. And if the truth is not heard, then the light cannot shine in the darkness. And if the light doesn't shine in the darkness, then darkness will continue to dominate. So, ask yourself: am I okay with being uncomfortable or unpopular? Is what I'm fighting for worth the fight? The answer is "yes!"

Nebuchadnezzar

Hitler represents Nebuchadnezzar in Bonhoeffer's story. He was the leader of the Nazi party, and he controlled the armed forces that carried out the horrors of the Holocaust. German church leaders also represent Nebuchadnezzar because many of them either aligned with Hitler or swore an outright allegiance to him. Bonhoeffer was both a Christian and a German; he loved the Church, and he loved his country, but his strong biblical convictions compelled him to stand in opposition to these two groups. In this section, you'll see a heavyweight bout between Hitler's evil laws and Bonhoeffer's biblical responses.

Biblical Leadership vs. Worldly Leadership (mid-1930s)

In the years leading up to Hitler's reign, Bonhoeffer made two distinct observations: Germans were desperately searching for a strong leader, and Hitler's popularity was growing among young Germans. Then, just a few days after Hitler was installed, Bonhoeffer gave a speech over the radio to discuss the problems with the Fuhrer Principle (Hitler's rule) as it concerned young Germans; this speech would mark the beginning of Bonhoeffer's public opposition to Hitler's extreme Nazi beliefs. The word *fuhrer* simply means "the leader." There's nothing wrong with leadership, but simply being a leader doesn't make one virtuous. For example, Jesus was a righteous leader, because He always submitted to the will of God the Father. In contrast, under the Fuhrer Principle, Hitler made himself the supreme leader and a god, which led to wickedness and idolatry.

In Bonhoeffer's radio speech, he hoped to draw a distinction between biblical leadership and worldly leadership. Bonhoeffer argued the problem with having a fuhrer of Hitler's type is that it eventually leads to idol worship — man worshiping man. Bonhoeffer believed that God was the governing authority on earth and that man was to worship God, not other men. With these statements, Bonhoeffer directly challenged Hitler's authority, and shortly into his speech, Bonhoeffer was stopped and shut down. It's unclear whether this stoppage was Nazi censorship or just coincidence. Either way, Bonhoeffer didn't panic; he simply pivoted and published his full speech in the newspaper. In fact, his speech received so much attention that he was asked to give a lecture on it at Berlin University.[20]

Whether directed at Hitler or not, Bonhoeffer's statements were very bold. Not only did he challenge Hitler's authority, but he also challenged German church leaders to support his biblical stance. Bonhoeffer's bold speech threw a wrench in the spokes of the church leaders who supported Hitler, which didn't make him many friends. But the truth needed to be spoken and Bonhoeffer spoke the truth with courage and conviction.

Application --

Bonhoeffer was one of the few Christians in Germany capable of delivering such a powerful message against Hitler's leadership. God had equipped him and given him the platform to speak. But if Bonhoeffer hadn't spoken out, then he would've given up all that God had prepared for him. Similarly, there may come a time when you're the only person in the room willing to defend God's Word, and if you don't speak out, then it's possible that you will give up all that God has prepared for you. God gives each of us unique assignments, or "platforms." For some, it may be teaching little children in Sunday school classes. For others, it may be speaking at a school board meeting, in a church, or in a youth group meeting. But that's the thing with inspiration and courage — it's contagious. One of the major themes in this book is encouraging yourself in the Lord and strengthening those around you. When you act on your faith and take courageous stands on

---

20. Ibid., p. 139.

God's Word, there may be an earthly cost to serving God, but the benefits are eternal.

Hitler's Radical Laws

Hitler's minister of propaganda was a man named Joseph Goebbels, who paved the way for the persecution of the Jews in Germany. Goebbels used the press to portray Jews as rats, inferior, impure, and deserving of death. Goebbels even recorded his thoughts on Christianity in his personal diary. Keep in mind, this is the man who had control of Germany's press for over a decade. He said:

> "The insanity of the Christian doctrine of redemption really doesn't fit at all into our time…. It is simply incomprehensible how anybody can consider the Christian doctrine of redemption as a guide for the difficult life of today."[21]

Within days of Hitler becoming Germany's chancellor, Goebbels devised a plan to help the Nazis quickly install a totalitarian government with Hitler as their leader. The plan was simple: create a crisis and stoke fear among the people, then implement a radical law under the guise of providing safety. It started by burning down the main government building, the Reichstag; and since Goebbels had control of the press, the Communists were blamed for burning the Reichstag and accused of attacking the German government. The crisis created enough panic among the people that they were willing to allow the government to implement temporary safety laws. Goebbels' plan to strengthen the Nazi regime by making the people less free worked like a charm. Some examples of these radical "temporary safety laws" are given below.

- *The Reichstag Fire Edict* was signed one day after the Reichstag fire. This edict was a knee-jerk response to the fear and threat of communism; it suspended individual liberties and civil rights in exchange for government protection.

---

21. Ibid., p. 166.

- *The Enabling Act* was signed days after the Reichstag Fire Edict; it allowed Hitler to pass laws quickly and unilaterally, effectively making Hitler a dictator. Immediately after this act was signed, Nazi stormtroopers began paroling the streets; political opponents were then hunted down, beaten, arrested, or killed; there was a boycott on all Jewish stores in Germany; citizens lost their right to assemble; and none of it was covered in the press because the press was completely controlled by Goebbels and his Nazi propaganda machine.

- *The Aryan Paragraph* went into effect on April 7, 1933, and was the third radical policy enacted within the first 70 days of Hitler's reign. Under the Aryan Paragraph, Jews were banned from government jobs and positions in the ministry. These rules were presented by the Nazi propaganda machine as the "Restoration of the Civil Service."[22]

- *The Nuremberg Laws of 1935,* also known as the Nuremberg Race Laws, were sold to the public as protecting and preserving the purity and superiority of the German race, or what Hitler called the Aryan race; these laws placed Jews as the lowest, most inferior race. As such, Jews were prohibited from marrying Germans, employing German females, or holding German citizenship. By writing Jewish discrimination into law, the groundwork was being laid for the horrors of the Holocaust.

Application -

This section speaks to the importance of defending our civil rights and preserving our individual liberties; this applies to all Americans. Goebbels used a tactic of creating a crisis to stoke fear, and then exploiting that fear to enact radical laws. This tactic is neither new, nor extinct; it is very much alive today. If we fail to know our history, then we are in danger of repeating it. Remember what Dr. Marlene McMillan said in the introduction of this book: "What you don't know about history will hurt you."[23] In fact, every story in this book deals with this very problem — ungodly leaders issuing evil decrees to bring people into bondage.

Bonhoeffer's Responses to Hitler

Nebuchadnezzar always gives an evil decree. And just as the three young Hebrew men had to decide if they would bow to the golden idol, Bonhoeffer had to decide if he would comply with Hitler's evil laws. He chose not to comply, and instead published essays responding to them using the Bible and theology. Below are a few of Bonhoeffer's biblically sound responses to Hitler's edicts.

The Church and the Jewish Question was Bonhoeffer's response to Hitler's Aryan Paragraph. With this essay, Bonhoeffer presented church leaders with three scriptural duties of the Church. First, the Church was obligated to question the actions of the state; second, the Church was obligated to help any victims of the state (including non-Christians); and third, the Church was obligated to work against the state if the state was perpetrating evil. In the middle of Bonhoeffer's presentation, some church leaders got up and left, while virtually every other leader felt overwhelmed at the prospect of helping the Jews, given Hitler's anti-Jewish laws. Again, Bonhoeffer stood alone and said:

> "It is rather the task of Christian preaching to say: here is the church, where Jew and German stand together under the Word of God, here is the proof whether a church is still the church or not."[24]

The Aryan Clause in the Church was a pamphlet Bonhoeffer wrote and distributed explaining that, scripturally, Jews should have the same rights as Germans in the clergy and that anyone who was not willing to work with the Jews was not part of the true Church. This

---

23. McMillan, Marlene. *Mountains of Deceit.* (Forth Worth: Liberty View Media, 2011), 13.
24. Ibid., p. 150.

was a bold stance for Bonhoeffer to take, considering that Reinhold Krause, the leader of the Berlin German Christians (a group loyal to Hitler), demanded that German Christians distance themselves from their "Jewishness," that they swear allegiance to Hitler, and that they remove all Jews from their churches.

The Confessing Church and the Ecumenical Movement was an essay Bonhoeffer wrote in 1935, just before Hitler's Race Laws went into effect. In this essay, Bonhoeffer discussed the necessity for the Church to act on its biblical beliefs by condemning Hitler's anti-Semitic laws and the Nazi regime. Going back to his childhood, Bonhoeffer had no patience for professing Christians who made a mental assent to God's Word while refusing to act on their faith; Bonhoeffer would call this "cheap grace."[25] Bonhoeffer remembered the devastating effects of Jim Crow laws in the American south, and he, with this essay, was crying out for the Church to change course before it was too late.

The Prayerbook of the Bible was an essay Bonhoeffer published in 1940, at the beginning of Hitler's military advances throughout Europe. The essay examined the Book of Psalms and reiterated God's love for the Jewish people — which was an open rebuke of the Nazis. Additionally, Bonhoeffer urged Christians to return to the model prayers of the Bible, namely those prayed by Christ Himself. It paints quite a picture. Here, at the beginning of WWII, Bonhoeffer's boldness was on display as he issued biblical corrections to both the Nazis and the Church.[26]

"Every word of God is pure; He is a shield to those who put their trust in Him" (Proverbs 30:5).

Application -

Thankfully, we have God's Word as a shield, and we are not left defenseless when confronted with the fiery darts of spiritual

---

25. Ibid., p. 279.
26. Ibid., p. 368.

warfare (Ephesians 6:16). And because God's Word is pure and true, we don't have to rely on our own abilities and our own strength to stand against such intense persecution. Bonhoeffer's writings were public, which means he wasn't hiding his unpopular beliefs from peers, friends, family, or even the Nazis — everything he said was out in the open. Bonhoeffer here shows both obedience and courage by simply presenting God's Word despite the consequences. When we face a conflict or persecution in our lives, God may ask us to take a public stance in front of our peers, friends, family, and even those who wish to do us harm. But before we act, it's imperative that we begin by seeking God's guidance; only after we hear from God can we know when and how to put our faith into action. But what if we don't have enough time to seek God for an answer? What if we only have a moment to respond? I address these important questions in chapter 10.

Hitler's View of Christianity

Hitler was a politician and often positioned himself as a friend of Christianity by claiming to be a Christian himself. He made such claims early in his career while trying to present himself as a moral German, but privately he regularly mocked Christians and Christianity. Hitler once stated:

> "It's been our misfortune to have the wrong religion. Why didn't we have the religion of the Japanese, who regard sacrifice for the Fatherland as the highest good? The Mohammedan religion too would have been much more compatible to us than Christianity. Why did it have to be Christianity with its meekness and flabbiness?"[27]

For the most part, Hitler's pandering to the Germans worked, and his anti-Jewish laws crept into the German church. Many German church leaders felt obligated to support their new fuhrer, so with hopes of appeasing Hitler, they decided to go along with his anti-Jewish plans and policies. While they may not have agreed with Hitler morally,

27. Ibid., p. 165.

their hope was to get on his good side and eventually change his mind. To show the level of support Hitler eventually received from the German church, I'll quote the German Reich Church's celebratory publication on Hitler's 50th birthday in 1939:

> "We celebrate with jubilation our Fuhrer's fiftieth birthday. In him God has given the German people a real miracle worker.... Let our thanks be to the resolute and inflexible will not to disappoint ... our Fuhrer and the great historic hour."[28]

Hitler's goal was to eventually replace Germany's traditional Protestant Christian churches with a National Reich Church. For years and years, Hitler spoke publicly in favor of Christianity, while secretly, behind closed doors, he plotted to remove Christianity and replace it with a new religion where he was a god; and when the timing was right, Hitler intended to make the transition. Part of Hitler's plan was to remove all Bibles from churches and replace them with his book *Mein Kampf*, which was to be regarded as the greatest of all documents. He also planned to replace all crosses with swastikas; then, he planned to ban the Bible from being printed altogether.[29] The shocking thing is that many German churches, due to spiritual blindness, supported Hitler's efforts for over a decade.

Application -

There is a real enemy ruling in our world, the devil, who seeks to steal, to kill, and to destroy. The world is not a neutral place where opposing sides can live in harmony; rather, there are evil forces in this world that seek to destroy our faith and destroy our lives. Ephesians 6:12 says it this way, "For we wrestle not against flesh and blood, but against principalities, against powers, against the rulers of the darkness of this world, against spiritual wickedness in high places." Yes, Christ has overcome this world,

---

28. Metaxas, *Bonhoeffer: Pastor, Prophet, Martyr, Spy*, p. 325.
29. Ibid., p. 171.

and we can rest assured that our victory is secure in Him; but we should not be ignorant to the evil that is present in our world, so that we can guard our hearts and protect our faith (Proverbs 4:14–23). This is a war between light and darkness, between good and evil, and we know there is an enemy seeking to destroy us. The enemy we are fighting is clever, evil, and has one goal — our destruction. We are all engaged in this war. How do you suggest choosing the side you're on?

Bonhoeffer's Powerful Preaching (late 1930s)

Since Hitler's regime had total control of the German press, it was almost impossible to know what was truly happening inside Germany and German churches. Only the churches that were aligned with Hitler were free to hold regular services, while free thinkers like Bonhoeffer were heavily censored or silenced altogether. Bonhoeffer developed the reputation of being a troublemaker among certain church leaders, so a plan was schemed to keep Bonhoeffer quiet by sending him to preach in London. But what those German church leaders failed to consider was that Bonhoeffer would not be censored in London, which meant he could freely preach the truth of God's Word and he could teach the truth about the Nazis. He was in a perfect position to point the church back to the Bible while simultaneously subverting Hitler's Nazi regime. He was such an effective preacher and teacher that he caused thousands of Christians throughout Europe to join two prominent anti-Nazi groups: the Pastor's Emergency League and the Confessing Church. Both organizations supported Jewish clergy and opposed Nazi efforts to infiltrate the Protestant Church. By boldly proclaiming sound doctrine, Bonhoeffer was able to spearhead an effective opposition movement against Hitler's Nazi regime.

> "I believe that the Bible alone is the answer to all our questions, and that we need only to ask repeatedly and a little humbly, in order to receive the answer.... That is because in the Bible God speaks to us.... Only if we

seek Him, will He answer us.... If God determines where
He is to be found, then it will be in a place which is not
immediately pleasing to my nature and which is not at
all congenial to me. This place is the Cross of Christ. And
whomever would find Him must go to the foot of the
Cross, as the Sermon on the Mount commands. This is not
according to our nature at all, it is entirely contrary to it.
But this is the message of the Bible, not only in the New but
also in the Old Testament."[30]

—Dietrich Bonhoeffer in a letter to his brother-in-law in 1936

Bonhoeffer played a key role in the establishment of the Confessing
Church, which promoted a return to sound doctrine, and rejected
the anti-Semitism that was being promulgated in Germany and
German churches. Bonhoeffer's view was that the Confessing
Church wasn't a new Church, neither was it a piece of the Church
that had broken away. To Bonhoeffer, the Confessing Church
was part of the true Church, because it was committed to sound
doctrine. Really, the German Reich church had broken away from
the true Church and was obligated to return to the Word of God.
In just a short time, England became the only country in Europe
where thousands of German Christians took a stand against the
Nazis — all because of Bonhoeffer.

However, there was a cost to Bonhoeffer's effective leadership. The
Gestapo became aware of Bonhoeffer's ministry and began hunting
down and arresting members of the Confessing Church. Then,
in January of 1938, Bonhoeffer and 30 members of the Confessing
Church were arrested by the Gestapo; and after being interrogated
and released, Bonhoeffer was banned from Berlin.

Application ------------------------------

There will be real and formidable adversaries in our life, and
taking a courageous stand against them will be extremely

---

30. Ibid.

difficult. But what would've happened if Bonhoeffer had succumbed to cowardice? What if he had stopped preaching sound doctrine or stopped teaching against Nazism? Would there have been such a strong movement against Hitler's Nazi regime? Would the horrors of the Holocaust have been even worse?

The point is, Bonhoeffer felt called by God to preach, to teach, to say what he was saying, and to write what he was writing. Similarly, God has something for each of us to do and it's our responsibility to find out what that is and respond accordingly, no matter the consequence. But being obedient doesn't mean we'll be trouble free; Bonhoeffer was obedient, and he got arrested and banned from his hometown. Courage means acting despite the presence of fear. There's a price to pay for following the Lord; it's different for each of us, but it's a price we must be willing to pay. There is also a price to pay for not following the Lord, a price none of us can afford to pay.

Nebuchadnezzar's Final Decree: Allegiance to Hitler

On April 20, 1938 — Hitler's birthday — the head of the Reich church, Friedrich Werner, published new marching orders for every pastor in Germany. They were to swear allegiance to Hitler or be dismissed from the Church.

> "Anyone who is called to a spiritual office is to affirm his loyal duty with the following oath: "I swear that I will be faithful and obedient to Adolf Hitler, the Fuhrer of the German Reich and people, that I will conscientiously observe the laws and carry out the duties of my office, so help me God."...Anyone who refuses to take the oath of allegiance is to be dismissed."[31]

This is the exact situation Bonhoeffer had been warning of and working to prevent. Five years earlier in his 1933 radio speech,

---

31. Ibid., p. 308.

Bonhoeffer reasoned from Scripture that the Fuhrer Principle would eventually lead to the fuhrer becoming held up by the church as "god," and that's exactly what happened.

The head of the German Reich church demanded faithfulness and obedience, not to God, but to Hitler; and if anyone refused, they were dismissed from the church. Many German pastors simply lost heart in the fight against Hitler, or lacked the courage to stand up for what was right, and they gave in to the oath of allegiance. As a result, the German church suffered even more fractures. With this oath, Germany had reached the point of no return, having essentially made Hitler their god.

Bonhoeffer Seeks God's Will

By the end of 1938, Hitler's Gestapo began destroying Jewish homes and Jewish businesses, and Jews were being publicly beaten and eventually killed;[32] this was taking place while many German church leaders were swearing allegiance to Hitler. Then, as WWII was imminent, Hitler enacted a military draft and Bonhoeffer's number was up. Bonhoeffer was a patriot who loved his country, but he would not serve Hitler's evil Nazi regime. Either by divine intervention or by pure happenstance, there was a behind-the-scenes effort to get Bonhoeffer out of Germany and away from Hitler's draft, and He was given a job offer to preach and teach in New York City; this was his ticket out of Hitler's army. Despite the appeal of safety in America, Bonhoeffer experienced an internal struggle about what to do. Eventually, though, Bonhoeffer accepted the job and moved to New York.

As soon as Bonhoeffer reached America, he found himself longing for his home country. He thought he was following God's leading by coming to America, but now he felt the pull to go back to Germany, especially because he didn't want to abandon his countrymen to fight a war without him. Bonhoeffer wasn't sure if

---

32. Ibid., p. 315.

he was standing in God's will or his own. Did he make a mistake in coming to America? Is this what God really wanted for him?

After wrestling with the issue, Bonhoeffer finally received the clarity he was looking for, but only after spending time in prayer and fellowship with God — that's the key. Ideals, values, and principles can only take a person so far. At some point you must hear from God for yourself.

> "I have had the time to think and to pray about my situation and that of my nation and to have God's will for me clarified. I have come to the conclusion that I have made a mistake in coming to America. I must live through this difficult period of our national history with the Christian people of Germany. I shall have no right to participate in the reconstruction of Christian life in Germany after the war if I do not share in the trials of this time with my people."[33]

Since childhood, Bonhoeffer did his best to walk the path of obedience to God's Word, and he often paid a price for doing so. Bonhoeffer rejected Hitler's race laws, and he rebuked the segment of the German church that swore allegiance to Hitler. When it came to the Christian's responsibility to act, Bonhoeffer wrote:

> "Mere waiting and looking on is not Christian behavior. The Christian is called to sympathy and action, not in the first place by his own sufferings, but by the sufferings of his brethren, for whose sake Christ suffered."[34]

Basically, Bonhoeffer was saying, "If Jesus loved the Jews so much that He died for them, then shouldn't followers of Jesus also love the Jews?" It's one thing to believe it, it's another thing to live it. This is the struggle that all Christians will face at one time or another: Do I stand and fight, or do I bury my head in the sand? Do I stand on God's

---

33. Ibid., p. 321.
34. Ibid., p. 447.

Word, no matter the consequences, or do I bow to the pressure and let darkness roll over me? It's not that big of a deal, right?

Application ------------------------------

Every Christian, at one time or another, is required to follow a rule or a policy that contradicts the Word of God; knowing what's right and doing what's right can be very difficult. The difference is we have the privilege of going directly to God in prayer; we can hear directly from God on what path to follow. Hebrews 4:16 says, "Let us therefore come boldly to the throne of grace, that we may obtain mercy and find grace to help in time of need." Bonhoeffer said he made a mistake, as we all do, and it was only remedied when he went back to the throne of grace, back to God. We have this same access to our Heavenly Father, but it's up to us to choose to take advantage of it.

Bonhoeffer Becomes a Spy

"Being a Christian is less about cautiously avoiding sin than about courageously and actively doing God's will."[35]

—Eric Metaxas' explanation of the life of Bonhoeffer

Bonhoeffer realized he had to join the fight. So, in July of 1939, Bonhoeffer left the safety of America for the fiery furnace in Germany. He wasn't exactly sure what God wanted him to do in Germany, but he felt an overwhelming obligation to act. It was no longer acceptable to Bonhoeffer to be the person speaking the truth while taking no action; it was time for Bonhoeffer to get his own hands dirty. Eberhard Bethge, Bonhoeffer's close friend, fellow pastor, and fellow theologian wrote this:

"Bonhoeffer introduced us in 1935 to the problem of what we today call political resistance.... The escalating persecution of the Jews generated an increasingly hostile

---

35. Metaxas, Eric. *Bonhoeffer: Pastor, prophet, martyr, spy.* (Nashville: Thomas Nelson, 2010), 486.

situation, especially for Bonhoeffer himself. We now realize that mere confession, no matter how courageous, inescapably meant complicity with the murders."[36]

Bonhoeffer had developed many connections over his career across Germany and Europe, and with WWII on the doorstep, Bonhoeffer was invited to join a German Military Intelligence group called the *Abwehr*. The Gestapo and the Abwehr were both German military groups; they weren't exactly friends, but they weren't exactly enemies either. For Bonhoeffer, the benefit of joining the Abwehr was the ability to gain access to military intelligence while staying somewhat insulated from the Gestapo. Bonhoeffer's involvement in the Abwehr required him to have a secret role under the guise of being a traveling preacher. He was to travel to strategic locations to preach, and as he traveled, he would pass along sensitive information about a plot to assassinate Hitler.[37]

Bonhoeffer — the theologian, preacher, and Sunday school teacher — became a spy in a plot to assassinate Adolf Hitler.

Bonhoeffer's new affiliation with the Abwehr placed him in a bit of a tug-of-war between the church and the Gestapo. Some leaders in the church questioned whether Bonhoeffer had flipped and become a supporter of Hitler, and the Gestapo questioned whether he was really a preacher or a spy pretending to be a preacher. If church leaders found out Bonhoeffer was involved in a plot to kill Hitler, they would most likely condemn his actions. And if the Gestapo found out Bonhoeffer was a spy, he would be arrested and killed. Bonhoeffer gave his theological defense of his high-stakes involvement in the Abwehr.

> "Who stands fast? Only the man whose final standard is
> not his reason, his principles, his conscience, his freedom,
> or his virtue, but who is ready to sacrifice all this when he
> is called to obedient and responsible action in faith and in

---

36. Ibid., p. 358.
37. Ibid., p. 370.

exclusive allegiance to God — the responsible man, who tries to make his whole life an answer to the question and call of God."[38]

Bonhoeffer was convinced he was where God wanted him to be. However, his role as a conspirator, though done out of obedience to God, secured his place in Hitler's fiery furnace.

Application

Bonhoeffer never imagined he would be involved in a plot to kill Hitler. Murder is a sin; but this was war and Hitler was slaughtering people, gassing them to death, and burning their bodies in his death camps. Regardless of the situation, the example given by Bonhoeffer was to seek God, obey Him, and to put faith into action.

God might take us places we never thought we'd go, and He might ask us to do things we never thought we'd do. In the years and decades leading up to WWII, Bonhoeffer had many seemingly insignificant experiences as he traveled, worked, taught, and preached. But as life went on and Bonhoeffer gained new experiences, God used those experiences to prepare him for what was ahead. When Bonhoeffer became a spy, he was able to rely on the many connections and acquaintances he had made in Germany and London earlier in his life.

The point is this: if we are living our lives in faith and obedience to God, then He will lead us step-by-step into the place He has for us; it's entirely His doing and not at all our own doing. And if along the way you begin to feel like what you're doing is insignificant or unimportant, remind yourself that nothing escapes God's eye — no detail is too small for God. In Bonhoeffer's story — and every story in this book — God demonstrates His marvelous ability to weave together our seemingly meaningless and inconsequential experiences into

---

38. Ibid., p. 446.

something of eternal value. If we're intentionally seeking Him and acting in obedience, we should not discredit the work God has for us, no matter how small or unpleasant it may seem. God knows how to use our previous life experiences in unexpected ways in the future.

FIERY FURNACE

"We will have to move through a very deep valley, I believe much deeper than we can sense now, before we will be able to ascend the other side again." — Dietrich Bonhoeffer[39]

In September of 1939, hardly a month after Bonhoeffer's return from America, Hitler invaded Poland, and WWII officially began. In a matter of months, Germany took control of Poland, Holland, Belgium, France, Albania, Greece, Yugoslavia, and North Africa. Bonhoeffer received information about Nazi troops were forcing prisoners in Poland to do labor and then murdering them afterword. This soon turned into the mass murder of civilians.

It's difficult to comprehend just how fast the evil escalated under Hitler's Nazi regime. For example, 1933 is when restrictions were first placed on German Jews, but in less than one decade, Hitler's military began the mass murder of Jews, Polish civilians, those with disabilities, and even German citizens who resisted his authority. Hitler's regime streamlined its process of mass killings through its euthanasia program, which started in medical vans that were used to gas prisoners to death. This process evolved into the use of gas chambers and crematoriums in Nazi death camps. Quite literally, this was the fiery furnace Bonhoeffer faced.

---

39. Ibid., p. 374.

Application

In 2019, my wife and I traveled to Poland and visited the Auschwitz Concentration Camp. We saw the train tracks where prisoners arrived; we stood on the platform where the selection process took place; we walked through the barracks where the prisoners were kept; we saw the furnaces where dead bodies were burned; we saw the pile of shoes that had been taken off the feet of little children; we saw the mountain of human hair that had been used to make clothing. Our tour guide — whose family members had died in this camp — ended our tour with this haunting statement.

> "Auschwitz was preserved so others could learn from what happened here. But, as I look at society today, I realize we've learned nothing."

As soon as we left the tour, I realized it had been one of the most impactful experiences of my life. I started the day wanting to take pictures so I could remember the details. But after just a few minutes, I was hit with a palpable sense of the level of evil and the level of suffering that had taken place there, and I stopped taking pictures. I'm embarrassed I took any pictures at all. I gained a new understanding of evil. Now, I realize this evil is precisely what Bonhoeffer was trying to prevent. And we face such evil in various measures every single day.

Attempts to Kill Hitler

On March 13, 1943, Hitler flew to the eastern front to visit German troops. Through a series of harrowing events, and strategically placed German double agents (including from Bonhoeffer's group, the Abwehr), a bomb made its way onto Hitler's plane. But when the detonator was pressed and the mechanism fired, nothing happened — the bomb was a dud. The plane landed, and Hitler walked away none the wiser.

Soon after, Bonhoeffer participated in a second assassination attempt, only this time two bombs were to be carried in an overcoat worn by a German major. The major was to give a presentation to Hitler on weaponry, during which time the bombs in his overcoat would be detonated, killing Hitler and the major himself. For whatever reason, both bombs had a 10-minute fuse, so they would have to be armed ahead of time in anticipation of Hitler's location during the presentation. When the time came, the German major activated the bombs and proceeded with his weaponry presentation. Amazingly, everything was going according to plan. Then, in the middle of the weaponry presentation, Hitler abruptly and inexplicably ended the presentation and walked out of the room. The major quickly went into the nearest restroom and defused the bombs with seconds to spare. Hitler escaped death yet again.[40]

Bonhoeffer Arrested

On April 5, 1943, just days after the failed assassination attempts on Hitler, the Gestapo arrived at Bonhoeffer's home. Bonhoeffer was arrested, escorted to a black Mercedes, and taken to Tegel military prison in Berlin. He took nothing with him except his Bible. Bonhoeffer did not expect to be in prison very long, assuming a trial would quickly take place and he would soon be released. But for six months, no warrant was presented for his arrest and Bonhoeffer remained in prison. Oddly enough, Bonhoeffer eventually learned that his arrest wasn't because of his involvement in the plot to kill Hitler, but because of his involvement in a rescue operation to save seven Jews from Hitler's concentration camps. The Gestapo perceived this rescue operation as a money laundering scheme.[41]

---

40. Ibid., p. 431.
41. Ibid., p. 441.

Maria von Wedemeyer

In the middle of his involvement in the conspiracy to kill Hitler —
before he was arrested and imprisoned — Bonhoeffer fell in love.
In the fall of 1942, Bonhoeffer traveled to northern Germany to visit
an old friend named Ruth. While visiting Ruth, Bonhoeffer met
Maria von Wedemeyer, Ruth's granddaughter. In fact, Bonhoeffer
had been friends with Ruth and Maria's family for years, but his
only memory of Maria was of her as a child. But time had passed,
and Maria had become a woman. This time the two seemed to have
quite the chemistry.

Nothing came of the relationship for several months, mostly
because the two lived hours away from each other. They did,
however, write letters to keep in touch, and Maria's grandmother
pushed the envelope by suggesting the two get married. Maria's
mother was not a fan of the relationship, given Bonhoeffer was
36 years old and Maria was just 18. Plus, Bonhoeffer was an
established theologian and preacher while Maria was just out of
high school; the two seemed to be on different paths. If that wasn't
cause enough for concern, there was still the issue of Bonhoeffer
being a spy. It's safe to say that neither party wanted to rush into
anything.

Despite the many doubts and concerns, Bonhoeffer and Maria
were smitten with each other, only neither wanted to be the first to
admit it. Thanks to the persistence of Maria's grandmother, the two
were forced to address the elephant in the room — marriage. Maria
was the first to express her feelings in a letter she wrote on January
10, 1943. She gushed to Bonhoeffer:

> "Today I can say Yes to you from my entire, joyful heart."[42]

One week later, on January 17, 1943, Bonhoeffer returned the
sentiment and made their engagement official. He said:

---

42. Ibid., p. 420.

"I sense and am overwhelmed by the awareness that a gift without equal has been given me.... Let us now be and become happy in each other."[43]

The two declared their intentions to marry, though Maria requested a lengthy engagement due to upcoming obligations with the Red Cross. Bonhoeffer happily agreed to wait. It's unclear if Bonhoeffer told Maria about his involvement in the plot to kill Hitler, but to keep Maria and her family safe, it seemed best to keep their engagement a secret. That decision proved to be wise, as Bonhoeffer's arrest took place just a few months later. The two spent their entire engagement separated, with Bonhoeffer stuck in Nazi prisons.

Bonhoeffer and Maria kept in touch while he was in Tegel prison. He was able to receive visitors, as well as write and receive letters — though all letters were screened by German guards. Even so, Bonhoeffer and Maria wrote many letters to each other over the next two years, and the letters have since been compiled and published in a book titled, *Love Letters from Cell 92*. Most of the letters read like love letters, even love poems, showcasing the deep admiration Bonhoeffer and Maria shared for each other. The letters also give a sense of their humanity, their struggles, their hopes, and even their imperfections. However, through it all, never lost was their mutual love of God and their submission to His will for their life together. Sadly, Bonhoeffer never left the Nazi prisons, and he was executed before the two could marry.

Bonhoeffer Imprisoned for Two Years and Martyred

While at Tegel, Bonhoeffer learned of the *Valkyrie* operation, which was another attempt to kill Hitler, along with Heinrich Himmler (Hitler's top military officer), and Joseph Goebbels.[44] On July 20, 1944, the Valkyrie operation was executed almost perfectly, and a

43. Ibid., p. 420-421.
44. Ibid., p. 481.

bomb was successfully detonated just a few feet from Hitler. Again, inexplicably, Hitler survived the blast. This failed assassination attempt enraged and emboldened Hitler, who viewed his survival as proof that his leadership was a divine appointment. Hitler, now knowing there were conspirators among his top officers, began to hunt down and kill every conspirator in Germany — this spelled the end for Bonhoeffer.

In the days following the failed Valkyrie operation, Bonhoeffer learned that many of his fellow conspirators had been arrested, tortured for information, and killed along with their families; these were Bonhoeffer's friends. Bonhoeffer knew he would likely be interrogated, tortured, and killed at any time; if he was ever going to make it out of prison, he had to do something now — so he plotted a prison-break.[45] However, Bonhoeffer's escape efforts kept getting delayed for various reasons, the biggest reason being that his escape would've caused the Gestapo to interrogate and possibly torture his family for information — a consequence Bonhoeffer was unwilling to accept. So, Bonhoeffer gave up his plans of escaping.

In total, Bonhoeffer spent 18 months at Tegel prison before being transferred to a Gestapo prison in Berlin called *Prinz-Albrecht-Strasse*. He was kept in an underground cell, as were some of his fellow conspirators, including his brother-in-law. Most prisoners were tortured by the Gestapo. During this time, Allied forces were making their way through Europe and the area around Bonhoeffer's prison in Berlin had been attacked. The war would soon be over, and Hitler's days were numbered, but the Nazis still had prisons and death camps full of prisoners to deal with. Whenever the Allies got closer, the Nazis would either transfer prisoners to another location or kill them.

By February of 1945, Bonhoeffer had been in prison for two years. He never imagined he would be in prison so long. After four months in Prinz-Albrecht-Strasse, Bonhoeffer was transferred to the Nazi concentration camp at *Buchenwald*. Transferred with

---

45. Ibid., p. 493.

Bonhoeffer was a former chancellor, an admiral, generals, and a judge. It's hard to imagine such a distinguished group of men being packed up like cattle and shipped to their death. Buchenwald was a place of death — that was its function — but Bonhoeffer never lost hope that the war would end or someone on the outside would advocate for his release. After two months in Buchenwald, Allied forces continued to close in and Bonhoeffer was transferred yet again; only this time, he was taken to *Flossenburg,* an extermination camp.

Bonhoeffer arrived at Flossenburg only to learn that the prison was at capacity, and that he and his fellow prisoners would have to be taken elsewhere. Finally, after an arduous and disorganized transport, Bonhoeffer arrived at a town called Schonberg. The town had been ravaged by the war, and supplies were so scarce that a schoolhouse was being used as a makeshift prison. Bonhoeffer shared his cell (which was just a classroom) with others, and on his final morning in Schonberg — which happened to be a Sunday — Bonhoeffer's cellmates asked him to preach a Sunday sermon. Bonhoeffer obliged and preached from Isaiah 53:5 and 1 Peter 1:3.

"But He was wounded for our transgressions, He was bruised for our iniquities; the chastisement for our peace was upon Him, and by His stripes we are healed" (Isaiah 53:5).

"Blessed be the God and Father of our Lord Jesus Christ, who according to His abundant mercy has begotten us again to a living hope through the resurrection of Jesus Christ from the dead" (1 Peter 1:3).

These details were recorded by one of Bonhoeffer's cellmates who survived the war and wrote about his experiences with Bonhoeffer. Moments after he gave his closing prayer, German guards opened the door and called for Bonhoeffer. This could only mean that it was his turn to be executed. As he left his Sunday sermon, Bonhoeffer's last words were:

"This is the end. For me the beginning of life."[46]

46. Ibid., p. 528.

Bonhoeffer left the schoolhouse prison and was immediately taken back to the extermination camp at Flossenburg. It turns out that, through many arrests, interrogations, and tortures, Hitler's henchmen had confiscated diaries and documents of Bonhoeffer's fellow conspirators. More than likely, Hitler read these diaries and documents, he saw Bonhoeffer's name, and he ordered Bonhoeffer to be killed — that's most likely why Bonhoeffer was taken from his Sunday sermon and executed.[47] Bonhoeffer spent approximately 12 hours at Flossenburg before he was murdered. On April 9, 1945, Dietrich Bonhoeffer was hung to death, and his body was thrown on a pile of bodies and burned. The Allies marched on Flossenburg two weeks later, Hitler killed himself a week after that, and the war ended four months after that.

Application

We might wonder whether it was God's will for Bonhoeffer to engage in an assassination attempt to kill Hitler, and that might lead to questions. Why would God allow someone so clearly dedicated to serving Him to die such a tragic death? Was Bonhoeffer really in God's will? Why does God allow Christians to suffer? Why would God allow such evil to persist? These are questions that've been asked whenever and wherever evil and suffering have existed. But in studying the Bible — and human history — we see that God has used those who were willing to suffer for Him to make the greatest impact for good. In one way or another, every hero of faith has experienced suffering. Jesus was the greatest example of all.

Bonhoeffer's journey wasn't perfect, and you could argue his death wasn't fair; some might even say Bonhoeffer's ministry wasn't worth him dying in a Nazi death camp. But for Bonhoeffer, the deciding factor was that God's Word compelled him to work against Hitler. And Bonhoeffer, desiring to be an obedient servant of Christ, was willing to lay down his own life for others. And he

---

47. Ibid., p. 529.

lived that out through his ministry — whether as a preacher, a theologian, a Sunday school teacher, or as a spy — Bonhoeffer humbled himself and submitted his life to God.

The Bible instructs us at times to show mercy (which Bonhoeffer did) and it instructs us at times to stand, fight, and destroy the enemy (which Bonhoeffer did); knowing the difference can be difficult. This is why we must hear from God for ourselves.

Bonhoeffer's story may seem tragic to us, but I doubt God sees it that way. God was involved in Bonhoeffer's life from the very beginning, and Bonhoeffer was in fellowship with God until the end. Bonhoeffer's perspective on life was that we must fully submit ourselves to God. Everything, including the simple joys of life and the miserable pains of death, must be given over to the Lord. For Bonhoeffer, it was all or nothing.[48] His life and story has inspired countless numbers of people to live as truly committed followers of Christ.

In this section, I'll discuss just a few ways that God was with Dietrich Bonhoeffer, not just in prison or in death, but throughout his life. Let's go chronologically.

His Parents

Bonhoeffer was a combination of attributes from both of his parents; he was a rational, measured thinker like his dad, and he was a doer of God's Word like his mom. When Hitler was elected in 1933 and began to enact his racial laws, Bonhoeffer always seemed ready to give a theologically sound response that was well thought out. He wasn't known to make snap judgments or to let his emotions get the best of him; he learned that from his father. Additionally, Bonhoeffer was constantly compelled to act on his faith, whether that meant showing kindness to a person in need

48. Ibid., p. 457.

or participating in an operation to rescue seven Jews from Nazi concentration camps. And no matter his station in life — whether as a student, a preacher, a spy, or a prisoner — Bonhoeffer was diligent in his prayer life and his daily Bible reading; he learned that from his mother.

"Train up a child in the way he should go, and when he is old he will not depart from it" (Proverbs 22:6).

The impact of Bonhoeffer's parents is a testament to the validity of God's Word; what the Bible says will happen is precisely what happened through Bonhoeffer's upbringing. He was raised to prioritize the Bible and to live out his Christian faith, and that's what happened. The disciplines that were instilled in him as a child were evident in his life as a theologian, as a preacher, as a pastor, as a spy, and even as a prisoner. If Bonhoeffer's parents simply taught him to read the Bible, but never taught him to act on his beliefs, would he have become such a service-minded preacher? Would he have stood up to backslidden congregations and warned them to return to sound doctrine? Probably not. In this way, God's Word did not return unto Him void; this is one way that God was with Bonhoeffer.

Willingness to Stand Alone

For a true follower of Jesus, obedience and standing alone often go together. Bonhoeffer likened himself to the prophet Jeremiah in the sense that God gave them both a specific message which they knew would not be well received; in fact, both men knew their message would be rejected. But Bonhoeffer understood the Christian's obligation is to obey God; it's not the role of the Christian to worry about what happens next or to try to control the outcomes. Bonhoeffer's obedience to God was evident throughout his life. Here are some examples:

◆ He committed to studying theology despite pressure from his family not to.

+ He shifted his focus from theology to preaching despite his parents' wishes.

+ He spoke out against Hitler's Fuhrer Principle even though he knew it would be unpopular.

+ He refused to align with the German Reich church and its required allegiance to Hitler even though it made him an enemy of the Nazi regime.

+ He defended the Jews and rebuked church leaders for their compliance with Hitler's Race Laws even though he was ostracized for it.

+ He chose to leave the safety of America and return to Germany even though it meant he may have to fight in WWII.

+ He decided to join the Abwehr's plot to assassinate Hitler even though it put his life at risk.

+ He was committed to fervent prayer even as he was led to the gallows at Flossenburg.

These are just a few examples of Bonhoeffer's obedience to God's Word. These examples also demonstrate Bonhoeffer's boldness and courage to take difficult stands in the face of intense conflict. Each example is encouraging on its own, but together they tell a remarkable and awe-inspiring story. So, while Bonhoeffer did often stand alone, he was never truly alone because he was where God wanted him to be.

Ready in Season and Out of Season

"Preach the word! Be ready in season and out of season. Convince, rebuke, exhort, with all longsuffering and teaching. For the time will come when they will not endure sound doctrine, but according to their own desires, because they have itching ears, they will heap up for themselves teachers; and they will turn their ears away from the truth,

and be turned aside to fables. But you be watchful in all things, endure
afflictions, do the work of an evangelist, fulfill your ministry"
(2 Timothy 4:2-5).

"But sanctify the Lord God in your hearts, and always be ready to give
a defense to everyone who asks you a reason for the hope that is in you,
with meekness and fear" (1 Peter 3:15).

God's Word instructs us to always be ready to explain why we're so
hopeful, and to preach sound doctrine — Bonhoeffer excelled at
this. Theologically, Bonhoeffer was highly regarded as a brilliant
thinker and analyzer of Scripture, but he approached his theology
with his father's scientific mind, and his mother's thoughtfulness,
intentionality, and humility. These unique characteristics helped
Bonhoeffer issue some of the most, if not the most, timely and
effective messages of his day. Here are a few examples of how
Bonhoeffer was always ready to give a biblical defense.

◆ Hitler's *Aryan Paragraph* persecuted Jews in Germany.
  Bonhoeffer responded with The Church and the Jewish
  Question, which outlined the Church's scriptural duty to
  support the Jews.

◆ When German church leaders were required to swear allegiance
  to Hitler and remove all Jews from their churches, Bonhoeffer
  responded with *The Aryan Clause in the Church* which explained
  that, scripturally, anyone who is not willing to work with the
  Jews is not part of the true Church.

◆ When Hitler's Race Laws went into effect, Bonhoeffer's essay *The*
  Confessing Church and the Ecumenical Movement instructed the
  Church to act on their biblical beliefs, and to condemn both the
  Nazi regime and Hitler's anti-Semitic laws.

◆ In the middle of WWII, while many church leaders were
  aligning with Hitler, Bonhoeffer wrote *The Prayerbook of the Bible*
  which reiterated God's love for the Jewish people and urged

Christians to return to the model prayers of the Bible. This was an open rebuke to both the Nazis and German church leaders.

Again, these are just a few of the many examples of how Bonhoeffer was always ready to give an account, to share his hope, and to preach sound doctrine. This is an easy concept to understand, but it's extremely difficult to live out. Just consider how Bonhoeffer faced pressure from all different directions — his family, his friends, his peers, the church, and the Gestapo — it's enough to make anyone want to run and hide. But this is what's so inspiring about Dietrich Bonhoeffer: he was just a man like any other man. He didn't have superpowers and he didn't like to draw attention to himself; he simply submitted to God's will and placed his life in God's hands. God did the rest.

A Living Faith

Bonhoeffer's mother taught her children to have a living faith, which means to put your faith into action. It's important to understand and believe the doctrines of the Bible, but it's also important to allow those beliefs to change the way you live your life. One of the most powerful testimonies of Bonhoeffer's living faith came from the camp doctor (if you can imagine such a thing) who oversaw Bonhoeffer's execution at Flossenburg. Years later, the doctor described Bonhoeffer's final moments.

> "On the morning of that day ... I saw Pastor Bonhoeffer, before taking off his prison garb, kneeling on the floor praying fervently to his God. I was most deeply moved by the way this lovable man prayed, so devout and so certain that God heard his prayer. At the place of execution, he again said a short prayer and then climbed the steps to the gallows, brave and composed.... In the almost fifty years that I worked as a doctor, I have hardly ever seen a man die so entirely submissive to the will of God."[49]

---

49. Ibid., p. 532.

"Entirely submissive to the will of God." That's how Bonhoeffer was described by this camp doctor. Certainly, there are many examples of how Bonhoeffer modeled Christlike behaviors — volunteering in Barcelona, rescuing Jews from the Nazis, preaching the Gospel — but the account given by this camp doctor is arguably the most impactful example of how Bonhoeffer's faith impacted the way he lived.

It Matters What You Believe

What if most Germans in the 1920s, '30s and '40s believed what Bonhoeffer believed? And what if, instead of electing Hitler for his strength, they elected a leader who shared Bonhoeffer's biblical worldview? Would WWII have ever happened? Would the Holocaust have ever happened?

It matters what one person believes, it matters what a church believes, and it matters what a nation believes — Bonhoeffer's story proves that. The atrocities perpetrated by the Nazi regime were not evidence of a political problem or a military problem; they were evidence of a spiritual problem, which required a spiritual answer.

Bonhoeffer's entire ministry was based on sound doctrine. But when Bonhoeffer's knowledge of God's Word made its way into his heart, a living faith sprang up that not only changed his understanding of the Bible, but it changed the way he lived his life. Imagine how different things would've been if the German church leaders, instead of swearing allegiance to Hitler, had lived out what the Bible says and let God's Word change their hearts and lives. The German church disagreed with almost all of Hitler's radical laws and policies, but Nazism was able to grow and infiltrate German churches because so few church leaders lived out their faith — and they lacked the courage to stand for God's Word.

This is emblematic of the spiritual problem I'm talking about. Bonhoeffer, along with every other person featured in this book, stood in the minority. Their message, their beliefs, their convictions were not popular and few people, if any, stood with them. Sadly, this is why cowardice is so common and courage is so rare — though both are contagious. In short, the answer to every spiritual problem is Jesus, *"the Way, the Truth, and the Life" (John 14:6).*

Application

Try to place yourself in Bonhoeffer's shoes and connect to his life experiences, the struggles along with the victories. Bonhoeffer was 39 years old when he died, but he lived enough to fill two lifetimes. A life lived in obedience to God is an eventful life that's full of both great challenges and great joys. However, there's no greater joy than being in the presence of God.

"Where can I go from Your Spirit? Or where can I flee from Your presence? If I ascend into heaven, You are there; if I make my bed in hell, behold, You are there" (Psalm 139:7–8).

I heard it said once in a sermon, and rightly so, "One moment in the presence of God can do more for you than one thousand sermons." Ultimately, that's the message I hope the readers of this book take with them. Yes, the major themes of this book are having courage to stand on God's Word, obedience, seeking God, and hearing from God — but these are all different ways of saying the same thing: I want to be in God's presence. Being in God's presence not only brings us peace, but it can bring strength, it can bring healing, it can bring forgiveness, it can bring joy, and it can definitely bring courage.

chapter four

The Apostle Paul

Other than Jesus, the Apostle Paul is arguably the most well known and most influential figure in the New Testament. Before his conversion, Paul (then Saul) led the persecution against the early church and even consented to the stoning and death of Stephen (Acts 8:1). But after his conversion on the road to Damascus, Paul wrote more New Testament books than any other author, and he did more to spread the Gospel than perhaps any other human in history. Paul is a marvelous example of just how far God can bring even the most heinous sinner.

But this story isn't about any of that. This story — which comes from the Book of Acts — is about relationships, the pain of saying goodbye to those we love, and obeying God no matter how bleak things look. This story compels us to lay aside our own desires and our comforts, to obey God's call, even if it means walking into one fiery furnace after another. In this chapter, I'll be dealing with a lesser-known story in Paul's life: his gut-wrenching farewell to his beloved elders at Ephesus.

In this story, the Holy Spirit called Paul to go preach in Jerusalem. But Paul knew that meant he would be attacked and mistreated for what he said. Not only that, but Paul's obedience also meant he had to leave his home, leave his friends, and leave his Christian community. He would have to leave the life he built and risk watching it all be undone and perverted in his absence. Paul let go of all these things, not because there's anything wrong with having a home or caring about friends, but because the unique and specific call God placed on his life required him to do so.

Application –

This story hits home for me because in 2021 — after 13 years of teaching and coaching — I felt led by God to leave the career I loved. Being a teacher and a coach was a natural fit for me and I saw it as my ministry in life. In my role as a teacher, I wanted to consistently reflect Christ and model godly attributes in front of my students, my athletes, their parents, and my colleagues. I met some of my closest friends through teaching and coaching; most of my mentors were teachers and coaches; it's how I made a living, and I was getting good at it. My whole life revolved around teaching and coaching. That's why I relate to this story of Paul's, because walking away from the job I loved, the people I knew so well, and the foundations I had labored to establish, was an excruciating decision.

This story also makes me think of my parents. In the early 1990s, 30 years before I made the decision to leave my teaching career, my parents made their own difficult decision to withdraw my siblings and me from the public school system and to homeschool us instead. Many other parents at that time considered my parents to be "weird" or "on the fringe," but what I remember most about my parents' decision to homeschool is that they prioritized the Word of God. And 30 years later, when I faced my own difficult decision, I continued to follow my parents' example and chose to go God's way. Who has been such an example in your life?

 BABYLON

Paul was always within an arm's reach of spiritual persecution, whether he was persecuting Christians as Saul, or whether he was being persecuted as Paul. Later in his ministry, Paul described the many persecutions he endured.

"In labors more abundant, in stripes above measure, in prisons more frequently, in deaths often. From the Jews five times I received forty stripes minus one. Three times I was beaten with rods; once I was stoned; three times I was shipwrecked; a night and a day I have been in the deep; in journeys often, in perils of waters, in perils of robbers, in perils of my own countrymen, in perils of the Gentiles, in perils in the city, in perils in the wilderness, in perils in the sea, in perils among false brethren; in weariness and toil, in sleeplessness often, in hunger and thirst, in fastings often, in cold and nakedness—besides the other things, what comes upon me daily: my deep concern for all the churches" (2 Corinthians 11:23–28).

It's safe to say that Paul was no stranger to hardship. But why was that the case for such a great man of God? One reason Paul was persecuted so frequently is because he was obedient to God's call on his life. Much of Paul's ministry was spent addressing errors within the Church — which often meant rebuking his peers to their face — and he endured persecution because of it (2 Timothy 4:2); this was the life Paul lived. Paul's obedience and persecution were directly related, in fact, together they represent Paul's Babylon in this story.

Application -

Typically, when we obey God and do the right thing, we expect a positive outcome — this was not the norm for Paul. Over and over, Paul obeyed God's call on his life, which was to spread the message of "Jesus Christ and Him crucified" (1 Corinthians 2:2), and Paul was consistently persecuted for it; we will be persecuted in our lives as well. Despite all that, the detail I hope to inspire you with is how Paul remained obedient to God's call, even though he knew it would lead to persecution. He was willing to leave his dear friends, his home, and all the comforts of a beautiful city, knowing he would be persecuted.

Can you relate? How many times have you done the right thing and were still mistreated? Would you stand up and do the right thing if it meant leaving your friends, your home, and your livelihood, all while knowing you'd be mistreated on top of it? That's a hard sell, but that may be what God asks us to do at times. For Paul, it seems like that's what God asked him to do over and over again. But as I hope to point out in this chapter, Paul was willing to respond to God's call no matter the cost; this is the inspiring and encouraging message.

In this story, the Holy Spirit tells Paul to leave his roots in Ephesus and to go to Jerusalem where he will be persecuted. Even though the Holy Spirit's message is clear, Paul is urged by his dear friends — who were fellow Christians — to disobey God's call and instead choose safety and comfort. The pressure to disobey God to avoid pain and to please others represents Paul's Nebuchadnezzar.

Ephesus

The city of Ephesus was a wealthy and prominent city, and it was the closest thing to a home that Paul had. Compared to all the suffering Paul had already experienced (as explained in the previous section), Ephesus was practically a five-star resort. Paul spent close to three years preaching and teaching in Ephesus, which is the most time he spent in any single location during his entire ministry. And while Paul's preaching caused some in the city to hate him, it also caused many to believe on the Lord Jesus (Acts 19:18).

The impact of Paul's ministry in Ephesus is immeasurable, and he also built many meaningful and lifelong relationships there. Given that much of Paul's time in Ephesus was spent in synagogues and lecture halls, it makes sense that his closest friends would've been the elders of the church — those who sat under his leadership, supported his ministry, and strengthened the church. Paul and the elders went through many spiritual battles together, they shared many stories of faith, and together they witnessed many of God's wonderful works. There was a mutual respect, admiration, and love between them. And when you're in the middle of a spiritual Babylon, which Paul continually was, having the support of close friends and a community can mean the world.

At the peak of Paul's ministry in Ephesus, the Bible says, *"the Word of the Lord grew mightily and prevailed" (Acts 19:20)*. By all accounts, Paul's ministry was thriving in this great city. But just as Paul was beginning to see the fruits of his labor, the Holy Spirit called him away to Jerusalem — a city that was hostile toward Paul's ministry (Acts 19:21). God instructed him to leave, to travel to a city where he would certainly be persecuted. This was a pivotal moment for Paul's ministry.

Application -------------------------------

The spiritual conflict presented here is in the decision to obey God or not. It's a decision that must be made on the front end, no matter what happens afterward. Because we are so distant from this story, it's easy for us to lose sight of the price Paul paid for his decision to obey God. In this case, obeying God meant guaranteed persecution and suffering. But Paul decided from the start that, no matter the cost, he was going to live his life in surrender to God. In fact, Jesus foretold Paul's suffering to Ananias when He said, *"I will show him how many things he must suffer for My name's sake" (Acts 9:16)*.

It's not wrong to build relationships or to plant roots wherever God has placed you, that's what we're supposed to do. Paul was excellent at building and maintaining relationships — these are good things. But it's wrong when these good things cause us to lose sight of God's priorities. Jesus said, *"He who loves father or mother more than Me is not worthy of Me. And he who loves son or daughter more than Me is not worthy of Me. And he who does not take his cross and follow after Me is not worthy of Me" (Matthew 10:37–38).* The life we are called to live is not a self-centered life, but a Cross-centered life.

Are we expecting to suffer? If we don't make the decision up front that we're willing to suffer to follow God's leading, we'll be easily discouraged when we're inevitably blindsided. It's a good thing to ask ourselves if our faith is securely placed in the work Christ did at the Cross, and to think about what that means in our lives.

Paul's Farewell

Paul wasted no time in answering the Holy Spirit's call to go to Jerusalem; in fact, the Bible says Paul was *"hurrying to be at Jerusalem" (Acts 20:16).* Even though Paul had been rooted in Ephesus for years, he knew his time there had come to an end. Paul's eagerness to go to Jerusalem meant he didn't have enough time to make a final stop in Ephesus, so Paul sent a message to the elders there and requested they make the trip to come see him. It was a lengthy trip for the elders and required them to walk at least a portion of it, but their willingness to endure this difficult journey demonstrated their love and respect for the Apostle Paul. This was an extremely important meeting for Paul and the elders because it was the last time they would ever see each other; it was Paul's farewell.

"I go bound in the spirit to Jerusalem, not knowing the things that will happen to me there, except that the Holy Spirit testifies in every city, saying that chains and tribulations await me. But none of these things

move me; nor do I count my life dear to myself, so that I may finish my race with joy, and the ministry which I received from the Lord Jesus, to testify to the gospel of the grace of God" (Acts 20:22–24).

Paul shared his heart with his dear friends and reflected on their time together in Ephesus. He recalled their daily interactions with one another, how they supported each other in their labor for the Lord, and the persecutions they endured together to serve God. Paul explained to the elders how the Holy Spirit had assigned him to Jerusalem and that persecution awaited him there. Paul gave an awe-inspiring response to the unpleasant news saying, "none of these things move me."

"And indeed, now I know that you all, among whom I have gone preaching the kingdom of God, will see my face no more" (Acts 20:25).

There is a cost to living for Jesus Christ, a cost which Paul had been paying for years, and was determined to keep paying; this time, however, the cost was more than persecution or shipwreck, but fellowship with his dear friends.

Paul's Forewarning

Paul's permanent departure wasn't the only painful part of this meeting. In the same breath as his final farewell, Paul gave a dire warning to his dear friends that as soon as he left for Jerusalem, enemies would come in his place and try to pervert the Word of God. The responsibility of standing up and defending God's Word in Ephesus would now shift from Paul to the elders.

"For I know this, that after my departure savage wolves will come in among you, not sparing the flock. Also, from among yourselves men will rise up, speaking perverse things, to draw away the disciples after themselves. Therefore, watch and remember that for three years I did not cease to warn everyone night and day with tears" (Acts 20:29–31).

This was a serious warning from Paul, spiritual warfare was coming — no doubt about it. I imagine that also would have made it incredibly difficult for Paul to leave; he had been investing in the spiritual well-being of the Church in this city for years, protecting it from evil and spiritual attacks, pouring into it every single day. And now he had to walk away from it all and trust that God and those staying behind would be able to continue to protect the church — without him.

"And when he had said these things, he knelt down and prayed with them all. Then they all wept freely, and fell on Paul's neck and kissed him, sorrowing most of all for the words which he spoke, that they would see his face no more. And they accompanied him to the ship" (Acts 20:36–38).

This was more than just a sad goodbye for Paul. There was a finality to this goodbye, and danger was implicit. There was grief mixed with gratitude, sadness mixed with love, and prayer mixed with spiritual warfare. But Paul was so faithful and so committed to being used by God however and whenever God wanted, that he was willing to set the inevitable difficulties aside so that he could gain the Lord.

Application ------------------------------

Think about how we make decisions. Do we make decisions based on the perceived outcome, or based on God's Word? Do we assume that if an outcome will be painful, that it's probably not from God? Do we assume that God will only lead us into comfortable and enjoyable situations? If we make decisions based only on how we think things may turn out, we'll continually be confused. *"He is a double-minded man, unstable in all his ways"* (James 1:8).

Paul's decision to obey God was painful, but it was also necessary. And even though he was doing the right thing, Paul's life was about to become more difficult as a result. Nowadays, when we make difficult decisions, we expect instant gratification; that wasn't always the case for Paul, neither will it always be the case for us. Paul's situation went from bad to worse, even though he was being obedient and going where God wanted him to go. Similarly, your difficult decision may lead to further difficulties, and it may even impact the people you love.

Paul knew he was walking into an unrelenting battle, and he knew the elders he was leaving behind in Ephesus would also be walking into a battle — this time without his insight and guidance. This is like a parent watching their child grow up into a young adult, and slowly being forced to loosen the grip on their life and trust God to protect them. The parent might ask themselves, "Did I teach them well enough? Are they ready to be on their own? Will they be okay?" These are all good and reasonable questions, and perhaps Paul thought the same things about the church at Ephesus. It's human and normal to be afraid in situations like this, but the bigger question is whether we will allow that fear to rule our lives, or will we be able to trust God despite that fear?

Paul Is Pressured to Disobey God

Paul parted with the elders and immediately set sail for Jerusalem. During his journey, however, he came across certain disciples — followers of Jesus — who urged him not to go into Jerusalem.

"And finding disciples, we stayed there seven days. They told Paul through the Spirit not to go up to Jerusalem" (Acts 21:4).

These Christians, through the Spirit, were also made aware of the troubles awaiting Paul in Jerusalem, so they warned him not to go. They meant well, of course, but their advice was based on their own concern for Paul's safety, not God's direction to Paul; but Paul remained steadfast in his determination to go to Jerusalem as the Spirit compelled him (Acts 20:22).

The bigger point here is that, as followers of Christ, we're in desperate need of discernment and having a relationship with God to the point where His voice transcends every other voice. While it's good and wise to seek counsel from other Christians, especially when a serious decision needs to be made, it's imperative that other opinions give way to what God has already spoken to us.

The Holy Spirit gave Paul clear instructions to go to Jerusalem, but it seemed like there were hurdles popping up everywhere. And if we try to put ourselves in Paul's shoes, we might gain a better understanding of the level of conflict Paul was facing. Here are examples of Paul's conflicts:

* Obeying God meant leaving home.

* Leaving home meant he would never see his friends or his church again.

* Never seeing his friends and church again meant they would face spiritual attacks without him.

* Obeying God and going to Jerusalem meant he would suffer spiritually, physically, and emotionally — and probably alone.

* His fellow Christians were telling him not to go, so if Paul was even the least bit hesitant about going, these comments from the other disciples must have certainly exploited that doubt.

This wasn't just one fork in the road; it was multiple. And once again it all came down to one main question: did Paul really trust God?

Paul's Response

Paul's response to these disciples sums up the whole message of this chapter, and of the whole book, really.

"Then Paul answered, 'What do you mean by weeping and breaking my heart? For I am ready not only to be bound, but also to die at Jerusalem for the name of the Lord Jesus'" (Acts 21:13).

We can see the emotion in Paul's first statement. He was heartbroken by the disciples begging him to stay. But he set his and their emotions aside, too, and instead set his resolve. God told him to go to Jerusalem and he was going — even if it meant he would die.

"So, when he would not be persuaded, we ceased, saying, 'The will of the Lord be done" (Acts 21:14).

This last verse is very important because it shows Paul's absolute and immoveable commitment to serving God no matter how much pain and suffering he may endure. And once the disciples realized Paul would not be persuaded — meaning he would not compromise his convictions — they relented and said, "The will of the Lord be done." In the end, Paul's courage to stand against any and all opposition to God's Word and his commitment to walking the path God laid before him have given us much of the New Testament.

Application

What if Paul did what the disciples were urging him to do? What if he compromised God's call when things started to get difficult? What if Paul avoided Jerusalem and took the more comfortable path? More than likely, the Gospel would not have been preached in Jerusalem and it would not have been spread throughout the world. Did Paul know the letters he wrote to churches from prison would transform Christianity? Did he know his letters would be recorded in the Bible, translated into virtually every language spoken on earth, smuggled into countries where the Bible was banned, and used as the foundation for millions of sermons over the last two thousand years?

While our decision may not be as impactful as Paul's, we can understand how the impact of our decisions can extend beyond our comprehension. We can't be Paul, but that doesn't mean the impact of our decisions won't impact the lives of other people.

God uses people like Paul, who are obedient to the leading of His Spirit, to impact the world.

God's path may be difficult, and advice from your friends, family, and even your church family may point to a much easier path. But this story is a good reminder that even Christians can be wrong, no matter how well-meaning they are. That's why it's so important for us to hear from God for ourselves and to make sure what we're hearing is lining up 100% with His Word. When God asks us to do something (especially something hard), we face a fork in the road and need to decide if we really trust him, or not — no matter what anyone else says.

FIERY FURNACE

Paul ultimately made the courageous, yet difficult, decision to go to Jerusalem. It wasn't pleasant when he arrived; in fact it was harder than he suspected. I want to make known some of the trials, conflicts, and persecutions Paul endured after obeying the Holy Spirit's call and after he sailed to Jerusalem. Below is an abbreviated list:

- He was lied about, dragged, beaten, and arrested (Acts 21:28–33).

- He was threatened with torture (Acts 22:24).

- He was falsely accused and wrongly imprisoned for years (Acts 24, 25).

- He was mocked and called insane (Acts 26:24).

- He was shipwrecked (Acts 27).

- He was bitten by a poisonous snake (Acts 28:3).

As you can see, Paul's fiery furnace wasn't just a single consequence, but many consequences over multiple years. For Paul, serving God came at a heavy cost. He faced incredible challenges, arrests, beatings, and life-or-death situations — all because of his relentless commitment to obey God and stand on His Word.

Application

This book is all about having courage to take a biblical stand, knowing full-well that you'll be persecuted for it. This applies to all Christians who are brave enough to take such a stand. As Christians, we are in Babylon and face Nebuchadnezzars constantly; there are many forks in the road and different paths laid out before us. Sometimes it's easy to take God's path; sometimes it's not. But experiencing resistance or conflict doesn't mean you're on the wrong path; in fact, it's often confirmation that you're on the right path.

One of the questions I can't help but ask when confronted with Paul's story of leaving his beloved community is how many times throughout our daily lives do we compromise our convictions out of convenience or comfort? How many times do we let ourselves get talked out of important situations because of how someone else feels — or because it's just easier? That's part of what is so inspiring about Paul; he was completely sold out for God's purpose no matter what, or who, seemed to stand in the way. And with that level of conviction, it is no wonder that God used him in incredible, world-changing ways.

4ᵀᴴ Man in the Fire

"At my first defense no one stood with me, but all forsook me. May it not be charged against them. But the Lord stood with me and strengthened me, so that the message might be preached fully through me, and that all the Gentiles might hear. Also, I was delivered out of the mouth of the lion. And the Lord will deliver me from every evil work and preserve me for His heavenly kingdom. To Him be glory forever and ever. Amen!" (2 Timothy 4:16–18).

When everyone else deserted Paul, the Lord stood with him as the fourth man in the fire; this is a powerful glimpse into how God works in us and through us. God doesn't call us and then leave us on our own. He stands with us in the face of opposition, and in every situation he strengthens us so that His message will be heard.

How did Paul come to the point where he could have such great courage to stand against such intense conflicts and heart-breaking losses? To answer those questions, let's look back at Paul's relationship with God before his time in Ephesus, before he was called to Jerusalem, and before he faced the persecution mentioned in the previous section.

Paul's Early Ministry

The first time we read about Paul in the Bible was before his conversion. He was named Saul then, and he was a well-known persecutor of Christians, including the murder of a Christian named Stephen (Acts 7:58). After Stephen's death, Saul traveled down the road to Damascus searching for more Christians to arrest. That's when Saul met Jesus, who asked him this famous question:

"Saul, Saul, why are you persecuting me?" (Acts 9:4).

Saul fell to the ground, trembling and afraid, and asked a question back:

"Lord, what do you want me to do?" (Acts 9:6).

Instead of issuing out judgement on Saul, Jesus showed mercy and sent him to the city where he was to be baptized. This interaction, though seemingly short, shows the true character of God — merciful, redemptive, and compassionate — which Paul trusted throughout the rest of his life.

Paul's Experiences and Preparations

This Damascus Road experience prepared Paul in many ways to have the courage to leave behind the comfort (and love and joy) of his community at Ephesus in order to be used by God in Jerusalem. But it is just the first of several; in many ways, God had been preparing Paul to trust Him on his journey to Jerusalem for years. Below are just a few examples:

- He became blind, but he was healed (Acts 9:8–9, 18).

- He suffered great things, but he was a chosen vessel of God (Acts 9:15–16).

- He would've been killed, but the disciples saved his life (Acts 9:23, 25).

- He was feared by the disciples, but Barnabas defended him (Acts 9:26–27).

- He would've been killed again, but his brethren saved his life again (Acts 9:29–30).

- He was confronted by evil spirits, but being filled with the Holy Spirit, he rebuked them (Acts 13:9–11).

- He was contradicted and blasphemed, but he spoke with boldness (Acts 13:45–46).

- He was persecuted and thrown out of the city, but he shook the dust off his feet and moved on (Acts 13:50–51).

- He would've been stoned to death, but he was provided with safety (Acts 14:5–6).

- He was stoned and thought to be dead, but he was miraculously healed (Acts 14:19–20).

- He had a heated conflict with Barnabas, but he continued his evangelistic work (Acts 15:39–41).

- He was confronted by a demon-possessed woman, but he cast the spirit out (Acts 16:16–18).

- He was beaten and thrown in jail, only to be set free by a divine earthquake and given an opportunity to lead the jailer to the Lord (Acts 16:23–34).

- His life was threatened, but his brethren protected him (Acts 17:5, 10, 13).

- He was mocked for his preaching, but he was given a greater audience (Acts 17:18–22).

- He was mocked for his preaching again, but he was left blameless (Acts 18:6).

- He was accused and brought before a judge, but his accusations were dismissed (Acts 18:12–16).

- He was contended with, but God performed many miracles through him (Acts 19:9–11).

- He was threatened by an angry mob, but he was protected by disciples (Acts 19:29–30).

- He was targeted to be killed yet again, but he reasoned to sail in the opposite direction (Acts 20:3).

This is an incredible list! Yes, Paul constantly found himself in the middle of conflict, persecution, or trials, but God was watching over him in every circumstance. These experiences proved over and over again that God is faithful and trustworthy, and Paul gained invaluable knowledge about God and deepened his relationship with God through each and every one of them.

"... what persecutions I endured. And out of them all the Lord delivered me. Yes, and all who desire to live godly in Christ Jesus will suffer persecution" (2 Timothy 3:11–12).

Earlier, I asked how Paul was able to have such great courage to stand against the most intense conflicts and heart-breaking losses. Here's my answer: Paul learned to trust God because God had proven Himself to be faithful and true, no matter what conflict he faced. Paul's entire biblical record proves that God honored his obedience, which strengthened Paul to be even more courageous.

Other than Jesus, Paul is perhaps the greatest example of how we are to live a Christian life. By simply obeying the Holy Spirit's call to go to Jerusalem, God initiated a domino effect that spread the Gospel of Jesus Christ around the world and through all generations. In this way, Paul's ministry did more to advance the Gospel than perhaps any other in human history.

Near the end of his ministry Paul said:

"I endure all things for the sake of the elect, that they also may obtain the salvation which is in Christ Jesus with eternal glory"
(2 Timothy 2:10).

Paul was willing to endure all these things — the conflict, the loss, the trials, the tribulations, the persecutions, and even death — so that others might be saved.

"I have fought the good fight, I have finished the race, I have kept the faith. Finally, there is laid up for me the crown of righteousness, which the Lord, the righteous Judge, will give to me on that Day, and not to me only but also to all who have loved His appearing
(2 Timothy 4:7–8).

Application

It's important to remember that, while Paul's example is commendable and we are blessed to learn from his ministry, the purpose of this story isn't to elevate Paul but to glorify God and to inspire all of us to walk whatever path God has laid before us.

Paul was a highly educated and brilliant man, but he also made a living as a tentmaker; he was also a skilled laborer who worked with his hands (Acts 18:3). It may be surprising to think that such a respected and revered man of God worked as a tentmaker to support his ministry. While Paul had a much greater calling on his life, he didn't let his day job as a tentmaker discredit his greater calling.

The same is true for us. We would be foolish to discredit or belittle the position in which God has placed us. If Paul had been like some of us and given up because, "God can't use me, I'm just a tentmaker," the impact of that loss would've been catastrophic! Similarly, think of what you, your family, and your community could miss out on if you say, "God can't use me, I'm just a _____."

Paul's story is about obedience and courage, but it's also about God's ability to use anybody who is willing to follow Him, and the incredible relationship we can establish with Him when we allow ourselves to be used by Him. God took Saul and changed him from a murderer of Christians into the greatest evangelist in history! Paul was used by God over and over and over again throughout his life, and each time, he learned more about God and himself — and that knowledge gave him the courage he needed the next time. It was a dynamic relationship that changed Paul's life — and ours — forever.

chapter five

William Tyndale

William Tyndale was an Englishman, Bible scholar, master linguist, translator, author, and leader of the Protestant Reformation. He had a keen ability for communication and possessed a mastery of eight languages: Hebrew, Greek, Latin, Italian, German, Spanish, French, and English. Tyndale, though you may not have heard of him previously, is the man most responsible for the greatest contribution to mankind in the last 2,000 years. To put it plainly, Tyndale gave us the King James Bible.

Tyndale's story is so captivating that even a poorly written paragraph about his life is still inspiring. But the story of William Tyndale begs the telling, at least briefly, of the stories of John Wycliffe and Martin Luther — Reformers on whose shoulders William Tyndale stood. All three men lived under the auspices of the Roman Catholic Church, which meant they lived under the rule of the pope, the church, and its common use of indulgences during this time.

John Wycliffe

John Wycliffe was an Englishman who earned a doctorate in theology from Oxford in 1372. Wycliffe lived during a time when the Roman Catholic Church operated under cannon law and regularly practiced the sale of indulgences as literal payment for sins. The common belief during that time was the pope was the religious authority and thus the common man had no business reading or interpreting the Bible. This stringent belief would be the source of Tyndale's conflict over 150 years later. At the time, Bibles were written only in Latin; they were very difficult to obtain and even more difficult to understand. Consequently, virtually no lay person owned a Bible, let alone a Bible written in his native tongue. This meant the commoner had to rely on the often twisted, inaccurate, and corrupted versions of the Bible told to them by their local priests.

Wycliffe believed that the Word of God — not the pope and not the church — was the authority over all things and that every person should be able to read the Bible daily. To Wycliffe, the only way to solve this dilemma was to translate the Bible from Latin into English, something that had never been done. And in 1384, Wycliffe gave the world its first English Bible. Tyndale's Bible differed from Wycliffe's in that Tyndale translated from the original Greek and Hebrew, while Wycliffe translated from Latin. Additionally, Tyndale's Bible was user-friendly, portable, and easy to read.

Wycliffe's accomplishment, of course, was met with vitriol and hostility by the religious leaders of that day who claimed that translating the Bible into English was the same as casting pearls before swine. They believed only church officials were qualified to read God's Word — a claim to which Wycliffe replied, "Englishmen learn Christ's law best in English. Moses heard God's law in his own tongue; so did Christ's apostles."[1]

John Wycliffe died of a stroke on December 31, 1384, the same year he completed his English Bible. His bold efforts to translate God's Word into English began a movement that sparked the Protestant Reformation. For these reasons, Wycliffe is commonly referred to as the "Morning Star of the Reformation." Wycliffe summarized his biblical worldview in this statement:

---

1. J. Nicholson and D. Swaggart, *Light of Liberty* (Baton Rouge, LA: Jimmy Swaggart Ministries, 2017), p.11.

"Faith in our Lord Jesus Christ is sufficient for salvation. There must be atonement made for sin according to the righteousness of God. The person to make this atonement must be God and man."[2]

Sadly, more than 30 years after his death, the Roman Catholic Church convicted Wycliffe of over 250 counts of heresy, and they banned his writings and burned all his works. Beyond that, Pope Martin V dug up Wycliffe's remains, burned them, and scattered his ashes in the River Swift. The River Swift, however, eventually carried Wycliffe's ashes into the Atlantic Ocean, symbolizing the spreading of God's Word across the world — something only God can orchestrate.

Application

Though separated by 140 years, Wycliffe and Tyndale shared the same passion for creating an English Bible. Tyndale's Bible, in many ways, was better that Wycliffe's, but if not for Wycliffe's original courageous stand against the most powerful leaders at the time, Tyndale's Bible may have never been created. The point is, we should not underestimate or belittle the work we do for God, because we never know who it will impact or when it will impact them, even 140 years later.

Martin Luther

In 1483, 99 years after John Wycliffe's death, Martin Luther was born in Germany and raised in the Catholic church. Luther studied law, theology, and philosophy. He had a great desire for spiritual truth and to learn of God and salvation, but he simply did not know how or where to begin. So, to fill the spiritual void in his life, Luther became a monk. He soon found that being a monk did not bring him peace with God, so he became a priest instead. Then, on one trip to Rome, he witnessed overwhelming wickedness and debauchery taking place under the Roman church's authority and

2. Ibid., p. 11.

decided he wanted no part of such a sinful system created by man.[3] Eager to find truth, Luther threw himself into Scripture, earned a doctorate in theology, and began giving lectures at the University of Wittenberg.

Through his studies, Luther began to understand the doctrine of justification by faith, as taught by the Apostle Paul. Luther saw the clear distinction between the teachings of the Catholic Church at the time and the Word of God, which really is the distinction between the doctrines of justification by works and justification by faith.

"For by grace you have been saved through faith, and that not of yourselves; it is the gift of God" (Ephesians 2:8).

Luther realized that true biblical salvation was the result of faith in Christ's substitutionary death on the Cross and was a gift of God's grace, not the result of church attendance or works. With this revelation, Luther suddenly became alive with the light of God's Word inside of him and he began to see the darkness that was being promulgated from the church.

To address these errors within the church, and to reveal biblical truth, Luther wrote down 95 points of contention that existed between the church and the Word of God; this list became known as "Martin Luther's Ninety-Five Theses." On October 31, 1517, Martin Luther famously nailed his Ninety-Five Theses to the door of the Castle Church in Wittenberg. This document, written with as much humility as biblical accuracy, was an open rebuke of the church and its leadership. And, thanks to the timely invention of the printing press, Luther's ideas were widely published. As more and more people began to agree with him, the Lutheran movement began.

In 1518, just a few months after he nailed his theses to the church doors, Luther was summoned by the pope to give an account for his accusations against the church. And when the religious leaders

---

3.   Ibid., p. 14.

realized they were unable to compete with the biblical accuracy of Luther's statements, they tried to hide their shortcomings by banning Luther from the church. Unshaken, Luther responded matter-of-factly and without compromise:

> "I deny that the pope is above scripture. His Holiness abuses scripture."[4]

Two years later, the pope issued an ultimatum to Luther: recant your statements or be excommunicated from the church. Luther responded to the threat by publicly burning the pope's letter. Though he was banished from the church, Luther was given yet another opportunity to appear before church, leaders to retract his Ninety-Five Theses. Luther, by now, had become famous for his courageous stand against the false teachings of the church, so this upcoming meeting was a must-see event; thousands of people crowded the streets and pressed against the doors of the town hall to hear what Luther would say.

Luther was labeled a heretic, like Wycliffe before him and Tyndale after, and the church expected him to crumble under the pressure and retract his previous statements about the church. But Luther did not take back what he said about the church and his testimony pulled no punches. He said:

> "Unless I am convinced by the testimony of Scripture or by plain reason, I am mastered by the passages of Scripture which I have quoted, and my conscience is captive to the Word of God. I cannot and will not recant, for it is neither safe nor honest to violate one's conscience. I can do no other. Here I take my stand, God being my helper. Amen."[5]

Luther and his writings were subsequently banned, he was declared a heretic, and sentenced to death. Luther, however, was able to flee into hiding before the sentencing. In 1534, while in hiding, Luther completed the first German translation of the New

---

4. Ibid., p. 19.
5. Ibid., p. 21.

Testament, an accomplishment that would play a major role in William Tyndale's New Testament. Luther died of a stroke in 1546.

Application -------------------------------

The Bible says, *"So then neither he who plants is anything, nor he who waters, but God who gives the increase. Now he who plants, and he who waters are one, and each one will receive his own reward according to his own labor" (I Cor. 3:7–8).*

We can apply that Scripture to Wycliffe, Luther, and Tyndale: Wycliffe planted seeds that were watered by Luther, and God gave the increase through Tyndale's English Bible. In fact, Tyndale and Luther met at least once in Germany in 1524 before Luther was forced into hiding. This meeting, no doubt, impacted the work on Tyndale's Bible.

The point is, while we're all given unique talents and abilities by God, none of us are above anyone else. How can you live this out? I heard in a sermon once: "The ground is level at the foot of the Cross." It's important to remember that while God has a special job for each of us, no one's work for God is more important that another's.

Tyndale's Unique Abilities

William Tyndale was born in England around 1494 and began studying at Oxford at the age of 12. Not much is known about his childhood other than he came from a reasonably wealthy family of merchants and landowners. As a writer, Tyndale benefitted from the printing press, perhaps more than Luther. Tyndale published many writings on Christianity and was known for printing booklets, pocketbooks, and pamphlets. He also gave us common phrases such as, "salt of the earth," "let there be light," and "the spirit is willing." Tyndale is frequently quoted today, though unknowingly, and it's said that Tyndale's work has reached more people than Shakespeare's.[6]

Tyndale was well-educated, a talented writer and communicator, and a remarkable translator. His understanding of languages, words, structures, rhetoric, and dialects was arguably the greatest of his time. Gifted as he was, his heart and mind were ever on the Holy Scriptures. John Foxe wrote about Tyndale's love of God's Word:

> "William Tyndale, the faithful minister and constant martyr of Christ ... brought up from a child in the University of Oxford, where he, by long continuance, grew up, and increased as well in the knowledge of tongues and other liberal arts as especially in the knowledge of the scriptures, whereunto his mind was singularly addicted.... His manners also and conversation being correspondent to the same, were such, that all that knew him, reputed and esteemed him to be a man of most virtuous disposition, and of life unspotted."[7]

So, not only was Tyndale extremely intelligent, but he especially loved God's Word, and it affected his lifestyle in such a way that those who knew him regarded him as a virtuous man. Every talent, gift, ability, and acquisition of William Tyndale's was concentrated and focused on God's Word, specifically the intent to make it accessible to the common man.

Think for a moment how difficult it must've been for Tyndale to translate the Bible from the original Greek and Hebrew into English, having had no blueprint to follow and no real guidepost from which to navigate. Here's what he did: Tyndale took the original Greek and translated it into common English vernacular. Then, he took the original Hebrew and translated it into common English, while simultaneously maintaining agreement between the Greek and the Hebrew languages. And if that wasn't difficult

6. D. Daniell, *William Tyndale: A Biography* (New Haven, CT: Yale University Press, 1994).
7. Ibid., p. 39.

enough, he translated from Latin to English as well. And for the cherry on top, Tyndale had to consider and implement the unique styles and habits of the original authors without losing continuity throughout the Old and New Testaments — a period that spanned thousands of years. It's an undertaking and an achievement that boggles the mind. But this is just one example of what God can accomplish through one willing person.

An English Bible for the Common Man

In Tyndale's time, most everything was written in Latin. From his time as a young schoolboy all through his graduate studies, Tyndale did his reading and writing in Latin. In fact, of the 6,000+ books that were in the Oxford University Library in the early 17th century, only 60 of those books (around 1%) were published in English.[8] Tyndale saw this as a problem because his countrymen spoke English, not Latin. If everything, especially the Bible, was printed only in Latin, that meant the common man was not able to read the Bible; and would be left to rely on the corruptible commentaries of church dignitaries. In *Foxe's Book of Martyrs*, Foxe wrote of Tyndale:

> "He perceived that it was not possible to establish the lay people in any truth, except the Scriptures were so plainly laid before their eyes in their mother tongue that they might see the meaning of the text: for else, whatsoever truth should be taught them, the enemies of the truth would quench it, either with reasons of sophistry, and traditions of their own making, founded without all good Scripture."[9]

Tyndale saw that people needed a Bible that was written in their own language and easy to understand. If the common man was to perpetually rely on the slanted stories and false doctrines of the priests, then the common man would also continue to live in

---

8.   Ibid., p. 45.
9.   J. Foxe, *Foxe's Book of Martyrs* (Philadelphia, PA: J.B. Smith, 1856).

perpetual darkness. Tyndale understood that an English Bible was the answer to this problem, and he happened to possess the set of skills that could make a practical English Bible a reality. He was the right person, in the right place, at the right time to create a reader-friendly, word-for-word, English translation of the Holy Bible.

So, in 1522, Tyndale began his work on translating the Bible into English, starting with the New Testament. Since Tyndale was able to read Greek, Hebrew, and Latin, he could read the words in the Bible as they were written by the original authors; he wasn't restricted to reading someone else's thoughts on the Book of Romans. For example, he was able to read the exact words the Apostle Paul had written.[10] This allowed Tyndale to create an English translation more accurate than any other.

For Tyndale, though, his Bible had to be as scholarly as possible, meaning it had to be a word-for-word translation. Not only that, but it needed to be easy to understand so that the common person could read it and grasp its meaning. It's one thing to understand a concept, but it's another thing being able to communicate that concept in such a way that a child can understand it — this was Tyndale's goal. In fact, when discussing the Bible with an educated individual, Tyndale stated:

> "If God spare my life ere many years, I will cause a boy that driveth the plough shall know more of the Scripture than thou dost."[11]

Tyndale was committed to the prospect that even a simple ploughboy could read the Word of God, in his own language, and read it with such ease as to gain as much knowledge as the most learned man.

Tyndale's life presents quite the dichotomy: he was a wealthy man whose intellect and academic achievements were unparalleled, yet he dedicated his life so that even the most uneducated, poorest

10. Daniell, *William Tyndale: A Biography*, p. 40.
11. Ibid., p. 1.

ploughboy could have the same understanding of God's Word that he possessed. He would rather labor for the lost than revel in his money or boast of his high intellect. Such blessings and virtue can come through a gifted, talented, and consecrated man only when that man yields those gifts as an instrument in God's hands. Tyndale was not a perfect man, of course, but his life's achievements and his readiness to forsake all his earthly gain for the cause of Christ, highlight the eternal good that can be accomplished through God's grace.

Application

Since the day I met my wife, the thing I admire most about her is her commitment to use all her gifts, talents, and abilities to serve God. She's incredibly talented. She graduated valedictorian of her class in Law school, she's a talented pianist, and has a wonderful sense of humor; not to mention, everyone loves her, and she can relate to absolutely anybody. But she's not prideful about it, she wants to honor God with her gifts.

This is how I see William Tyndale, in a way. He was an incredibly gifted and talented man with a capacity to do amazing things. But despite all that, his eye was singularly focused on putting God's Word in the hands of as many people as possible. This is an admirable and inspiring quality that we should strive to emulate. God used Wycliffe, Luther, and Tyndale in ways that were similar, and He also used them in ways that were very different. Similarly, God will use each of us in ways that are similar, and He will use each of us in ways that are very different — as long as we're willing to be used by Him.

BABYLON

William Tyndale lived in a time when the church was believed to be the authority over men, a price tag was placed on salvation, and only church leaders were considered worthy of reading the Bible. Nowadays, if we don't like a church or a pastor, we can just leave and go to a different church. Tyndale's experience wasn't like that. The religious leaders of Tyndale's era held all the power, even the political power, and rejecting their leadership was essentially an act of treason. So, reformers like Tyndale — who believed God's Word was the authority over man, that salvation was a gift through faith in Jesus Christ, and that every person should be able to read the Bible — were labeled heretics and troublemakers who were to be arrested, tried, convicted, and executed.

As a young man, Tyndale experienced the corruption and mishandling of God's Word at the university level. In his work, *The Practice of Prelates,* he discussed the brainwashing process he witnessed while at Oxford. Mind you this was over 500 years ago, and it still resonates today:

> "In the universities they have ordained that no man shall look in the Scripture until he be nursed in the heathen language eight or nine years and armed with false principles with which he is clean shut out of the understanding of scripture."[12]

Even in the culture of his day, Tyndale recognized the indoctrination that was taking place in schools and churches; Tyndale saw this, but most people didn't. The result was the people who were "educated" and "churched" were the ones who impacted the culture; business, politics, education, and religion were all influenced by the brainwashing Tyndale described. These were the people running the country, which meant Tyndale's thoughts and ideas were not at all mainstream. So, for anyone willing to stand up to such spiritual darkness, like Tyndale was, courage was a prerequisite, and conflict was a certainty. This was William Tyndale's version of Babylon.

---

12. William Tyndale. *The Works of Tyndale* (London: Ebenezer Palmer, 1831).

Application ------------------------------

Tyndale lived in an upside-down world, especially regarding the church. The church was wrong on leadership, they were wrong on salvation, they were wrong on almost everything. While this caused the people to live in great darkness, it made the light of God's truth shine even brighter!

We have the same opportunity today to be lights in our upside-down culture of darkness, where good is called evil and evil is called good, even within some "Christian" churches. It's not that we are the lights, but that we have the Light living inside of us — Jesus is the Light that shines in the darkness and it's incumbent upon us to carry His Light with us wherever we go — no matter the consequence.

Nebuchadnezzar

Because the Latin Bible was so difficult to use and understand, Tyndale found that even the priests lacked understanding in the Word. The need for an easy-to-read, easy-to-understand English Bible had never been greater. And as already mentioned with Wycliffe and Luther, Tyndale was not the first person to translate the Bible into another language. Before Tyndale's English translation, the Bible had already been translated into French, Catalan, Spanish, Portuguese, German, Czech, and Dutch — the most popular translation having been Luther's German New Testament[13]; but even Luther's Bible was not a word-for-word translation, having been a more vernacular, or dynamic equivalent translation.[14] The Bible had been translated into different languages all over Europe, so why not in England? And why not in English?

---

13. Ibid., p. 92–93.
14. https://www.1517.org/articles/luthers-german-bible.

Conflict

The king of England and the Catholic Church held opposing views to William Tyndale. For example, Tyndale believed the Bible should be printed in English; the king and Church did not. Tyndale believed the Bible should be read by the common man; the king and Church did not. In England, these beliefs were so strong that it was actually illegal to translate the Bible into English. Tyndale's English Bible, if completed in England, would make him a criminal.[15] To Tyndale, the king and the Church of that day were his Nebuchadnezzars.

To make matters worse for Tyndale, the Lutheran movement had driven fear into the king of England and the Catholic Church; they feared what would happen if the people no longer relied on clergy to explain God's Word. If the people could read the Bible themselves and see the errors that plagued the church, then the church would lose control of the people. To the king and the Church, translating the Bible into English was not an academic or scholarly undertaking; to them, it was an act of subversion.

Reformers like Wycliffe, Luther, and Tyndale were seen as threats to the king and the Church, which meant they must be stopped. Tyndale understood that his mission to create an English Bible would be met with conflict and opposition.

A Marked Man

Tyndale was well-acquainted with noblemen, clergymen, politicians, doctors, and merchants, with whom he often found himself in theological debates. Whether at Oxford, Cambridge, around the dinner table, or at the local pub, Tyndale was known to open the Bible and go to certain passages, showing those in his company what God had to say on a matter. This habit, of course, made Tyndale more enemies than friends, and he solidified his reputation as a bit of a troublemaker. His belief that every person

---

15. Daniell, *William Tyndale: A Biography*, p. 94.

should be able to read the Bible for themselves did not make him many friends either. Tyndale's persisting burden to give the common Englishman an English Bible had always come with a heavy cost, and the cost would only grow heavier.

As soon as Tyndale began translating the New Testament, he encountered more difficulty from detractors than help from his friends. According to many, particularly the noble and religious elite of the time, the Bible was not meant to be given to the masses. Tyndale was labeled a heretic for his beliefs, as was anyone who helped him; this forced Tyndale to leave his home if he was to complete his English translation. So, Tyndale set off for London hoping to find help there. While in London, he observed the rotten state of the church and its church leaders; he witnessed how the priests and preachers had elevated themselves and instituted a litany of man-made rules, heaping burdens onto the backs of the people; these observations only reinforced his belief in the need for an English Bible.

Unfortunately, Tyndale's reputation as a heretic and troublemaker preceded him in London, and he was unable to find help there. Tyndale found that the entirety of England was not conducive to his work, and he had no choice but to leave his home country; so, he headed to Cologne in Luther's Germany.

Tyndale's Bible Printed and Burned

Having endured mostly difficulties and setbacks in London, Tyndale finally saw a bit of progress in Germany where, in 1525, the first pages of his English New Testament rolled off the printing press.[16] But before the Book of Matthew was completely printed, authorities caught wind of Tyndale's work and determined to arrest him and confiscate his work. So, Tyndale picked up and fled to Worms, Germany, taking his work with him. And in 1526, after four years of labor, Tyndale completed his translation of the entire New Testament; several thousand English New Testament were printed

16. Ibid., p. 108.

there in Worms. Tragically, a wealthy bishop decided to buy up all Tyndale's Bibles just to burn them; as quickly as they were printed, they were destroyed. Tyndale had sacrificed so much and worked so hard, and completed such an honorable and righteous work, only to have his Bibles bought and burned.

Thankfully, Tyndale did not let these setbacks stop him. He revisited his work, making corrections and adding commentary as needed, which resulted in his English New Testament being reprinted and distributed yet again. While Tyndale's English New Testament provided a light to the English people, it also fixed the eyes of the enemy directly on him.

Shipwrecked

Once he had completed the New Testament, Tyndale immediately began working on the Old Testament. During this time, Tyndale traveled to Germany where he met with Martin Luther, among others. Tyndale left his meeting with Luther and sailed from Germany to Holland. On this trip Tyndale suffered a shipwreck and lost all his possessions — his books, his writings, his money — and most tragically he lost his nearly completed translation of the Old Testament.

To recap: First, he had to relocate multiple times to complete his New Testament, which was immediately burned, and then his Old Testament was lost at sea. Despite these heavy blows, Tyndale was committed to completing an English Bible no matter how long it took, so he started the Old Testament all over again. And by 1530, while living in Antwerp, Holland, Tyndale successfully completed the first five books of the Old Testament (the Pentateuch) into English. The English-speaking world now had easy access to the Gospels, the Words of Christ, and Paul's Epistles; and with Tyndale's Pentateuch, they could also read the story of creation, God's covenant with Abraham, Israel's deliverance from Egypt, the

Red Sea miracle, and the instructions for the Tabernacle and the Sacrificial System.

Despite his many trials, tribulations, setbacks, and conflicts, Tyndale refused to give up on his work of translating the entire Bible into English. Tyndale had many opportunities to give up on the massive responsibility of translating the Bible — his New Testament Bibles were burned, his Old Testament books were lost in a shipwreck, he was labeled a heretic, and few people would work with him. Not to mention he was forced to leave his home country just to get started on his translations. He sacrificed much, but complaints and gripes and regrets never seemed to be on his lips. His thoughts and words were ever on the Word of God and the people who must be given the chance to read it. Tyndale's vision was singular, his convictions were immovable, and his resilience was strong.

Application

Tyndale was a marked man, and nobody seemed to want to associate with him. You might feel like you've been marked or mistreated for a stand you've taken — or maybe that's something keeping you from taking a stand. People may call you judgmental, bigoted, homophobic, or a radical, and it may even affect your ability to find work. Tyndale experienced this treatment in his home country when nobody would help him, so he went elsewhere. But by being pushed out of his home, Tyndale was given the opportunity to witness the spiritual debauchery in London, which only strengthened his resolve. So, what seemed like a negative became a positive.

At times, God instructs us to stay put where we are and go through the fire with Him; other times, God instructs us to pick up and leave, as He goes before us. Neither of these instructions are easy to follow, but whatever path God has prepared for us, we can be encouraged to know that others, like Tyndale, have gone on before us. And as we know already, and will see again, Tyndale would eventually accomplish his work, despite the hindrances along the way.

It seems like Tyndale's work was always taking two steps forward and one step back. And though it may not have seemed like it at the time, he was still making progress despite the resistance, conflicts, and setbacks he faced. Similarly, we sometimes feel like we're working incredibly hard, but we're just not seeing the results we'd hoped for, and it feels like we're just spinning our wheels. On top of that, outside influences may be hindering or even destroying our work; it seems completely unfair. But we can learn from Tyndale that, as time passes and we look back, we'll be able to see that God was helping us the whole time and we really did accomplish a great deal.

FIERY FURNACE

Tyndale's story is incredibly and uniquely inspiring, but it ends very differently than most of the other stories in this book. Tyndale clearly had a marvelous mind and a brilliant capacity to communicate, which is inspiring in itself; but most impressive was his commitment to, and love for, sharing God's Word — even to his dying breath. He never let his constant conflict discourage him, and he refused to bow to the pressure of the corrupted king and Church. He chose to stand on the truth of God's Word.

Though he did complete the entire New Testament and most of the Old Testament (about 80–90% of the entire Bible), William Tyndale was betrayed, arrested, imprisoned, convicted, and ultimately killed for his work before he could finish translating the entire Bible.[17]

---

17. J. Foxe, *Foxe's Book of Martyrs*, p. 121.

Betrayal

While translating the Old Testament in Antwerp, Holland, Tyndale met and befriended a man named Henry Philips.[18] Henry Philips studied at Oxford, like Tyndale, and came from a relatively wealthy family, also like Tyndale; the two men had at least a few things in common. Through various personal and social interactions, Philips gathered a fair amount of personal information about Tyndale and became well acquainted with his work, his home, and his studies. Considering Tyndale's reputation, allowing Philips into his home was quite trusting, and quite dangerous.

Tyndale had only known Philips a few days and was unaware of his character and ill repute. Philips had previously squandered whatever money he had and had become a conman to get by. He was simply using Tyndale as a means to collect some sort of bounty. Tyndale, remember, was a marked man; he had defied the king of England and the Catholic Church by translating and publishing his English Bible against their law and against their wishes, so there would've been many authorities interested in arresting him and seizing his work. Like Luther and the Reformers before him, Tyndale had long been labeled a heretic and had escaped numerous attempts at his arrest, so the sensitive information Philips had gathered about Tyndale could easily be used against him. And that's exactly what happened; Tyndale was set up, trapped, and betrayed by Philips.

After days of spying on Tyndale, Philips left town and presented his scheme to the Court at Brussels. Philips soon returned to Antwerp and brought with him the procurer-general (the emperor's attorney) and a team of officers to arrest Tyndale. Philips had either been sent to Antwerp by a nameless employer to spy on Tyndale, or he simply stumbled upon Tyndale by chance and saw an opportunity for personal gain. Either way, Tyndale and his work had reached their stopping point. Tyndale was arrested and taken

---

18. Ibid., p. 122.

to Vilvorde, Belgium, where he spent the next 16 months in prison. While in prison, Tyndale was questioned, interrogated, and tried by a group of theologians, lawyers, and various other councils. Tyndale was formally condemned as a heretic, sentenced to death, and executed on October 6, 1536.[19]

Tyndale's Execution

Before his execution, Tyndale was made into a public example — humiliated, discredited, and denigrated. His accusers publicly stated that Tyndale was a heretic worthy of death, and his priesthood (Tyndale was a minister) was ceremonially stripped. This, to them, was an open show — undeniable proof — that Tyndale's English Bible was a farce and that the church was indeed the supreme authority. The theatrics of it all were meant to strike fear into anyone else who would dare to go against the church.

On the morning of his execution, William Tyndale was led by guards and marched through a crowd to the center of town. He made his final stop at two large wooden beams that were surrounded by brush — this was his execution site. Tyndale had his back positioned against the logs that were in the shape of a cross, his hands and feet were bound, and a chain was secured around his neck. Before the hangman tightened the chain to kill him, Tyndale was given one last opportunity to pray. And as he approached the final moment of his life on earth, Tyndale's last words rang out across the town-center:

> "Lord, open the King of England's eyes!"

Tyndale was then strangled to death and his body burned at the stake.[20]

---

19. Ibid., p. 123.
20. Daniell, *William Tyndale: A Biography*, p. 383.

Tyndale's Resolve

Tyndale could have prevented a lot of his difficulties, conflicts, and setbacks if he had obeyed the king and the Church. He also had plenty of excuses to stop along the way: his Bibles were burned, he lost his Old Testament in the shipwreck, and he was run out of his home country. He could have just said, "Well, the timing just isn't right, maybe God can use someone else to translate the Bible into English." Or he could have just apologized for violating the king's laws and begged the Church for forgiveness. If he had done that, then he could've stayed alive and written other important books. Did William Tyndale really have to be the one to translate the Bible? Couldn't someone else have done it? Did William Tyndale really have to be the one to take such a courageous and uncompromising stand against the king and the Church? All these questions are understandable, even relatable, but Tyndale's actions were different than most, and that's what's inspiring.

Tyndale was just a man, like any other. Yes, he was uniquely gifted and used by God in a way that few have ever been used, but he was still just a man. Yet, as he reached the final seconds of his life, and he felt the cold chain pressed to his throat while the hangman readied himself, Tyndale's heart and mind were on the Bible. He didn't cry out for his books, his home, his wealth, or even his own life. Facing death he proclaimed, "Lord, open the King of England's eyes." He wasn't asking God to open the king's eyes to stop his execution. He was asking God to open the king's eyes to see the importance of placing an English Bible in the hands of every Englishman.

Application -

Think of Tyndale's journey from beginning to end: as a young man he saw the mishandling of the Bible at Oxford, he witnessed the preachers proclaiming false doctrine in London, he was marked as a troublemaker in his own country, his Bibles were burned, he lost all of his possessions when he was shipwrecked, he had to start all over again from scratch, he was betrayed by a friend, he was humiliated and persecuted, and finally, he was strangled to death and burned at the stake — publicly.

Now, considering all that, think of the absolute, unwavering commitment Tyndale must've had to translate the Bible into English. I wonder, have I ever been so committed to anything in my life? Have I ever held such a strong conviction to endure what Tyndale endured? Have I ever been so courageous as to stare death in the face and ask God to have mercy on my accusers? Tyndale modeled all these attributes, which inspires us to stand on God's Word as he did.

As Christians, we know that the Word of God is inexhaustible, it's life giving, it's our Daily Bread — where would we be without it? Even so, would any of us be willing to die just to have a Bible in our hands? My prayer and hope is that God would place a greater desire and a greater love for His Word in our hearts. I'm so thankful for the Bible; I've had multiple Bibles my entire life and I know I've taken it for granted at times. But Tyndale's life shows how important and how valuable God's Word is. It's worth taking a stand for.

4TH Man in the Fire

Tyndale gave us the entire New Testament and Pentateuch in English. He also left behind substantial work on other Old Testament books before he was executed. Three years after Tyndale's execution, King Henry VIII used Tyndale's translations to create his "Great Bible," which was the foundation for what would become the King James Bible. Tyndale's prayer, "Lord, open the King of England's eyes," was answered. Finally, 75 years after Tyndale's death, King James assembled a group of Bible scholars to complete the work that Tyndale had started, and the 1611 King James Bible was the result. It's believed that 90 percent of the King James Bible is attributed to Tyndale's work, which has since lasted over 500 years (nearly 600 if we date back to Tyndale's New Testament).[21] This is why Tyndale, through God's providence, is credited with giving us the King James Bible.

A Bible in Every Hand

One of the ways that God used Tyndale's unique talents was through his knack for creating booklets, pocketbooks, and pamphlets. Prior to Tyndale, Bibles were not practically made, meaning they were large, bulky, difficult to transport, and difficult to read. Tyndale's English Bibles were superior because they weren't weighed down with personal commentary; they were smaller books, easier to carry, and easier to read. So, not only did Tyndale bring God's Word to the masses, but his more practical Bibles made it possible for every man, woman, boy, and girl to carry God's Word with them everywhere they went.[22]

United and Strengthened

Think of how the modern smartphone connects people around the world; Tyndale's Bible was even more impactful than that, because his Bible didn't just connect people, it united a nation. Tyndale's Bible was printed in plain English, and it could be carried in a pocket, which meant it could be read and discussed by the masses. This not only united people with other people, but it united people with God.

Tyndale's Bible, for the first time, provided a great source of strength and encouragement to the common man who no longer had to reside under the thumb of the Catholic Church. At the beginning of Tyndale's New Testament, he wrote the following personal paragraph to the reader, sharing his heart and intention in translating God's Word.

---

21. J. Nicholson and D. Swaggart, *Light of Liberty*, p. 25.
22. Daniell, *William Tyndale: A Biography*, p. 134.

"I have here translated (brethren and sisters most dear and tenderly beloved in Christ) the New Testament for your spiritual edifying, consolation, and solace.... For we have not received the gifts of God for ourselves only, or for to hide them, but for to bestow them unto the honoring of God and Christ, and edifying of the congregation, which is the body of Christ."[23]

Tyndale understood that the light of the Gospel is not to be hidden under a bushel but held up high so that others may see and believe. He wrote these words while being forced to leave his home country, being hunted by authorities, and being called a heretic. Tyndale didn't say, "Hide your Bibles and don't discuss God's Word in public, otherwise you'll be arrested and convicted." In fact, Tyndale encouraged people to do the exact opposite; he said to share God's gifts and use them to strengthen each other.

Application

I grew up playing sports, and I was a teacher and a coach for 13 years, so when I read Tyndale's words of encouragement, I envision myself as a coach giving an encouraging speech to my team before a competition; I'd pump them up and reassure them that all their hard work was going to pay off. And I'd also urge them to speak up and encourage their teammates as well. In a way, Tyndale is coaching us and encouraging us to read God's Word, to receive salvation through faith in Christ, and to share it with others.

Tyndale translated the Bible for our spiritual benefit, that we might be encouraged and strengthened. Then he said not to hide these things but to share them with others so they too can be encouraged and strengthened. And really, that's the whole purpose of this book. As I explained in the Introduction, David encouraged himself in the Lord, Jesus commanded Peter to

---

23. Ibid., p. 120.

strengthen his brethren, and God instructed us to teach His wonderful works to our children. This is what it's all about!

Every story and every chapter in this book emphasizes the importance of the Bible and taking a stand on the truth of God's Word, but without Tyndale, would we even have an English Bible? Would anyone else have ever translated the original texts into a common English vernacular? Maybe, maybe not. This goes to show just how important Tyndale's convictions, obedience, and courageous actions were. What does this mean for us and our convictions? What will be lost if we quit the work God has called us to accomplish?

chapter six

Joshua and Caleb

Joshua and Caleb begin their inspiring story of faith and courage as slaves in Egypt. You're probably familiar with the story of the great Exodus and how Moses led God's people out of Egyptian bondage. Joshua and Caleb were part of that group. The Exodus story is usually seen from Moses' perspective — how he talked with God, stood before Pharaoh, led the Exodus, and parted the Red Sea — but the account in this chapter will focus on the perspectives of Joshua and Caleb. These two men experienced God's deliverance from Egypt and they witnessed many miracles in the wilderness. This chapter discusses how those experiences influenced their future decisions.

God's Promises

Egypt's evil pharoah had grown afraid of God's people, so he enslaved them so he could control them. God's people were treated brutally while in bondage, which caused them to cry out to God for help. And after hearing their cries, God promised to deliver His children from their suffering and to bring them into a good land, which was currently occupied by enemy armies.

"And the Lord said, 'I have surely seen the oppression of My people who are in Egypt, and have heard their cry because of their taskmasters, for I know their sorrows. So, I have come down to deliver them out of the

hand of the Egyptians, and to bring them up from that land to a good and large land, to a land flowing with milk and honey, to the place of the Canaanites and the Hittites and the Amorites and the Perizzites and the Hivites and the Jebusites"' (Exodus 3:7–8).

After God gave these promises to Moses, He sent Moses to tell Pharaoh, *"Thus says the Lord God of Israel: 'Let My people go.'"* Pharaoh's response was, *"Who is the Lord, that I should obey His voice?" (Exodus 5:1–2).* So not only did Pharoah reject God's Word, but he severely increased the burden on God's people — which included Joshua and Caleb (Exodus 5:6–7).

"And I have also heard the groaning of the children of Israel whom the Egyptians keep in bondage, and I have remembered My covenant.... I am the Lord; I will bring you out from under the burdens of the Egyptians, I will rescue you from their bondage, and I will redeem you with an outstretched arm and with great judgments. I will take you as My people, and I will be your God.... And I will bring you into the land which I swore to give to Abraham, Isaac, and Jacob; and I will give it to you as a heritage: I am the Lord" (Exodus 6:5–8).

Pharoah's wickedness wasn't going to stop God from keeping His promises to deliver His children from slavery and to bring them into a good land; so, God began to move on behalf of His children. The story goes that as Pharoah's heart was hardened, God brought plagues upon Egypt until Pharoah finally released God's people.

"And it came to pass, on that very same day, that the Lord brought the children of Israel out of the land of Egypt according to their armies" (Exodus 12:51).

This was the fulfillment of God's first promise, which Joshua and Caleb experienced along with all of the Israelites. But just because God was able to keep promises to His children, that doesn't mean things were going to be easy for them. Pharaoh soon regretted his decision to release God's people and decided to chase them down and drag them back into slavery once again (Exodus 14:9). But as

Pharaoh caught up to God's people and had them trapped against
the uncrossable Red Sea, Moses responded with an encouraging
message:

*"And Moses said to the people, 'Do not be afraid. Stand still, and see the
salvation of the Lord, which He will accomplish for you today. For the
Egyptians whom you see today, you shall see again no more forever.
The Lord will fight for you, and you shall hold your peace'"*
(Exodus 14:13–14).

It's difficult — even impossible at times — to see how God is
moving while we are going through our trials, and we easily fall
into the trap of thinking we could handle the situation better than
God. However, we learn from God's Word and from His wonderful
works that have been passed down from generation to generation,
that God can make a way when there seems to be no way.

*"Then Moses stretched out his hand over the sea; and the Lord caused
the sea to go back by a strong east wind all that night, and made the
sea into dry land, and the waters were divided. So, the children of
Israel went into the midst of the sea on the dry ground, and the waters
were a wall to them on their right hand and on their left.... And Moses
stretched out his hand over the sea; and when the morning appeared,
the sea returned to its full depth, while the Egyptians were fleeing into
it. So, the Lord overthrew the Egyptians in the midst of the sea. Then
the waters returned and covered the chariots, the horsemen, and all the
army of Pharaoh that came into the sea after them. Not so much as one
of them remained" (Exodus 14:21–28).*

Just as the three Hebrew children walked out of the fiery furnace
without even smelling like smoke, God's children walked across the
Red Sea without getting a drop of water on them (Exodus 14:28–31).
And not only that, but Pharoah and his army were totally defeated.

*"Then sang Moses and the children of Israel this song unto the Lord,
and spoke, saying, I will sing unto the Lord, for he hath triumphed
gloriously: the horse and his rider hath he thrown into the sea. The*

Lord is my strength and song, and he is become my salvation: he is my God, and I will prepare him a habitation; my father's God, and I will exalt him" (Exodus 15:1-2 KJV)

We should take note and always remember to praise the Lord in all things. When the Israelites walked across dry land and were saved from their enemies, the first thing they did was praise God. But delivering His people from Egypt was only the first half of God's promises; now, He would make good on His second — bringing His children into a good land.

Application

In this section, God proved Himself faithful to His promises and a protector of His people. And after witnessing all these wonderful works, God's children responded appropriately with praise, saying, "The Lord is my strength." This is a key message: we will certainly face hard times and fearful situations in life, and we will have little strength of our own to rely on (if any). Thankfully, we don't need to rely on our strength, because the Lord is our strength — and an endless source of it.

In this incredible story, Joshua and Caleb were among the people who saw God move in miraculous ways. They lived these miracles! And because of those experiences with God, they had every reason to trust Him with their futures — this is the lesson we can apply to our lives. Whether we experience God's miracle-working power, or we hear about it or read about it, we have every reason to trust Him with our futures. So, the next time we face a conflict at work, home, school, or even at church, we can act with courage and trust God.

It's important to remember that Pharaoh chased after God's people and tried to enslave them again; this is something that can (and will) happen in our lives too. If we live for the Lord, we will experience victories and blessings. And while the devil may be defeated, the Bible says that he is still active and intentionally seeking opportunities to bring God's children back into bondage, back into sin. So, while we have every reason to hope and trust in God, we shouldn't be ignorant of the things that seek to destroy our faith.

 **BABYLON** After being freed from Egypt and experiencing the Red Sea miracle, the Israelites wandered in the wilderness. While being in the wilderness doesn't sound great, the good news is they were no longer being ruled by an evil taskmaster; they were being ruled by God. In fact, the wilderness is where the pillar of cloud (God's presence) had brought them. God did not want His children to wander aimlessly, so He gave them instructions on how to live. But God's instructions were very different from Pharoah's, because God didn't punish His children or increase their burdens. Rather, God's instructions were simple and loving.

"If you diligently heed the voice of the Lord your God and do what is right in His sight, give ear to His commandments and keep all His statutes, I will put none of the diseases on you which I have brought on the Egyptians. For I am the Lord who heals you" (Exodus 15:26).

The Israelites experienced many ups and downs in the wilderness; they committed many failures, but they also saw many victories. For example, they complained because the water was bitter, then they saw the miracle of the bitter water being made sweet (Exodus 15:25). They complained about the lack of food, then God gave them manna from Heaven (Exodus 16:3–4). And when they slid into idolatry, God gave them the Law, the Commandments, and the guidelines for the Tabernacle (Exodus 20–32). God's children had every reason to trust in Him, but they continually resorted to unbelief.

Every conflict the Israelites faced provided them with two choices: they could either complain or they could trust God. God had promised His children on multiple occasions that He would bring

them into a good land — the Promised Land. But because of
unbelief, every single Israelite — except for Joshua and Caleb —
died in the wilderness before they could experience God's promise
of a good land. In this way, the wilderness of unbelief represents
Babylon in Joshua and Caleb's story.

Joshua

In the wilderness, coincidently, is where Joshua is first mentioned
in the Bible. Moses called on Joshua to go and fight against Amalek,
which indicates Joshua was an experienced warrior, trustworthy,
and held in high regard.

*"Choose us some men and go out, fight with Amalek.... So, Joshua did as
Moses said to him, and fought with Amalek.... Joshua defeated Amalek
and his people with the edge of the sword. Then the Lord said to Moses,
'Write this for a memorial in the book and recount it in the hearing of
Joshua, that I will utterly blot out the remembrance of Amalek from
under heaven'" (Exodus 17:9–14).*

Joshua's first recorded act in the Bible was his victory over Amalek
— that's quite the first impression. After Joshua's triumph, the Lord
told Moses to record the details of the victory, and to repeat them
to Joshua so he would never forget. This directive is important
because it reinforces our biblical instructions to strengthen
ourselves in the Lord, to strengthen others by sharing in God's
victories, and to recount God's victories to the next generation.

In addition to being a great warrior, Joshua was also a faithful
servant. One example of Joshua's faithfulness can be found when
God called Moses up into Mount Sanai and Moses brought Joshua
with him (Exodus 24:12–14). The Bible says that while Moses was
with God in the mountain for 40 days and 40 nights — receiving
the Law and the Commandments — God's children slid into
idolatry and forged a golden calf to worship. But Joshua did not
partake in the idol worship; he stayed on the mountain and waited
patiently for Moses to come back down (Exodus 32:17).

Caleb

Caleb is introduced at one of the most critical points in this story — when God's people reached the edge of the wilderness and sat on the outskirts of the Promised Land. Moses selected 12 rulers to go and search out the land — one ruler from each of the 12 Tribes of Israel; Joshua was chosen by Moses to represent the Tribe of Ephraim; Caleb was chosen to represent the Tribe of Judah (the lineage of Christ). The Bible doesn't say much about Caleb or give much of his backstory, but we know that he held a prominent position in the Tribe of Judah. We will learn that Caleb — much like Joshua — was also a faithful servant of God. The next section will demonstrate Caleb's sincere desire to serve the Lord and to encourage others to serve the Lord as well.

Application -

The wilderness is both literal and symbolic. It symbolizes a time in our lives when we are constantly tested — and perhaps never quite satisfied. It's not the "promised land" we want, but it's a crucial part of the journey to get there. In the wilderness is where we must decide whether we want to stay on God's path and continue to trust Him, or if we want to wander off track, backslide, and complain. It's the same battle of faith vs. unbelief that Joshua, Caleb, and the Israelites faced in their wilderness.

God never promised that we wouldn't spend time in the wilderness; in fact, it's almost guaranteed that we will. And while the Bible portrays a frustrating picture of the Israelites constantly failing in the wilderness, it also presents the inspirational stories of Joshua and Caleb, who remained faithful. Not only did Joshua and Caleb remain faithful in the wilderness, but they actually gained prominence and experienced blessings in the wilderness because of their trust in God. So, if God has brought us to a wilderness, then He's already prepared a way to get us through that wilderness if we're willing to trust Him.

Finally, just as Joshua was called on to fight against Amalek, there may come a time when God calls on us to join the fight as well. But the hard part is knowing when it's time to join the fight and when it's time to stand still and watch the Lord do the fighting; that's why seeking Him and hearing from Him personally are imperative. At the Red Sea, God fought for His children. But in the wilderness, God's children joined the fight. Simply put — when He says fight, fight; and when He says stand still, stand still.

Nebuchadnezzar

In the wilderness, most of God's children succumbed to complaining, murmuring, idolatry, and unbelief — even after the many miracles God had recently performed for them. Even though the Israelites knew God's Word and witnessed His power, continuing to obey Him wasn't easy for them. In this section, Joshua and Caleb are faced with two choices: follow the crowd and choose fear and unbelief or take a bold stance and trust God's Word despite the consequences. This difficult choice represents Joshua and Caleb's spiritual conflict, their Nebuchadnezzar.

The Twelve Spies

"See, I have set the land before you; go in and possess the land which the Lord swore to your fathers — to Abraham, Isaac, and Jacob — to give to them and their descendants after them.... Look, the Lord your God has set the land before you; go up and possess it, as the Lord God of your fathers has spoken to you; do not fear or be discouraged" (Deut. 1:8, 21).

The story of the 12 spies takes place after Moses led God's children through the wilderness to the edge of the Promised Land. And on the outskirts of the Promised Land, Moses sent 12 spies to determine whether they would be able to possess it. But given that God had already promised to give this land to His children — and God keeps His promises — the act of sending spies into the land teetered on the edge of unbelief, if not outrightly so. It's like receiving a diagnosis from a doctor, but then seeking a second opinion just to make sure the first diagnosis was accurate — there's not much confidence in the first doctor. God doesn't fail or make mistakes, so we either believe His Word or we don't; there's no such thing as a halfway faith.

The account of the 12 spies is given both in the Book of Numbers and in the Book of Deuteronomy. In both accounts, Joshua and Caleb are positioned as the examples of faith, conviction, courage, and strength. But before we get into the rest of this section, let's quickly remember what Joshua and Caleb — and the rest of the 12 spies — had witnessed up this point:

- God's power in Egypt through the plagues

- The Passover

- The parting of the Red Sea

- Their deliverance from Egypt

- The pillar of cloud by day and fire by night

- Manna from heaven

- Their victory over Amalek

All of God's children — including Joshua, Caleb, and the rest of the spies — experienced these miracles in the wilderness. So from here on out, they had every reason to believe God and to obey His command to possess the Promised Land.

Unbelief

After the spies searched the land, they brought their report back to Moses and found it to be exactly as God had described it: *"It truly flows with milk and honey" (Numbers 13:27).* But even though the land was everything they hoped for, and everything God said it would be, the stronghold of unbelief proved to be catastrophic.

"Nevertheless, the people who dwell in the land are strong; the cities are fortified and very large; moreover, we saw the descendants of Anak there" (Numbers 13:28).

The fearful spies were only focused on the difficulties, the problems, and the obstacles they saw — they did not have their eyes on the God who had already proved Himself to be greater than all these things. Moses recorded their complaints and unbelief in the Book of Deuteronomy:

"Nevertheless, you would not go up, but rebelled against the command of the Lord your God; and you complained in your tents, and said, 'Because the Lord hates us, He has brought us out of the land of Egypt to deliver us into the hand of the Amorites, to destroy us. Where can we go up? Our brethren have discouraged our hearts, saying, 'The people are greater and taller than we; the cities are great and fortified up to heaven; moreover, we have seen the sons of the Anakim there'" (Deuteronomy 1:26–28).

God promised to give this land to His children, but their rebellion made them think God somehow wanted to destroy them. These doubters became so twisted by unbelief that they heard the exact opposite of what God was saying. Unbelief is an outright attack on God's character and a rejection of His Word.

Joshua and Caleb's Response

Joshua and Caleb saw things differently than the other spies, and they chose to stand alone in their response to God's command; in fact, this was Caleb's shining moment. Just as his peers were toiling in fear and causing others to be discouraged, Caleb stood on the Word of the Lord and spoke with boldness.

"Then Caleb quieted the people before Moses, and said, 'Let us go up at once and take possession, for we are well able to overcome it'" (Numbers 13:30).

This was the attitude and language of faith and courage! But despite the faith of Joshua and Caleb, the rest of the people gave up and were full of excuses: the enemy is too strong, the walls are too big, and doing what God wants is just too hard. Ultimately, they allowed fear and doubt to control them.

"But the men who had gone up with him said, 'We are not able to go up against the people, for they are stronger than we. And they gave the children of Israel a bad report of the land which they had spied out..." *(Numbers 13:31–32).*

A clear line had been drawn in the sand: on one side stood Joshua and Caleb who were ready to act, and on the other side stood everyone else who chose comfortable slavery over uncomfortable victory. Joshua and Caleb were the outsiders, the oddballs, the misfits, and the troublemakers. Who would want to join them? We'll see in the next section how Joshua and Caleb were punished for their faith and even threatened with death.

Application -

The eyes of man and the eyes of God do not see the same way. Joshua and Caleb weren't blind; they saw the giants in the land, just like everyone else did. The difference was — for whatever reason — Joshua and Caleb were resolved to trust God at His Word. God's eyes saw victory for His children, but the doubtful eyes of the spies saw only defeat. I wonder how many times God has prepared a victory for His people that was forfeited because all they could see were the problems.

God may have something good for us up ahead, but to get there we'll have to endure some conflicts. But just as most of the Israelites were discouraged after seeing the giants, we might be intimidated or discouraged because of the obstacles that are in our way. This is the spiritual conflict for many, if not all, Christians. The task may feel too difficult, the waiting period may seem too long, and the people on the other side of the conflict appear to be too strong; there are always a million reasons to quit when we're faced with a spiritual conflict — but it's especially easy to quit when everyone around us has already quit.

The opposite is also true: if we don't quit, then it becomes easier for others to not quit; if we trust, it inspires others to trust as well.

FIERY FURNACE

Joshua and Caleb were the only two people who chose to follow God, and they faced a ton of pressure to change their minds; it was a classic case of peer pressure. Obeying God's Word and doing the right thing usually aren't the popular things to do; in fact, ignoring God's Word is easy, and it may even be comfortable or fun for a while. Joshua and Caleb made their decision to trust God, which placed them in opposition to their unbelieving peers. Joshua and Caleb found themselves facing not one but two fiery furnaces:

First, by standing alone and obeying God's Word, Joshua and Caleb were rejected by the group and threatened with being stoned to death.

Second, if they decided to change their minds or ignore God's Word, they would be accepted back into the group, but they would die in the wilderness.

So, why would Joshua and Caleb continue to obey God, knowing they would be excluded from their community and possibly killed for it? I'll attempt to answer that question in the next section.

Consequences

Sadly, the Israelites had become so discouraged by fear and doubt that they wanted to either return to slavery or die in the wilderness.

"And all the children of Israel complained against Moses and Aaron, and the whole congregation said to them, 'If only we had died in the land of Egypt! Or if only we had died in this wilderness! Why has the Lord brought us to this land to fall by the sword, that our wives and children should become victims? Would it not be better for us to return to Egypt?' So, they said to one another, 'Let us select a leader and return to Egypt'" (Numbers 14:2–4).

In the middle of this sad display, Joshua and Caleb once again went against the grain and spoke the truth about God, His character, and His promises.

"The land we passed through to spy out is an exceedingly good land. If the Lord delights in us, then He will bring us into this land and give it to us, 'a land which flows with milk and honey.' Only do not rebel against the Lord, nor fear the people of the land, for they are our bread; their protection has departed from them, and the Lord is with us. Do not fear them" (Numbers 14:7–9).

Joshua and Caleb's inspiring speech caused the Israelites to lash out and threaten to kill them (Numbers 14:10). But what could've been the demise of Joshua and Caleb turned out to be the demise of the doubters, who God referred to as an "evil congregation."

"'I the Lord have spoken this. I will surely do so to all this evil congregation who are gathered together against Me. In this wilderness they shall be consumed, and there they shall die.' Now the men whom Moses sent to spy out the land, who returned and made all the congregation complain against him by bringing a bad report of the land, those very men who brought the evil report about the land, died by the plague before the Lord" (Numbers 14:35–37).

Application -

Whenever we're faced with a moral or spiritual conflict, we're usually faced with multiple fiery furnaces as well. If we do the right thing, then we may be ostracized from our community or fired from our job, but if we choose to do nothing and say nothing, then maybe we'll save our job or our reputation, but we'll certainly forfeit what God has in store for us. The doubters surrounding Joshua and Caleb wanted to go back into Egypt and back into slavery, even though the wonderful blessings of God were right in front of them. That's how wildly impactful fear can be in our decision making.

Even though God's promise of victory was made abundantly clear, Joshua and Caleb were way outnumbered by the doubters and complainers. The Bible says the whole congregation wanted to stone Joshua and Caleb for their stance; it would've been much easier for them to join the group and let some other army fight the giants. Similarly, if God has given us clear instructions on what to do in our situation, we can also expect there to be many doubters and complainers who will stand against us — even among our closest friends and family. This is not an easy situation; it may break our heart and it may even cause us to reconsider our course of action. We might come to the point of asking God, "Why must I go through all this? What's the point?" But it's important to remember how that evil congregation of unbelief died in the wilderness; the path of faith, obedience, and boldness is a better path to follow.

 Joshua and Caleb chose the difficult and unpopular path, the path of obedience and faith. Their beliefs were so unpopular and offensive their peers were literally ready to kill them. But at the very last second — just before the people were about to kill Joshua and Caleb — God showed up.

"Now the glory of the Lord appeared in the tabernacle of meeting before all the children of Israel" (Numbers 14:10).

Not only did God step in and save Joshua and Caleb from the murderous mob, but He rewarded their faith; in fact, of the 12 original spies, Joshua and Caleb were the only two who didn't die of a plague in the wilderness.

"Now the men whom Moses sent to spy out the land, who returned and made all the congregation complain against him by bringing a bad report of the land, those very men who brought the evil report about the land, died by the plague before the Lord. But Joshua the son of Nun and Caleb the son of Jephunneh remained alive, of the men who went to spy out the land" (Numbers 14:36–38).

In the end, just two men — Joshua and Caleb — inherited the land which God had sworn to multiple generations, simply because they had the courage to stand up to peer pressure and obey God. Inheriting the Promised Land never required a strong army, the only requirement was faith.

"Surely not one of these men of this evil generation shall see that good land of which I swore to give to your fathers, except Caleb the son of Jephunneh; he shall see it, and to him and his children I am giving the land on which he walked, because he wholly followed the Lord.... Joshua the son of Nun, who stands before you, he shall go in there. Encourage him, for he shall cause Israel to inherit it" (Deuteronomy 1:35–38).

Earlier I asked why Joshua and Caleb would choose to obey God, knowing they would be excluded from their community and possibly killed. Every indication is that they were ready to die for their beliefs; if that wasn't true then they would've given in to the threats and gone along with whatever the group wanted. But that's not what happened. Joshua and Caleb weren't motivated by a life of ease or a land that flows with milk and honey. Every indication is that Joshua and Caleb were committed to serving God simply because they knew who He was, and they knew His character based on their past experiences. We too can come to the same conclusions.

Application -

We don't know the names of the ten spies who doubted and depressed a generation, but we do know the names of Joshua and Caleb. The point is, it matters what we believe, and it matters what we do with our faith. *"I have set before you life and death, blessing and cursing; therefore, choose life, that both you and your descendants may live" (Deuteronomy 30:19).* The choices we make today will not only impact our life, but the lives of our descendants as well. So, if God's Word is true (which it is), and God does what He says He will do (which He does), then we can trust that choosing the path of life will cause us to live.

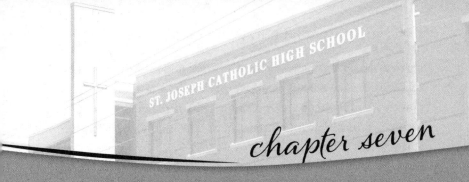

Josh Alexander

Josh Alexander was born in 2006 and by the time he was 17, he was a well-known public figure and speaker in Canada. Josh is an outspoken Christian and spends his time distributing Bibles, attending political and cultural rallies, organizing protests, and speaking out against ungodly and morally bankrupt political ideologies. He's an intelligent, poised, respectful, and well-spoken young man — it's no wonder his message resonates with young people. Even though he's barely old enough to drive, Josh is no stranger to spiritual persecution. In fact, he's been arrested more times than some criminals and he's been assaulted for quoting the Bible on more than one occasion.

Josh's Upbringing

Josh was homeschooled until the 7th grade, at which point he and his parents decided he would enroll in a local public school in Canada. In the public school system, Josh was an award-winning student who had never been disciplined or reprimanded in school. His parents were intentional about teaching him to become independent and respectful, and to have strong morals and traditional values. For example, Josh worked several days a week during the school year and was responsible for closing the building at night. He bought his own clothes, paid for his own gas, and bought his own food; he even made his own decisions regarding his education and his health, and by all accounts, Josh was thriving under this level of freedom. But no matter how much independence or responsibility Josh had, he maintained a loving relationship with his parents, and he highly valued their input and advice.

Something Sparked a Change in Josh

In January 2022, Josh was a 15-year-old student in 10th grade. He had always been a model student, but he was getting fed up with his public school's Covid mask mandates. Then, Josh started to notice the negative impacts that Canada's extreme Covid restrictions were having on his friends and kids his age. For example, there were reports of increased suicide rates, increased instances of substance abuse, increased porn consumption, and many other negative effects of social isolation. Josh said it was a situation everyone was struggling with, but nobody wanted to speak up about it because they were afraid of public backlash.

At the same time Josh noticed the dangers of lockdowns, the Canada freedom convoy, better known as the Freedom Convoy, came to town. You may remember hearing about this in the news, but as a reminder, the Freedom Convoy created a series of protests and blockades in response to Canada's Covid vaccine mandate for cross-border truckers. One day, Josh and some friends decided to check out the Freedom Convoy. When they arrived, they were amazed that life seemed so normal there — there were no Covid restrictions, no masks, no lockdowns. But when Josh returned home, everything was still locked down; it felt like a prison. Then on February 14, 2022, Prime Minister Justin Trudeau invoked the Emergency Act for the first time ever and shut down the Freedom Convoy. Nearly two years later, a Federal Court Judge ruled that Trudeau's use of the Emergency Act was unconstitutional.[1]

---

1. Christopher Nardi, January 24, 2024: https://nationalpost.com/news/politics/a-judge-ruled-trudeaus-use-of-the-emergencies-act-unconstitutional-so-what-happens-next.

Josh's experience at the Freedom Convoy was the spark that changed everything. After experiencing the courage of the Freedom Convoy, and their stance against extreme Covid mandates and the unconstitutional use of the Emergency Act, he realized he was done complying with unlawful policies and requirements at school. Josh returned from the Freedom Convoy and immediately began organizing school walkouts to protest his public school's Covid mask requirements. At Josh's first protest, which was the first time he ever took a public stand on his convictions, Josh was suspended from school.[2]

 **BABYLON** This section will give some background information on Josh and his school. It'll set the stage for Josh's conflict and will discuss how his collective school system defended gender ideology and shunned Christianity. In this way, the school system represents Babylon in Josh's story.

Josh's story, much like Jessica Tapia's story, deals with gender ideology in schools, but Josh's story is different in a few ways. First, Josh was a teenage student, while Jessica was a wife, mother, teacher, and coach. Second, Josh's conflict came mostly from adults in positions of authority who were much older than him, while Jessica's conflict came from peers, colleagues, and even some students much younger than her. Regardless of how similar or how different their stories are, it's important to relate to, and connect with, the dynamics of their conflicts so we can draw inspiration and be encouraged.

One thing I want to point out from this opening section is that Josh held very strong biblical convictions and he was committed to obeying God's Word; as a teenager, he held stronger convictions than most adults. Not only that, but he was willing to stand on his

---

2. Jordan B. Peterson, 2023, *Creeping Tyranny in Canada*, https://www.youtube.com/watch?v=zQ97LSG_qXQ.

beliefs, no matter the consequence. How often do we see something going wrong in our daily lives, but we ignore it or turn a blind eye? Maybe we think there's nothing we can do or that the problem is just too big for us to make a difference. Maybe we're afraid. Maybe we're so wrapped up in our own lives that we can't be bothered to notice. But as we've discussed already in this book, if we're sincerely following God and living out our faith, God may position us to take a stand that may bring real consequences. However the situation may play out, we know that God will show us the way through, and He will be with us.

Josh Goes to St. Joseph's Catholic High School

In the fall of 2022, just a few months after the Freedom Convoy and his first suspension, Josh entered the 11th grade at St. Joseph's Catholic High School in Ontario, Canada. Josh, a born-again Christian, transferred to St. Joseph's over the summer, assuming a parochial school would be more aligned with his values than his former public school. Spoiler alert: he was wrong. Within a few months of attending his new Catholic school, Josh was suspended twice, kicked out of school twice, and arrested on school grounds. His crime: taking a stand on his Christian beliefs in opposition to his school's transgender bathroom policy.

One of the most gripping elements of Josh's story is how strong his convictions were at such a young age. Josh's convictions were such that he couldn't turn a blind eye or ignore a situation he believed was truly wrong — he took action. Josh's Christian convictions will be on display throughout this chapter as he repeatedly took courageous stands based on his belief that the Bible is truly God's Word. Josh spoke the truth of God's Word in the middle of confusion, and he refused to bow to ungodly directives in the face of persecution. While it can be very difficult to stand up for God's Word without compromise, it's what Josh excels in.

Josh's collective school system, or Babylon, is made up of three main parts: his high school, his school board, and the Ontario Catholic School System (OCSS).

St. Joseph's Catholic High School is governed by the Renfrew County Catholic District School Board (RCCDSB).

RCCDSB, which is governed by OCSS, oversees 25 Catholic schools with the mission of, "Educating hearts and minds in the way of Christ."[3]

OCSS promises students "a spiritual, faith-based learning environment, where the teachings of Christ are central to the mission and vision of the educational experience."[4]

Thirty-one out of 37 school boards in the OCSS recognized Pride Month in 2022.

Ontario School Policies

The school policies in Ontario represent the governing laws in Josh's Babylon. Josh was required to follow his school's policies, several of which violated Josh's Christian beliefs. But where do these policies come from and what did Josh's Babylon look like?

Ontario's Catholic school system is unique because it's a part of the public school system and draws from the same public funds. But like America's public school system, Canada's schools follow a hierarchy in terms of funding and policies. For example:

America's public school system: state > district > school

Canada's public school system: province > district > school

Josh's Babylon: OCSS > RCCDSB > St. Joseph's Catholic High School

3. https://rccdsb.ca/.
4. Alexandra Ellison, April 7, 2023, https://wng.org/roundups/canadian-student-arrested-at-catholic-school-for-biblical-beliefs-on-gender-1680883437.

Every school policy in Ontario must adhere to the Ontario Human Rights Code, which prohibits discrimination "based on a protected ground in a protected social area." Under this code, gender identity and gender expression are listed as "protected grounds."[5] Gender ideology, as discussed in Chapter 2 of this book, rejects the biblical account of God's creation model, argues there are an infinite number of genders, and that each person is free to decide their gender for themselves. Isn't this essentially the clay telling the potter how it should be formed (Isaiah 45:9)?

Under this code, Josh's school implemented a transgender bathroom policy which allowed students to use the facility that aligned with their gender identity as opposed to their biological sex. Josh saw this policy as a clear rejection of God's Word because it denied God's creation model and promoted confusion and delusion instead.

> "The philosophy of the school room in one generation will
> be the philosophy of government in the next"
> — Abraham Lincoln.[6]

Wherever transgender policies like this are implemented, girls are the ones who suffer most. For example, under St. Joseph's transgender bathroom policy 18-year-old boys were given permission to share the same facilities with 14-year-old girls, as long as they identified as female. In this way, boys were permitted to view girls while at their most vulnerable, behind closed doors and with no adult supervision. This policy wasn't just implemented by Josh's principal; it was fought for and defended by the school board and the entire school system and set the stage for Josh's conflict with his school system.

---

5.   The Ontario Human rights Code, https://www.ohrc.on.ca/en/ontario-human-rights-code.
6.   https://www.brainyquote.com/quotes/abraham_lincoln_133687.

Sexuality Debate in Religion Class

In October of Josh's first semester at St. Joseph's, he was approached by several female classmates who confided in him about their feelings regarding the school's transgender bathroom policy. The girls told Josh they felt uncomfortable with male classmates using their facilities, especially (and predictably) while girls were changing clothes.[7] Josh felt compelled to defend these girls and to speak up on their behalf.

Josh was given the opportunity to advocate for his female classmates in a class debate on the topic of sexuality. During the debate, which took place in Josh's Religion class, students took turns sharing their opinions while the teacher facilitated the discussion; in this case, Josh's teacher also chimed in on the topic. As expected, there was overwhelming support for the school's transgender policy and the belief that a person's gender identity should always be affirmed. Josh's teacher claimed there were an infinite number of genders, and that everyone should be encouraged to explore their own unique gender identity.[8] At this point, Josh decided to join the debate and share his opinion, even though it stood out from everyone else's. Josh respectfully disagreed with his teacher and supported his argument by quoting Mark 10:6 which says:

"But from the beginning of the creation, God made them male and female."

Josh then mentioned the distinguishing characteristics between men and women, such as having different sexual reproductive organs. He argued that according to biology, a man cannot become a woman and a woman cannot become a man. And when Josh made that statement, his classmates began to call him a

---

7. Dylan Dyson, November 25, 2023, https://ottawa.ctvnews.ca/protest-over-gendered-washroom-use-at-renfrew-high-school-1.6169276.

8. Madeline Coggins, May 23, 2023, https://www.foxnews.com/media/canadian-student-speaks-out-after-detained-while-handing-free-bibles-protest-no-coincidence.

"misogynist," a "racist," and a "homophobic transphobe." Josh's teacher allegedly nodded along in agreement. Josh naturally assumed this new school — a Catholic school — would be more aligned with his biblical views, but to his utter surprise, it was not only hostile toward his biblical views, but zealous over gender ideology.

Application

Gender ideology took center stage during the Covid lockdowns of 2020–2021, but the seeds had been growing for generations. The "research practices" and theories of Alfred Kinsey and John Money had paved the way for today's concepts of gender identity and gender expression. Never mind that these theories, when put into practice, were complete failures and ended disastrously. But the culture created in and around these theories made it unsafe to have an opinion that differed from the group or differed from those in authority over the group. It became a test of courage to simply question such an obviously confusing and destructive ideology. The fact that public, private, and parochial schools are teaching these ideologies as fact (not merely presenting them as theory) in classrooms where children are in the most formative stages of life is a critical moral issue we face today. Josh's response, however, was based on the Bible and resulted in him being slandered, called names, and ostracized.

So, when we experience a culture that so openly opposes what God has laid out for us in His Word, we have several paths to choose from:

We can remain quiet and practice our faith privately while "loving the sinner and hating the sin." This approach will keep us out of trouble and will cost us nothing. Josh considered this approach and the moral direction it would inevitably produce in the lives of the students, and he decided against it.

We can try to avoid public pushback by saying, "Who are we to judge?" But when Josh's female classmates told him how the transgender policy was affecting them, Josh couldn't just turn a blind eye to the conflict and take a posture of pseudo-humility; he felt a responsibility to speak up on their behalf.

Another approach would be to chalk it up as just one more thing that's wrong with the world, so there's no advantage to speaking up about it. Besides, the world is full of people (and always has been) who are living in contradiction to God's Word. Speaking up won't change that. Josh didn't think this way. He believed that NOT speaking up, in actuality, was what's wrong with the world. After all, he was in a supposed Christian environment! Where were all the Christians speaking up for God's Word? Josh's voice gave support to the young women who were struggling with this policy, and it also gave a voice to God's truth in a "Christian" school.

Have you ever thought about standing up for someone but decided not to say something out of fear of being reprimanded or rejected? What does it take for someone to be willing to take such an unpopular and intimidating stand? It takes courage. Josh's courage was rare for anyone, but especially for someone his age.

Perhaps that's why Josh is admired so much by fellow Christians. Who do you and I want to be admired by?

Josh Stands up for His Classmates

Later that fall, after the heated classroom debate, Josh met with his school principal to explain that many female students were uncomfortable sharing facilities with male students. Unfortunately, Josh's principal was a roadblock rather than a support for these female students and chose not to address any of his or his female classmates' concerns. This was frustrating for Josh because he followed the appropriate protocol: he spoke to his classmates, he spoke to his teacher, and he spoke with administration, but it all fell on deaf ears.

After being ignored by his school administration, Josh felt compelled to take further action. So, he joined up with some classmates and used social media to organize a protest over the school's transgender bathroom policy. One of Josh's social media posts stated:

> "It is time to expose the perverted agenda in our education system ... males do not belong in female washrooms. Protect the girls from this evil narrative. Stop depriving our students of a healthy and natural environment. 'God made them male and female: Mark 10:6'...."[9]

Not only were Josh's social media posts open to the public, but the protest was open to the public as well. Josh even notified school administrators of the protest, informing them that it would take place during the school day, across the street, and off school grounds.

> "As a young man I feel an obligation to take action against something like that. I know there's a lot of misinformation posted online that this is an anti-trans rally, that's not the case. We just simply want male students removed from the female washrooms."[10]

Josh is Pre-emptively Punished

Josh's protest was scheduled to take place on November 25, 2022, but two days before the protest, Josh was given an "indefinite suspension" and placed under investigation for his alleged "bullying" of transgender classmates. As we'll discuss in the next section, these bullying allegations against Josh were not based on

9. Bruce McIntyre, February 12, 2023, https://www.pembrokeobserver.com/news/local-news/st-josephs-student-who-led-rally-against-open-bathroom-use-is-banned-from-attending-classes.
10. Dylan Dyson, November 25, 2023, https://ottawa.ctvnews.ca/protest-over-gendered-washroom-use-at-renfrew-high-school-1.6169276.

any of his actions, as he hadn't issued any threats or insults toward anyone; he was simply being punished for saying out loud what's been written in the Bible for thousands of years. And Josh's pre-emptive suspension, which was most likely meant to intimidate him into canceling the protest, only drew more attention to the issue.

> "My issue wasn't with the individual students. I have an issue with the system that is going to encourage this form of misbehavior.... I do sympathize with the confused transgender students ... because they've been wronged by their parents and by society and by the education system that has pushed this indoctrination on them. But at the same time, that doesn't mean I'm going to condone their wrongful behavior, especially when it's a violation of my female peers' privacy."[11]

This is an amazing statement. Josh's school system, their transgender bathroom policy, the class debate, the name calling, the principal's refusal to respond, the pre-emptive suspension — all these things together show the level of hostility toward Christianity that exists in Canada's culture. And at just 16 years old, Josh Alexander was willing to stand up to all of it, while at the same time showing compassion for his peers who'd fallen prey to gender confusion. Josh's boldness, conviction, and courage are rare and desperately needed today.

Application -

The more pushback Josh received, the louder and more visible his message became. We see this happen over and over in this book — how one person standing up can, surprisingly, result in others being encouraged to also stand up. And when Josh was

11. Peter Pinedo, February 23, 2021, https://www.catholicnewsagency.com/news/253702/canadian-catholic-school-student-who-was-suspended-for-protesting-transgender-bathroom-policy-speaks-out.

ignored, turned away, or shouted down, he didn't get discouraged; he simply shook it off and pressed forward.

This is reminiscent of when the Apostle Paul was imprisoned for preaching the Gospel. He told the church in Philippi: "... *most of the brethren in the Lord, having become confident by my chains, are much more bold to speak the word without fear" (Philippians 1:14)*. Putting Paul in prison was intended to stop the Gospel from spreading, but those efforts ended up having the opposite effect as more people were emboldened to speak without fear — the same is true in Josh's story.

What an interesting and counter-intuitive result! When faced with prison, as in Paul's case, who would anticipate it having such a positive effect? And yet, that's exactly what happened. Paul's persecution emboldened others to follow suit and speak the word without fear. Similarly, Josh's message wasn't popular or well received; that's the nature of being an outspoken Christian in Babylon. It would've been easier for Josh to disengage from the debate and let someone else take up the fight, but seeing Josh's courage can inspire us to have courage, and our courage, in turn, may give others courage as well. So, have courage! Because God stands with those who stand with Him.

If we have sought the Lord and are acting in obedience, we have cause to hope and believe that all things will work out for the good (Romans 8:28). Josh's resiliency reminds me of Matthew 10:14–15 which says, *"And whoever will not receive you nor hear your words, when you depart from that house or city, shake off the dust from your feet. Assuredly, I say to you, it will be more tolerable for the land of Sodom and Gomorrah in the day of judgment than for that city!"* We won't always get the response we hope for, but instead of allowing that to hinder us, we must shake the dust from our feet and soldier on.

 **Nebuchadnezzar**

If the collective school system (OCSS, RCCDSB, St. Joseph's Catholic High School) represents Josh's Babylon, then the leaders of the collective school system (school board, administrators) represent Josh's Nebuchadnezzars. In this section, we'll look at the commands that were given to Josh and the pressure that was placed on him to bow to the golden idol of gender ideology. More importantly, we'll focus on Josh's bold responses to Nebuchadnezzar's ungodly commands.

Josh's Protest

It's clear that Josh was living in an environment that was hostile toward the Bible and Christianity. But despite Josh's unwarranted suspension, his protest took place as scheduled on November 25, 2022, and because the protest was across the street and off school grounds, Josh was still able to attend. Josh's side of the protest was made up of about 30 people who were holding signs of Bible verses such as Mark 10:6. On the other side of the protest were various LGBTQ groups who, predictably, labeled Josh's group as a "terror organization."[12] There was a heavy police presence, but there was no escalation of violence.

Josh Is Suspended, Labelled a Bully and a Hater

Josh continued to serve his indefinite suspension while being investigated for alleged bullying. Then a few weeks later, on December 20, Josh's principal finished the investigation and sent a suspension letter to Josh's parents concluding that Josh was guilty of the following offenses:

◆ Making inappropriate comments to trans students.

◆ Refusing to recognize his classmates' trans identities.

---

12. Pinedo.

- Using "dead names" for trans students (a "dead name" is a trans person's name at birth).

- Stating that allowing males in female restrooms is unsafe.

- Making inappropriate comments about trans students on social media.

- Using a derogatory term in reference to a trans student.

According to Josh's principal, referring to a male as "he" is bullying, as is addressing a person by the name on their birth certificate. This was the standard being used to punish Josh. Josh was given a 20-day suspension on the grounds his actions were "bullying and harassing ... injurious to the moral tone of the school or the physical or mental well-being of others in the school ... motivated by bias, prejudice, or hate based on ... gender identity, gender expression, or other similar factors."[13]

Josh's indefinite suspension turned into an official 20-day suspension, and on top of that — according to his school system — he was now a bully, a harasser, unsafe, biased, prejudiced, and a hater. These were serious accusations against Josh's character, and they carried serious consequences. But no matter how harsh or unjust his punishments became, Josh held an incredibly strong resolve for the truth, and he was determined in his decision to hold fast to his faith rather than be intimidated by the unfair and inaccurate judgements made against him.

Application -

It's important to understand that Josh was not motivated by a desire to hurt or shame his trans classmates. It's also important to understand the kind of courage we're talking about — the kind of courage Josh was demonstrating — was mixed with love and compassion for others; it wasn't about attacking or demonizing people. Josh made it very clear the issue was not

---

13. *Alexander v. RCCDSB.*

with his classmates, but with an unjust system that was forcing an ungodly ideology on its students.

If we lash out in anger or make emotionally charged decisions, it can become difficult to know the line between hating evil vs. hating people. This is the case with every person highlighted in this book. The Apostle Paul clarified the confusion by saying, *"We do not wrestle against flesh and blood, but against principalities, against powers, against the rulers of the darkness of this age, against spiritual hosts of wickedness in the heavenly places" (Ephesians 6:12).*

Our job is to love people while proclaiming the truth, like the Apostle Paul did.

Josh Withdraws from Parental Control

After being suspended and having serious accusations leveled against him, Josh hired a lawyer to help appeal his suspension. Josh's appeal hit a snag because Canada's Education Act does not allow students under the age of 18 to make an appeal on their own behalf, which meant Josh's parents would have to speak for him — but Josh wanted to speak for himself. The law states that in Canada, a 16-year-old can be emancipated if they can demonstrate the ability to "live independently and support themselves financially."[14] So Josh, being a uniquely independent young man, capable of supporting himself and making his own decisions in life, qualified for legal withdrawal from parental control and became an independent minor, with the support of his parents. By doing this, Josh was be able to make his appeal and argue on his own behalf.

In the middle of perhaps the most difficult situation of his life, Josh made perhaps the most difficult decision of his life — to leave the protection of his parents and to stand on his own. This decision, however, would allow Josh to stand on his biblical convictions and to speak for himself, something that was core to Josh's values.

---

14. https://controlsafety.com.co/legal-age-to-leave-home-in-ontario-understanding-the-rules/.

For most teenagers, the reality of being independent may sound cool, but when the weight of responsibility and consequence sets in, most would rather let Mom and Dad handle things, and understandably so. But Josh was a different breed; he was built for this fight.

Nebuchadnezzar's Decree

Josh's 20-day suspension was served retroactively, meaning the days since his "indefinite suspension" on November 23 counted toward the 20 days. Josh was scheduled to return to school after winter break on January 9, 2023. In early January, Josh met with his principal to discuss his return to school, and he was given the following three conditions he must agree to or be excluded from school:

- Josh could not attend the two classes he shared with transgender students.

- Josh would have limited contact with students who identify as transgender.

- Josh was not allowed to use transgender students' birth names, a.k.a. "dead names."

Josh was presented with an ultimatum that required him to completely disregard his Christian convictions and adopt the principles of gender ideology. This was Nebuchadnezzar's decree: deny your God and bow or be kicked out of school.

Josh Refuses to Bow

Josh immediately rejected the conditions for his return, which he believed to be religious discrimination. On January 8, 2023, the night before he was scheduled to return to school from his suspension, Josh received an email from his principal stating he was being placed on a "non-disciplinary exclusion," which basically meant he was being held to his principal's terms whether he agreed or not. The letter asserted that Josh's mere presence would be detrimental to the physical and mental well-being of the transgender students.[15] By rejecting his principal's terms, Josh was forced into the fiery furnace.

"Shadrach, Meshach, and Abed-Nego answered and said to the king, 'O Nebuchadnezzar, we have no need to answer you in this matter. If that is the case, our God whom we serve is able to deliver us from the burning fiery furnace, and He will deliver us from your hand, O king. But if not, let it be known to you, O king, that we do not serve your gods, nor will we worship the gold image which you have set up'" *(Daniel 3:16–18).*

Even though he was bound for the proverbial fiery furnace, Josh wasn't willing to give up. He understood his school administrators were simply following the commands handed down from the school board and school system, but Josh had commandments of his own to follow that came from a much greater authority — the Word of God. So, despite being kicked out of his classes, Josh felt a sense of righteous indignation and decided, once again, to reject his school's unwarranted punishment. Josh's lawyer notified the school that Josh would not be complying with their "unlawful and discriminatory" exclusion of him from two classes; instead, Josh would be attending all his classes as usual.[16]

> "Josh believes he is called by the Lord Jesus Christ to proclaim the truth which includes telling those around him about the Lord's design for gender and to openly oppose the School Board's policy of permitting males to enter the girls' washrooms. Josh believes he would commit a sin if he disregarded the Lord's calling on his life and remained silent."[17]

So, on January 9, 2023, Josh returned to school for the first time since November and attended all his classes in person, including

15. McIntyre.
16. Ibid.
17. Coggins.

the two classes he was barred from attending. Though there were no incidents in any of these classes other than his mere presence, as a result of defying his first exclusion orders, Josh received a second "non-disciplinary exclusion," which meant that he was barred from school grounds and could not attend any of his classes in person; he would have to attend his classes online. Essentially, this was the school system's attempt at making the fire seven times hotter (Daniel 3:19).

Josh knew he would incur harsher punishments by bucking the system, but he was convinced holding his Christian beliefs did not constitute bullying, neither did they warrant him being suspended or excluded from school. In Josh's mind, complying with his principal's terms (Nebuchadnezzar's decree) would've been the same as denying his Christian beliefs.

> "I did this because I thought it was wrong to tacitly condone what I honestly perceived to be religious discrimination and to comply with directions that were unlawful."[18]

This one statement from Josh sums up the central message of his story, which is also the central message of this book: we must not cower in the face of spiritual conflict, but we must stand courageously on God's Word. Josh knew what his school expected of him, and he knew he would be punished for not complying with their discriminatory and unlawful exclusions. But Josh's defiance of the school's undue exclusions was not done out of rebellion, immaturity, or selfishness. Josh rejected the exclusions because, as he stated so well, going along with them was the same as "tacitly condoning" them, which he could not do while holding his Christian beliefs. If there's only one lesson to take away from Josh's story, this would be a good one.

---

18. *Alexander v. RCCDSB,* https://libertycoalitioncanada.com/wp-content/
    uploads/2023/01/Application_Josh-Alexander-v-RCCDSB_CV-23-00000025-0000_
    LCC-Website_redacted.pdf

Application ------------------------------------

Like Bonhoeffer, Josh had a biblical response to every ungodly policy. He received ungodly directives, and he responded with scriptural rejections. The key, however, is that Josh knew what he believed before he acted; he wasn't rebellious or anti-authority in his actions; he was simply living out his Christian beliefs. Some may look at Josh's refusals to comply as wrong or disrespectful to authority. But were the three Hebrew children wrong for not bowing to Nebuchadnezzar's golden idol? Was Josh's situation really any different?

Knowing when and how to act in the middle of conflict can be extremely difficult, and we don't always get it right; that's why we need to constantly seek God — in general, but certainly during times of conflict. Other times, God makes our path clear right away, and there's no looking back.

Josh's story, just like other stories in this book and just like our own story, is full of ups and downs and there's much to be learned from it all. But if your fiery furnace is getting hotter and you're thinking of giving up, just remember this is a crucial part of your story and that giving in now may be akin to tacitly condoning the wrong you are trying to stand against. Courage in the face of conflict isn't just a one-time decision but one that we must choose again and again as we walk towards — and walk through — the fiery furnace, no matter how much hotter it gets.

FIERY FURNACE

Josh was now in his fiery furnace, though in some ways, he stepped into the fiery furnace the moment he arrived at his new school. Christians everywhere carry a light inside them that's meant to be shared with others, but sometimes part of the conflict is that others want to snuff that light out — or they don't see it as a "light" at all. This section will discuss the continued punishments and persecution Josh endured because of his biblical stances against gender ideology and religious discrimination.

To this point, Josh had been suspended twice and excluded twice, and his conflict was about to reach its boiling point. What started as a difference of opinions in a class debate and Josh standing up for his classmates (who had asked him for help) had turned into an outright assault on Josh's religious liberty, his freedom of religious thought and expression, and Christianity in general. Josh was also losing course credits. Having just come out of the Covid lockdowns and the online learning debacle of 2020–2021, Josh knew from experience that online learning is inferior to in-person learning. Even though his school offered an online option, Josh turned it down because he felt he was being denied a quality education.

Josh Is Arrested and Kicked Out of School for the Year

If we know anything about Josh by now, it's that he wasn't willing to condone religious discrimination or unlawful directives. So, on the first day of the new semester (February 6, 2023), Josh attended his Automotive Mechanics class, despite being barred from school grounds — this was Josh's boldest stance yet. As soon as Josh walked into his Monday morning class, his teacher told him to leave the room and to go to the office. Josh was greeted in the office by two police officers, arrested, charged with trespassing, escorted out of the school, and placed in the back of a police car. Josh was then kicked out of school for the rest of the year. Does this sound like a fiery furnace? I think so.

> "I told the officer I should not be excluded from attending in-person classes because of religious discrimination against me."[19]

Josh, of course, was fully aware he was not allowed on school grounds, but he refused to "tacitly condone" religious

---

19. McIntyre.

discrimination and unlawful directives. Again, Josh expected to be punished for refusing to bow to his school's discriminatory rules, but his Christian beliefs, his faith, and his moral code all precluded him from condoning his school's actions. Even while being placed under arrest, Josh was clear in communicating his message and his beliefs. He knew what he was fighting for, and in fact, he'd been convinced of it all along. That's the key element in every spiritual conflict, isn't it? We must hear from God for ourselves as to what we are to do. Josh measured his responses against God's Word, acted on his convictions, and spoke the truth in love. Josh said it himself that he had compassion for the lost and the confused individuals, but he was against the systems that were perpetrating evil.

Public Persecution

A week after Josh's arrest, his school board wrote an open letter to the community saying the board "deeply respects religious freedoms.... While all our students are entitled — and encouraged — to share their beliefs — it cannot be at the expense of others.... No one should be made to feel unsafe or marginalized."[20] Statements like this come from the baseline perspective that merely holding Christian beliefs is threatening, oppressive, and abusive to non-Christians. Unfortunately, this baseline perspective is not rare, and we are seeing it gain increasing popularity in schools, workplaces, and our culture. That's part of why I am writing this book: the increasing hostility toward Christianity demands an increase in godly courage to stand against it. As confusion rises, truth must rise to meet it.

The school board's open letter to the community placed them in the position of moral superiority, while placing Christians in the "bully" category. The letter continued:

> "Bullying behavior that creates an unsafe space for our students is not tolerated.... A trans person should not be required to use a separate washroom or change room

20. Ellison.

because others express discomfort or transphobic attitudes, such as, 'trans women are a threat to other women.'"[21]

It's important to remember this whole thing started because a Catholic school — which claimed to place Christ's teachings at the center of its educational experience — implemented a transgender bathroom policy. And again, Josh wasn't just some rebellious teenager with an anti-authority complex. He was a Christian who'd never been reprimanded in school a day in his life. This whole time, Josh was simply living out his faith and doing what he believed was right in God's eyes, and he relied on God's Word to back him up. Josh said:

> "I did what I believe was right, what was right before God, so at the end of the day I'm happy with that."[22]

Josh maintained his compassion for the individuals who were confused about their gender, but he spoke out against and rejected the systems that were promulgating gender ideology. As a result, the same system that Josh stood against accused him of being a "bully" and a "hater." Josh responded to these labels saying:

> "I don't know what the next step will be. What I do know is I am being discriminated against for standing up for my personal and religious beliefs.... If you told me six months ago my life would have gone in this direction, I never would have believed you. This is not something any 16-year-old high school student could ever imagine, but here we are."[23]

Josh began with a simple biblical stance during a classroom debate, but it quickly turned into an intense spiritual crisis that would implicate his education, reputation, friends, public record — and even more. Not only did Josh get kicked out of school for the rest of the year but so did his parents. Josh's parents were both teachers in the public school district, but they were removed from their

21. Pinedo.
22. Ibid.
23. McIntyre.

teaching positions and placed under investigation during Josh's conflict with his Catholic school board.[24]

Application -

By now, Josh was fully committed to his path; if he was going to quit, he had plenty of opportunities already. Sometimes, we make it through a difficult trial and feel like we deserve a break, only to find that our sacrifices up to this point were just a precursor to the fiery furnace we were about to step into; this was Josh's experience. Everything up to this point had stayed inside Josh's school — his suspensions, exclusions, emails — but now he was being publicly disgraced by his school board, and his parents' reputations and livelihoods were threatened, too. Don't be surprised if, after you take a stronger stand, your Nebuchadnezzar turns up the heat on you.

Josh Is Assaulted and Arrested While Distributing Bibles

A few months after being arrested in school, Josh's legal representation (Liberty Coalition Canada) organized a protest on May 17, 2023, called the "I Stand with Josh Alexander Walkout." The protest was intended to garner support for defending religious freedom, keeping men out of women's restrooms, and promoting a return to a traditional culture. But just a few minutes into the event, Josh was assaulted while handing out free Bibles. The assault was caught on video and showed Josh holding his hands in the air while being pushed, shoved, and even choked by a mob of counter-protestors. Despite the video evidence of his non-violent response, Josh was the one arrested and removed from the protest.

"My goal isn't to run in there and fight with crazed activists. I want to get through to students, and I want to be a

---

24. Coggins.

responsible role-model to them and to be able to bring
them the truth in a way they will listen to it."[25]

Josh's persecution had now left the confines of the schoolhouse
and was taking place in the public square. Here Josh presents an
interesting picture in that he's in the middle of persecution, but
he didn't stop handing out Bibles; he didn't stop speaking the
truth; he kept on going, even though the fire was getting hotter all
around him. You might be asking yourself, "What's the point of
going through the conflict?" If you haven't found an answer to that
question yet, we will come back to it in the next section.

Josh's Appeal Is Delayed, Rejected, and Banned

Way back on December 22, 2022, Josh withdrew from parental
control and met the legal requirements to appeal his suspension
and argue on his own behalf. But for more than half a year, Josh's
school board refused to recognize him as an independent minor,
despite having received the proper paperwork from Josh's lawyer.
This intentional delay went on for as long as the school board
could get away with it. Then, in the spring of 2023, Josh filed a
complaint with the Ontario Superior Court of Justice, seeking an
opportunity to have his appeal heard. And finally, on August 31,
2023, a judge ruled that Josh indeed had withdrawn from parental
control eight months earlier on December 22, 2022, and his school
board must honor his right to have his appeal heard; it was a small
win that would be short-lived. Josh's lawyer commented on the
school board's delay tactics:

> "There needs to be accountability. From my perception, the
> school board's move here was to avoid that accountability,
> either through delay or hoping that Josh Alexander goes
> away because it is expensive to go to court. Thousands of
> dollars go into a motion like this — to do it right and to

25. Peterson, Jordan B. "The Future of Canada". The Jordan B. Peterson Podcast. https://
www.dailywire.com/podcasts/the-jordan-b-peterson-podcast/jbp-josh-and-nick.
November 22, 2023.

win. If the court followed the law as written, there was no doubt we were going to win."[26]

Josh's school board had no choice but to hear his appeal, and on November 15, 2023, Josh was finally given the opportunity to have his appeal heard. Josh's meeting, however, was not what he had hoped: he met in a private room with a three-person panel made up of school board trustees.[27] The panel promptly rejected Josh's appeal and placed its decision under a "publication ban," which meant no one could read it. James Kitchen (Josh's lawyer) responded to the publication ban:

> "They have sealed the entire file as if it was a case of a national security concern or some sort of criminal case.... Court proceedings are open to the public. The public has access to them. People have a right to use the fact that they have access to promote, advertise, and bring scrutiny or accountability to the decision-makers. It is also a free speech and fair trial right."[28]

The school board attempted to control the narrative by making repeated claims that Josh's suspension was never about his religious beliefs. To such claims, Kitchen responded:

> "This is pretty wild because it basically tells everyone who could read this decision to deny their eyes and ears. Any person who is honest and is using critical thinking would say, 'Obviously it is about his religious beliefs, and obviously it is about what he said.'"[29]

The board's decision to uphold Josh's suspension meant Josh was unable to receive his credits for that school year, he was still barred

---

26. Quinton Amundson, September 12, 2023, https://www.catholicregister.org/item/35861-student-suspended-over-gender-stance-wins-appeal.

27. Liberty Coalition Canada, December 21, 2023, https://libertycoalitioncanada.com/liberty-defense-fund/josh-alexander-v-rccdsb/.

28. Quinton Amundson, December 21, 2023, https://www.catholicregister.org/item/36285-renfrew-board-upholds-josh-alexander-s-suspension.

29. Ibid.

from school grounds, and he would have to complete his future course work from an off-campus site. The entire school system doubled down on everything. Josh was expected to accept this ruling and to deny his Christian faith.

Application -

If we stop the story there, it's a pretty discouraging message. By this time, most people would've called it quits, but this is one of Josh's defining qualities — he never called it quits. But, as God has proven over and over, He specializes in turning our trials and tribulations into more and greater opportunities. No matter how harsh the punishment seems, God is greater still.

Just having strong convictions and strong beliefs isn't the point. The point is knowing where our convictions and beliefs come from. What are they based on? It matters what we believe because what we believe impacts what we do with our time on earth, which impacts eternity. Ultimately, the big question is "Do my convictions and my beliefs line up with God's Word?"

Earlier I asked, "What's the point of going through the conflict?"

I addressed this question in the Introduction section of this book when I talked about encouraging ourselves in the Lord, strengthening our peers, and telling our children about God's wonderful works. So, one significant benefit to standing on God's Word through our conflicts is to grow in our walk with God and to help others do the same.

This last section of Josh's story will be a little different than in other chapters because Josh's story is still just getting started. At the time this was written (Spring 2024), Josh was 17 years old, and his lawyers were still deciding how to proceed after the school board's decision to bar him from school grounds. The fact that Josh's story is still unfolding means it's at a critical point; he's still walking through the fiery furnace. But every person featured in this book, at one time or another, was in the place Josh is in right now: walking through the fire, wondering when God will show up, and not sure if taking a stand was worth it. This is a critical point in the conflict for every Christian because it's where many people decide to give up.

Hopefully this book has shown how, time and again, God has walked through the fire with each person who stood with Him. But just wait! While Josh's story isn't finished, his story is much bigger than his high school dilemma. God is using Josh's story to draw attention from around the globe, not just to the stand he took, but to the Gospel itself.

Save Canada

Throughout his conflict, Josh has taken advantage of opportunities to preach God's Word and to shine a bright light in areas of darkness. One example of this has been Josh's involvement with the Save Canada movement, which is a national movement focused on restoring a traditional culture in Canada.

> "We have taken up the responsibility of igniting the Canadian youth by awakening them to the corrupt agenda being forced upon them. We are engaging in legal, political, spiritual, and ideological battles against the evil forces."[30]

Through this movement, Josh has been able to connect with, help, and learn from other young people who, like him, have taken courageous stands on God's Word in the face of spiritual conflict.

Man Rules, God Overrules

After Josh was assaulted and arrested at the "I Stand with Josh Alexander Walkout" in May of 2023, he was interrogated by the police and asked what Scriptures he was quoting at the protest. This was an attempt to charge him with hate crimes against the

---

30. https://savecanada.shop/pages/contact.

LGBTQ community. Josh was released from police custody and ordered not to return to his event; if he did return, he would be arrested immediately and charged with disrupting the peace. As soon as he was released, Josh gathered up his Bibles and began walking back to the protest. But just as Josh was about to step foot on the protest grounds, he was abruptly stopped and swarmed by hundreds of students who'd traveled to hear him speak. And since he had been stopped short of the police boundary line, Josh was able to stay for hours, handing out Bibles and talking to hundreds of Canadian youths.

A Larger Platform

Josh's story, particularly his arrests, has garnered national media attention in Canada and in the U.S., which has resulted in Josh appearing on national and international programs with Tucker Carlson and Jordan B. Peterson — both have huge audiences. Josh was also invited to speak at Turning Point USA's annual conference, AmericaFest, where he was given a platform to speak alongside prominent Christian and Conservative figures like Charlie Kirk, Glenn Beck, Riley Gaines, Dr. Ben Carson, Eric Metaxas, Allie Stuckey, and Candace Owens. Through these opportunities, Josh's story and message has been shared with people throughout North America and around the globe.

Parents Matter

I want to finish Josh's story talking about one of my favorite subjects: godly parents. Josh is an impressive and inspiring young man; that's why I chose to feature him in this book. But he didn't raise himself; his values and principles came from his parents. Here's a short story that shows just how much Josh loves, honors, and reveres his parents — a true testament to their success.

In December of 2023 Josh and his brother Nick appeared on Jordan B. Peterson's YouTube talk show. The boys were asked how their religious beliefs impact their political actions. Josh's brother spoke for the two and gave the following answer:

> "My political actions are based on my moral compass, and my moral compass is based on my biblical beliefs, the Bible."[31]

Josh agreed wholeheartedly with his brother's perspective and gushed how his parents have been excellent role models in a time when the nuclear family is under attack. Josh also credited his spiritual formation to the godly influence of his parents, who happen to be former pastors of a church in Arizona. And through the passing down of their godly heritage, Josh's parents modeled Proverbs 22:6 which says, *"Train up a child in the way he should go, and when he is old he will not depart from it."* Training matters. If Josh hadn't received a sound, biblical upbringing, then what would his moral compass look like now? What would his political actions look like? Yes, Josh deserves a lot of the credit in this chapter, but the influence of godly parents cannot be overstated.

Application

The most important thing about every person featured in this book is that they know God and have been willing to be used by Him, no matter the cost. There are many similarities, and some differences, in the ways God showed up in Josh's story compared to other stories in this book; each person and situation is unique. Not everyone will become a national figure at age 17 and be invited to speak at international events. Not everyone will be arrested for taking a biblical stand and have articles and books written about them. In fact, many of us might do the most courageous thing of our lifetime, only to have nobody know about it but you and God. And if that is the case, we'll be rewarded by God in His own way and in His own time. And we will have the satisfaction of knowing that we are people of

---

31. The Dr. Jordan B. Peterson Podcast, December 2023.

courage who responded obediently to what God has called on us to fulfill.

chapter eight

Corrie ten Boom

Corrie ten Boom was a Dutch clock maker, Bible School graduate, and social club leader — until the Germans invaded Holland and WWII began. During the war, Corrie became a leader for the Dutch underground operation that rescued Jewish families from Nazi concentration camps. Corrie was arrested in 1944 by the Gestapo and taken to prison, along with her family; she spent nearly a year in Nazi concentration camps. Corrie survived the Holocaust and went on to become a world-wide evangelist, a best-selling author, and an internationally renowned speaker. She also organized various Christian outreaches in Holland and Germany to help people recover from the trauma of WWII.

The ten Boom Family

Corrie's last name (ten Boom) is a rather uncommon Dutch surname which means "at the tree." The ten Boom family had such a godly heritage that when Corrie's grandfather, Willem ten Boom, opened the family clock shop in Holland in 1837, he often held prayer meetings there to pray specifically for peace in Jerusalem.[1]

Corrie's father, Casper, took up the family occupations of being both a devout Christian and a master clockmaker. Casper had

---

1. Corrie ten Boom, John Sherrill, and Elizabeth Sherrill, *The Hiding Place* (New York City, NY: Bantam, 1920).

a bushy white beard resembling Santa Clause, and he was well liked among the townspeople. And since the family clock shop happened to be on the main floor of their home, Casper's customers would often stop by his clock shop to receive a prayer, ask for advice, or just to chat. All through Corrie's childhood, her father would gather the entire family at morning and at night to read the Bible together. Casper's devotion to the Lord had a profound influence on all of his children, especially Corrie. Just as the Lord's door to salvation is open to all, the ten Boom's home was always open to those in need — Casper was adamant about that.

Corrie's mother, Cornelia, had always been a steady source of comfort and support for her. Cornelia was always busy tending to the rest of the ten Boom household, while Casper was kept busy tending to his clock shop. And if ever a family in their town was in need, it was common for the ten Booms to invite that family to stay with them in their home. At any given time, there could've been up to a dozen people living in the ten Boom house, including Corrie's parents, siblings, aunts, and any other guests in need; the ten Booms found that there was always someone in need. Sadly, Cornelia died in 1921 after a series of strokes.

Corrie had three older siblings — Willem Betsie, and Nollie. Corrie's brother Willem studied in Germany, held a doctorate in Philosophy, and became an ordained minister. Her sister Nollie was a teacher; and Betsie was the bookkeeper in their father's clock shop. All the ten Boom children were required by their father to learn to speak German and English, as well as Dutch, which made practical sense given that the Netherlands were geographically located between Germany and Belgium. The ability for Corrie and her siblings to communicate with people from different countries would prove to be a very useful skill, especially during WWII.

Corrie's Life Before WWII

Corrie was born in 1892 and gave her life to the Lord when she was just 5 years old. Whether she was living in her hometown or traveling the globe, Corrie spent the next 86 years of her life sharing the message of God's love and forgiveness.

When she was 17, Corrie developed tuberculosis and spent most of her time lying in bed. She began to wonder why God would allow an uncurable disease to come upon her at such a young age. Eventually, Corrie decided to focus on living each day to the fullest instead of constantly worrying about dying. Fortunately, Corrie found out that her tuberculosis was a misdiagnosed case of appendicitis, which was cured by an operation. So, what seemed like a death sentence was really a blessing in disguise. Now Corrie was committed to living her life to the fullest, and once she was healthy enough, she did just that.

With a new lease on life, Corrie began helping Nollie teach Bible lessons. Eventually, Corrie began teaching Bible lessons on her own and she even went on to earn a degree from Bible School. She also started a walking club that met before church on Sunday mornings. The club became so popular that membership grew to over 300 young girls. As one opportunity led to another, Corrie started more and more clubs — a gymnastics club, a drama club, and even a German language club. In 1919, at the age of 27, Corrie founded what was known as "The Triangle Club," where boys and girls could meet, socialize, and learn about God. Corrie had a real talent for working with people. She could identify their needs and then find the resources to meet those needs. She was so good at it that her clubs became known throughout all of Holland. And to top it all off, Corrie eventually followed in the footsteps of her father and grandfather and at the age of 32, she became Holland's first certified female clockmaker.

The Beje

The ten Boom home is an extremely important part of Corrie's story: in fact, it's so important that it's become a museum in her hometown of Haarlem. Corrie's home was located at 19

Barteljorisstraat in the city of Haarlem. It was affectionately
nicknamed the "Beje" (pronounced, Bay-yay). In many ways, the
ten Boom house was the town's social hub; whether business was
being conducted at the clock shop, people were stopping by to
pray with Casper, students were taking a Bible class with Nollie, or
young men and women were participating in one of Corrie's clubs
— people were constantly coming in and out of the Beje. For all
intents and purposes, the Beje was more than just a home; it was a
business, a hospital, a church, a kitchen, a town hall, and a haven,
and it had always been that way. It's as if the ten Boom family had
been preparing for a hundred years for what lay ahead.

The Angels' Den

One of the most unique features of the Beje is that it's actually two
separate houses that were joined together. The floors of the two
houses were uneven by a few feet, so there were some awkward
gaps, unusual nooks, and clever hiding places wherever the two
houses were connected.

Without a doubt, the most important room in the Beje was the
secret room where Corrie and her family would eventually hide
Jews from the Nazis. This hiding place, known as the Angels' Den,
was hidden behind a wall in Corrie's upstairs bedroom.

This room was created by a renowned European architect who
appeared at the Beje one day — out of the blue — with the skills
and desire to help the ten Booms during the Nazi occupation. Over
the course of several days, he and some fellow craftsmen snuck
supplies in and out of the Beje until this room, the Angels' Den,
was complete. And because the entrance to the room was not
noticeable to the naked eye, it became the perfect hiding place.

Application -

It boggles the mind to think that in the 1830s — over 100 years
before the Holocaust — Corrie's grandfather was holding prayer

meetings to intentionally pray for peace in Jerusalem in the very same home that became a safe haven for Jews during WWII! Willem ten Boom — a clock maker in 19th Century Holland — was moved by the Lord to pray for the Jews, a holy burden he would pass on to his son Casper, and eventually to Corrie and her siblings.

God blessed Corrie with gifts and talents (Bible studies, languages, prayer meetings, organizing clubs) that proved to be instrumental in her life, both during the war and beyond. In the same way God prepared Corrie, He is preparing each one of us for something specific. And just as Corrie never could have anticipated how God would use her everyday experiences to one day accomplish a seemingly impossible assignment, we may not see how God can use our everyday experiences to accomplish what He has called us to do.

Every life is full of unique details and every person has unique gifts, talents, and abilities. And sometimes, our imperfections or disjointed experiences are seen as flaws or quirks, but just as God was able to use the structural flaws of the Beje to achieve a divine purpose, He can use our perceived imperfections as well. As a master weaver creates a tapestry, God can take the smallest details of our lives and masterfully weave them into His plan. It's imperative that we see our lives through the lens of faith and God's Word, otherwise we may miss out on God's little masterpieces.

 BABYLON Babylon represents a world in opposition to God and His ways, and during the 1930s and early 1940s, Hitler and the Nazis forged a murderous and evil path that ran in complete opposition to God's ways. Many Nazis believed they were destined to be the "master race," and anyone that didn't fit the description of this "master race" was in imminent danger — the Jews were at the top of that list. And

since Hitler's army controlled most of Northern Europe during WWII, the Nazis posed a very serious threat.

The series of events that led up to WWII and the Holocaust are extremely important to understanding Corrie's (and so many others') story. For the sake of focusing on Corrie's unique life, it may be helpful to share a few examples of how Jewish persecution began in Germany years before the war started (some of this information was included in Dietrich Bonhoeffer's story). To be clear, Corrie was not Jewish, but she and her family were used by God to help Jewish families.

◆ 1933: Hitler banned Jews from holding public office, from working in civil services, and from being teachers and journalists.

◆ 1935: German Jews had their citizenship removed; they could not vote or marry non-Jews.

◆ 1938: Jews were not allowed to be doctors or lawyers in Germany.

◆ Around this same time, some Jews began fleeing to other countries to avoid persecution, but many Jews decided not to leave their homes, perhaps thinking that the worst of their persecution had passed. [2]

Hitler's persecution of the Jews rapidly increased during the 1930s, along with his thirst for power, and by 1940, Germany had invaded Holland, Corrie's homeland. Holland had remained neutral during WWI, and fully intended on remaining neutral during WWII as well. But Holland's neutrality did not stop Hitler's army from invading; neither did it stop them from occupying Dutch cities, raiding Dutch homes, or killing Dutch people. Since the ten Booms had been rooted in Holland for generations — and they happened to be Christians who loved the Jewish people — it was only a matter of time until they came face-to-face with this enemy.

2.   Janet and Geoff Benge, *Corrie ten Boom: Keeper of the Angels' Den* (Seattle, WA: YWAM Publishing, 1999).

Partly because of its neutrality and partly because of its lack of military power, Holland's prime minister had no choice but to sign a letter of surrender to Hitler, just days after being invaded, and it wasn't long until German soldiers took control of Corrie's hometown.[3] As Hitler's army took control of more and more countries in Northern Europe, only Great Britain remained free from German occupation. For a short time after invasion, it seemed that the German army intended to use Holland as a temporary base camp from which they would soon move on. Unfortunately for the ten Booms and for all of Holland, they did not soon move on.

Jews were being systematically isolated and eradicated from Northern Europe, and were forbidden from entering stores, restaurants, and public libraries. Jewish businesses were shut down and entire Jewish families began to disappear overnight; maybe they escaped or maybe they were taken to concentration camps — nobody knew for sure. Hitler, of course, believed the eradication of the Jews was essential, which meant forced compliance was also essential for the Germans to win the war.

As Jewish persecution reached a fever pitch, it was no longer taking place behind closed doors, but it began taking place out in the open — obvious and visible to the public. As German soldiers began openly mocking Jewish citizens in the street, it wasn't long until Dutch citizens followed suit and began to discriminate against their own Jewish neighbors. Even though Dutch Jews were being heavily persecuted, most Dutch citizens were still able to live their lives, albeit with certain restrictions, and since nobody wanted to lose any more of their privileges, they didn't ask questions or speak up. In fact, many Dutch people were eager to join the National Socialist Bond, a Nazi group, to gain preferential treatment from the German army.

Soon, the Jews had no freedoms whatsoever and any Jews who remained in Holland were forced into hiding. The German soldiers that occupied the town, along with the Gestapo, focused their

3. Ibid., p. 33.

attention on the Dutch citizens, especially those suspected of helping Jewish families escape. Church services around the country became increasingly full, which would've been a good thing except sermons became increasingly censored by German authorities, and speaking out against the German occupation was almost certainly a death sentence. In one church service, Corrie's nephew played Holland's national anthem on the piano, and he was arrested and taken to prison.[4] The ten Booms no longer recognized their home and — along with all of Holland and most of Europe — they were held under the thumb of an evil ideology.

Application

Not only did the Nazis hold very strong convictions, but they had the means to force others to comply with their worldview. The Hitler Youth had been formed as a strong, obedient, ideologically driven military force, and the German political infrastructure was also established and motivated. This allowed the Nazis to become very powerful and extremely dangerous. This was the world in which Corrie and the ten Boom family lived.

Elements of the Nazi's Socialist-Fascist ideology can be found in our current culture as well, especially in our government-run schools and universities. For example, one tactic that's used to implement a Socialist ideology is to begin the indoctrination process with small steps in ideological thinking and, over time, move toward a more radical result. Additionally, academics are then pushed aside (just look at our nation's scorecard), and the focus is increasingly placed on race and gender, revisionism takes place, and ideological wedges are then driven between children and their parents. The Fascist element in our schools and universities criticizes and shuts down anyone who opposes those ideals. If you haven't read my first book, *Conflicted*, I clearly lay out disturbing patterns in our own public education system

---

4. Ibid., p. 53.

that follow the pattern used by Hitler and the Nazis leading up to the Holocaust.

There is another commonly held (but erroneous) belief in our culture that education should be neutral when it comes to religion. I strongly contend there is no such thing as neutrality in education because there is always a default worldview! If an atheist teaches there is no God, that is not a neutral perspective. If a scientist teaches the earth was not created but was formed at the Big Bang, that is not neutral theory. If a philosophy teacher says there is no objective truth, that is not a neutral statement. Without God and without the Bible, the best that man can come up with is human secularism, where we are the center of our own universe (which, by the way, is also not a position of neutrality). Neutrality simply is not possible in education.

Holland tried to remain neutral during the war, but that just made it easier for the Germans to invade and take over. Dutch citizens were afraid to speak up or ask questions during German occupation, and eventually the Germans came for them, too. Over time, Dutch citizens started working with the German army by betraying their Jewish neighbors.

The German army was never neutral; they had a clear belief, and they acted on that belief. It wasn't until they were met by the Allied forces that the tide of evil began to be pushed back. Corrie and the ten Boom family weren't neutral either; they held strong biblical convictions on which they staked their lives, and through God's grace, they were able to save lives. Evil will overcome neutrality and lead to total corruption if it goes unchecked.

"A little leaven leavens the whole lump" (Galatians 5:9).

It matters what we believe, and it matters what we do with our belief as well. Hitler and the Nazi regime believed in their "master race" theory and they also believed the Jews were their great enemy. So, what did they do about it? They attempted to exterminate the Jews. The ten Boom family believed the Word of God declared the Jews to be a sacred people and, as such, should be protected and defended. So, what did the ten Booms do with their belief? They dedicated their lives to serving God, preaching the Gospel, and saving the Jews (and anyone else they could) from the Nazi death camps.

Nebuchadnezzar

Nebuchadnezzar can represent the ways and judgments of man, which are ungodly, in contrast with the ways and judgments of God, which are righteous. Nazism is a racist ideology that seeks to destroy the Jews along with anyone who helps the Jews; its ways and judgments are altogether evil. Corrie had two paths to choose from as she came face-to-face with this Nebuchadnezzar:

She could cooperate with the Nazis to save herself — her life, her comfort, her reputation, her family, and her freedoms — but in doing so, she would be consenting to the murder of her Jewish friends.

Or she could resist evil and help the Jews but risk her own life.

Corrie chose to resist evil and to help the Jews, a choice which put her life in jeopardy.

Nebuchadnezzar, in Corrie's story, is represented by different groups or individuals at different times; the groups are not necessarily interchangeable. They are:

- The German army: invaded Holland and carried out Hitler's mission; most soldiers would've been Nazis, but not all.

- The Gestapo: secret police who were used to spy, raid homes, and arrest Jews and Jew helpers; this would've been a mix of people such as German soldiers, Nazis, Dutch police, and regular citizens.

- The Nazis: members of the National Socialist political party that held control over Germany during WWII; not all Germans during WWII were Nazis.

- SS Guards: emphatic supporters of Hitler used to enforce his agenda; assumably most, if not all, were Nazis.

- Hitler: as the chancellor of Germany and leader of the Nazi Party, Adolf Hitler most closely represents Nebuchadnezzar in this story; he used others to carry out his evil commands.

Courage to Stand: The Underground

The first time Corrie was approached by a Jewish friend for help was in June of 1941, one year after Germany invaded Holland. Jewish people, especially men, were being hunted down, rounded up, and shipped off to concentration camps where they were either sentenced to slave labor, death, or both. With each passing week, more and more Jewish families, mostly women and children, were coming to the ten Booms for some kind of help — some needed a place to sleep that was safe from the Gestapo, some were trying to escape Holland, but all needed food. Corrie quickly realized that she didn't have enough food to feed all her guests, so she went to her brother Willem for help. Because Willem received his doctorate in Germany, he had always been Corrie's most trusted source for German news. Willem was also involved in the underground operation, he was a preacher, and Corrie knew she could trust his advice.

Willem and his wife ran an elderly care facility in Holland and many of their patients happened to be Jewish. Corrie explained her situation to Willem and said she didn't have enough food to feed all her guests. Willem's response came as a shock to Corrie. He suggested that she start stealing ration cards to get food for her guests. Initially, Corrie thought Willem's advice was outrageous, but as she traveled back to the Beje and thought about the people who'd risked their own lives just to get to her house, she began to change her mind. Corrie said:

"These desperate Jewish people had come to them for refuge, and they would not be turned away. Whatever it took, wherever it led, Corrie ten Boom promised herself she would find a way to help these people."[5]

By the time Corrie returned home from meeting with Willem, she had settled it in her mind that she needed to get more ration cards to help her guests stay alive. Fortunately, Corrie had many friends in the underground who offered to help. While it was a good thing that more and more people were offering to help, it also meant that more and more people were risking their own safety. At any moment, the Gestapo could raid the Beje and take everyone to the concentration camps; one mistake could cost all their lives.

Consequences: The Gestapo Raids Corrie's House

By 1943, there were very few Jews left in Holland. Most had been taken to concentration camps, some had escaped through the underground, and some were still in hiding. The German soldiers and the Gestapo were using more creative methods of finding Jews, such as using spies and raids. In fact, both Nollie's and Willem's homes were raided by the Gestapo and Nollie was arrested for hiding Jews.[6] Corrie was hiding four Jews and two underground workers, so it was only a matter of time until the Gestapo showed up at the Beje.

Corrie had developed the reputation for being the ringleader of the Beje's underground operation, and fear continued to mount that the Gestapo would raid at any moment. The ten Boom family asked themselves the same question they'd asked since the very beginning: "Should they go on with their underground activities and put themselves and their guests at risk?"[7] And despite the

---

5.   Ibid., p. 58.
6.   ten Boom, Sherrill, and Sherrill, *The Hiding Place*, p. 126.
7.   Benge, Corrie ten Boom: Keeper of the Angels' Den, p. 79.

inevitability of a Gestapo raid, their answer was the same as it had always been: a resounding "Yes!"

Eventually, the Gestapo caught wind of Corrie's underground operation and sent a spy to spring the trap. On February 28, 1944, a man named Jan Vogel came to visit Corrie at the Beje. Corrie had never seen this man before, but she was willing to hear him out. He claimed that his wife had been arrested for helping Jews and that a mutual friend in the underground had sent him to Corrie for help. Corrie happened to be battling an illness at the time and her head was spinning, but since nobody used their real names in the underground anyway, Corrie assumed the man was telling the truth. Corrie assured Jan Vogel that she would help him, but she asked him to come back later so she could rest a bit first. A few hours later, Corrie woke up to a commotion as her six guests sprinted up the stairs, through her bedroom, and into the hiding place. The Gestapo were raiding the Beje. Apparently, Jan Vogel was the spy who betrayed the ten Boom family, and his plea for help was just a ruse.

Corrie, Betsie, Casper, and the rest of the ten Boom family were detained by the Gestapo during the raid. Corrie and Betsie were isolated, interrogated, and beaten by the German soldiers who were searching feverishly for Jews in the house. While the six guests who were staying at the Beje had safely made their way into the hiding place without being caught, everyone downstairs waited nervously, hoping and praying that the German soldiers would not find them. And even though Corrie and Betsie's faces began to swell and bleed from their beatings, they kept their secret safe.

Though just a few feet above their heads, the Gestapo never found the guests or the hiding place — but the whole ten Boom family was arrested anyway. Casper, Corrie, Betsie, Willem, Nollie, and Corrie's nephew Peter were all chained together, marched out of the house, and taken to prison. Those who had made it into the Angels' Den were safe, but Corrie and her family were in grave danger.

Application

If you knew you could die for doing the right thing, would you still do it?

It's hard to read Corrie's story without imagining yourself in her position and wondering how you might have responded in her place. But Corrie's entire life was a kind of preparation for this battle. Corrie's parents and grandparents lived their faith and instilled in Corrie the biblical values of self-sacrifice, love for others, and an absolute trust in God no matter the consequences. So, when Corrie was faced with this crucial decision, she was prepared for it.

Corrie wasn't deterred by real, life-altering consequences to her actions. As she was being brutally beaten by the Gestapo inside her home, her faith turned into conviction, which turned into courage, which turned into strength.

FIERY FURNACE

Prisoners at Nazi concentration camps were dehumanized in every single possible way; that was part of the purpose of the camps — to dehumanize prisoners, break them down, and kill them. Unfortunately, that purpose was achieved at the cost of millions of lives in a relatively short time period. Corrie and her family chose to live out their Christian beliefs, and in doing so, they willingly and knowingly put themselves in the position to endure this Nazi hellscape. The ten Booms' love for people was so deep and so radical that they considered themselves to be demonstrations of God's love in the world, in the same way that Jesus was.

Corrie and her family didn't have to get involved in any of this; many other Dutch families stayed away from the underground because the risks were just too great. The ten Booms could've chosen to keep their biblical convictions to themselves and kept their faith private. They could've stepped back and ignored what was happening to their Jewish neighbors. And if they'd chosen that path, they probably wouldn't have been arrested or beaten, and they likely would've enjoyed some measure of safety during the war. Either way, things could've been much easier for them if they weren't compelled to live out their Christian faith. But that wasn't how the ten Booms understood Christianity to work. True Christianity, they believed, required more than just words; it required action.

"What does it profit, my brethren, if someone says he has faith but does not have works? Can faith save him? If a brother or sister is naked and destitute of daily food, and one of you says to them, 'Depart in peace, be warmed and filled,' but you do not give them the things which are needed for the body, what does it profit? Thus, also faith by itself, if it does not have works, is dead. But someone will say, 'You have faith, and I have works.' Show me your faith without your works, and I will show you my faith by my works" (James 2:14–18).

Scheveningen Prison: Casper ten Boom Dies

After the raid, the six members of the ten Boom family were taken to Scheveningen prison in south Holland. The family members were separated upon arrival, and Corrie was placed in a tiny prison cell with three other women. There was just one cot and one bathroom bucket to share between them. Corrie was shocked to learn that one of her cellmates had been in that very cell for three years; three years in a prison cell seemed like an eternity to Corrie. Early in the war, Corrie hoped the German army would just be passing through Holland, but that clearly wasn't the case. Now, she was trapped in a prison cell wondering what would become of her and her loved ones. Would they ever see each other again? Would they even survive this prison?

After ten days in prison, Corrie received word that her father had died of pneumonia, and her memory immediately went to the final time she saw him. It was after they had all been separated the day they arrived at the prison. Corrie spotted her father, sitting peacefully in a chair in the prison courtyard. She shouted to him, "Father, God go with you!" And he replied with a shout, "And with you, too, my daughters!"[8] Corrie would never see her father again, but his words would stay with her the rest of her life.

Vught Concentration Camp: Corrie and Betsie are Reunited

Corrie spent nearly four months in the Scheveningen prison before she was abruptly transferred to Vught, a German concentration camp in south Holland. Vught was reserved for the most dangerous prisoners; disease and death were everywhere.

However, something wonderful happened to Corrie at Vught: she was reunited with her sister Betsie as they both were being transferred. Not only were two sisters reunited in this dark place, but two prayer warriors were reunited. Immediately, Corrie and Betsie fell right back into their old routine of praying together and reading the Bible together — other prisoners soon joined in. There was a light in the darkness, after all!

Betsie had battled an illness her whole life, but it had grown worse in prison. Corrie noticed during morning roll calls that Betsie had become so sick and weak that she could hardly stand on her own two feet. If Betsie were to pass out at the wrong time, she would be sent to solitary confinement where she would certainly die. Corrie kept a constant eye on Betsie and made sure to always take care of her.

Corrie and Betsie had arrived at Vught in June of 1944, which was the same month the Allied forces landed on the beaches of Normandy on D-Day. The Nazis began to scramble as their death camps became overcrowded and the German army began losing ground to the Allied forces — something had to give. It wasn't long before the concentration camp guards decided that gas chambers

---

8. Ibid., p. 100.

weren't killing Jews efficiently enough, so they started using firing
lines to kill prisoners, throwing their dead bodies onto piles or
into ditches.

Ravensbruck: "We must tell them, Corrie."

After nearly three months in Vught, all the prisoners were held
at gunpoint, forced onto boxcars, and shipped to a different camp
in East Germany. The boxcars had no windows, no chairs, and no
toilets; they weren't suitable for livestock, let alone humans. The
prisoners were packed in so tightly that they could hardly breathe,
and the only way to get any relief was for everyone to sit down
in straight lines with their legs straddling the person in front of
them, like in a bobsled. As the nightmare went on for days, the
women had no choice but to go to the bathroom where they sat.
You can imagine the horror, the shame, and the embarrassment
the prisoners must've felt, let alone the physical and psychological
suffering.

Corrie began to wonder why the Germans would dedicate so much
time and energy to move thousands of old, frail, dying women from
prison to prison. There were times during these transportations
that the prisoners outnumbered the guards by the thousands,
but the prisoners had become so weak that fighting back was
impossible — this is a common tactic of the enemy.

As the boxcars finally stopped and the doors opened, women began
to fall to the ground, crawling and gasping for air, dying for water.
Corrie was able to make it to a nearby pond, but Betsie was too
weak to move, so Corrie brought some water to Betsie. All around
them, women were dead and dying, not from being shot or beaten,
but from the conditions in the boxcars and from being imprisoned.
Corrie rested beside Betsie for a moment and thought how this
would be a good time to die. She was outside, she was with her
sister, and she had already survived one concentration camp.
But even though Betsie was sicker, weaker, and in worse physical

condition than Corrie, Betsie was always the one encouraging Corrie to keep going, to get up, to move forward. God helped Corrie, so Corrie could help Betsie. But God also helped Betsie, so Betsie could help Corrie.

After the three-day boxcar ride, Corrie and Betsie arrived at Ravensbruck, a Nazi death camp for women. Upon their arrival, Corrie could see dark gray smoke billowing out of the smokestacks. More than likely, Corrie saw the smoke and wondered if she and Betsie would end up like most of the prisoners at Ravensbruck, having smoke from their ashes spewed out of those smokestacks. It seemed that the ten Boom sisters had arrived at their last stop.

The women were left to sleep outside in the rain and cold and had to use a ditch as a toilet. They became covered in lice and had no other choice but to cut off their own hair. Upon being processed at the camp, they were reduced to a prison number, stripped of their belongings, stripped of their clothes, searched, and utterly humiliated.[9] Then came the slave labor — 12 hours a day of backbreaking work and only a slice of old bread or a bowl of watery soup to sustain them. At night, over a thousand women were crammed into a barrack that was intended for a few hundred; there were a couple toilets, but they didn't work. The stench and the fleas were so rampant inside the barracks that the Nazi guards wouldn't even step foot inside. This, however, provided Corrie and Betsie the opportunity to hold Bible studies and prayer meetings without getting caught.

Eventually, Betsie became too weak to go on. She collapsed at the morning roll call and was taken to the concentration camp's "hospital." Corrie snuck into the hospital to check on Betsie and as the two sisters embraced each other to say goodbye, Betsie said something that Corrie never forgot. As Betsie lay there dying in a hospital bed, in a death camp in Germany, she said, "We must tell

---

9. Ibid., p. 155.

them, Corrie. We must tell them there is no pit so deep that God's love cannot reach it."[10]

That was the last time Corrie and Betsie ever spoke; Betsie died a few days later. Two weeks after Betsie's death, and nearly a year after the Gestapo raided the Beje, Corrie was discharged from Ravensbruck and sent on a train toward the Dutch border. Corrie had survived the Holocaust.

Of the 115,000 Jews living in Holland before WWII, only 8,500 survived the Holocaust. It's believed that as many as 26 million Europeans died in the Nazi concentration camps, including six million Jews. In total, over 50 million people died during WWII.[11]

Application

There is a big difference between our lives and the lives of Corrie, Betsie, and every victim of the Holocaust. But it's important for us to be thoughtful and to consider the many lessons their lives — and their deaths — can teach us.

God knows the future (in fact, He's already there), and He knows how to prepare His people for specific roles and circumstances. While we often experience fear and anxiety over the dangers that lie ahead, God already knows the outcome and is ready to equip us for the roles He calls us to. *"For we are His workmanship, created in Christ Jesus for good works, which God prepared beforehand that we should walk in them" (Ephesians 2:10).*

God placed Corrie into a family that supported her, taught her, and inspired her to live for God. But if you didn't come from a family like the ten Booms, God is ready and able to bring the right people into your life at just the right time. And as often as God brings people into our lives to help us, He brings us into others' lives to help them, too; it's not all about us, but it is always about Him.

10. Ibid., p. 163.
11. Ibid., p. 184.

While Corrie showed boldness and courage, she was constantly being strengthened by her father and her siblings. Corrie had to come by these godly traits honestly, meaning she had to learn them, develop them, and contend for them. Corrie never forgot the example set by her father and sister of constantly pointing to God, even in their final and darkest moments, and that gave her the courage to do the same.

If the path God has placed before you leads to a fiery furnace, you can be certain that God is already there, waiting for you, and that He will give you what you need when you need it. If the courageous stance you've taken has cost your job, your career, your friends, or your reputation, you can be encouraged knowing you stand in greatly esteemed company.

"Therefore we also, since we are surrounded by so great a cloud of witnesses, let us lay aside every weight, and the sin which so easily ensnares us, and let us run with endurance the race that is set before us, looking unto Jesus, the author and finisher of our faith, who for the joy that was set before Him endured the cross, despising the shame, and has sat down at the right hand of the throne of God. For consider Him who endured such hostility from sinners against Himself, lest you become weary and discouraged in your souls" (Hebrews 12:1–3).

Encourage yourself in the Lord, strengthen those around you, and tell your children about God's great power and love. If we remain strong — which we can only do by remaining in Christ — then we cannot be defeated.

4TH Man in the Fire

A common question among believers and non-believers alike is: "How could God allow the Holocaust to happen?" That's an important question; it's certainly one that the victims of the Holocaust must've asked. And while it's difficult for many to comprehend how a loving God could allow something as evil as the Holocaust to take place, it's important to know that, in one way or another, God is always involved in the affairs of this world (Daniel 4:17).

My goal is not to answer deep theological questions but to encourage believers with a reminder that no matter how intensely the fire rages, God is with us through it all. In this section, I'll showcase some of the miraculous ways that God was with the ten Boom family a hundred years before WWII, during WWII, and nearly a hundred years after WWII.

A House of Prayer

More than 100 years before WWII began, the ten Booms had been a family of prayer. In the 1830s, Corrie's grandfather Willem began holding prayer meetings in his clock shop, specifically praying for peace in Jerusalem. Maybe — just maybe — God had a reason for placing this burden for the Jews on Willem ten Boom's heart 100 years before the Holocaust. Willem ten Boom, his son Casper, and Casper's children Willem, Nollie, Betsie, and Corrie dedicated their lives to saving the Jewish people.

The ten Boom family prayed constantly, both individually and as a family; they prayed for others and for themselves, for their friends and even for their enemies. Prayer was such an integral part of their lives that on the night Germany invaded Holland, Corrie's and Betsie's initial reaction was to pray. Through a window in their home, Corrie and Betsie could see the night sky being lit up red as German fighter planes dropped bombs on the Dutch airport. Corrie prayed for the people that were in harm's way, she prayed for their safety and protection, and of course she prayed for her father and her siblings. Betsie, however, did something radical: she began to pray for the German fighter pilots! Betsie prayed for those who were attacking Holland and killing her fellow countrymen. To Corrie this seemed ridiculous at the time — praying for the Germans?! But Betsie persisted and prayed out loud:

"God, we bring before You the German pilots up in those planes dropping bombs on us right now. We pray their eyes will be opened to the evil ways of Hitler. God, bless them and let them know You are with them always."[12]

Betsie's prayer for the German fighter pilots stuck with Corrie and greatly impacted her ministry for the rest of her life.

Application

God's timeline is bigger than ours and He sees everything, from eternity past to eternity future. God sees things that we don't see; He knows things that we don't know. But time and time again, we see in the Bible, and in accounts like this one, that God desires to prepare and strengthen us through prayer. Prayer is as important in the short-term as it is in the long-term; its effects can last well beyond our own lives.

A House of Provision

Corrie's goal wasn't to just avoid being captured by the Nazis or to save her own life, as important as those things were. Her goal was to be a living demonstration of God's love in the world; that was true for the entire ten Boom family. In this case, they served God by helping as many Jews as they could. Avoiding capture and staying alive were only important because it allowed them to tell more people of God's love.

One example of God's presence and help came during German occupation in Holland when families in Corrie's town were required to turn in all their radios to the Dutch police, most of whom were under German control. Corrie knew that if the German army controlled the radios, then they also controlled the news coming in and out of Holland. And if they controlled the news, then they would only release news that favored the Germans. Corrie was nearly 50 years old at the time, but her nephew

---

12. Ibid., p. 38.

suggested hiding one of the family radios in the loose floorboards by the family piano. That way they could still listen to the radio whenever important news was being broadcast while someone played the piano to drown out the noise.[13] This unique feature of the Beje allowed the ten Booms to receive important, life-saving information during the war.

The ten Boom house (the Beje) provided miracles well beyond hiding radios in floorboards. The ten Boom family used the unique, awkward, and "negative" spaces of the Beje, which had only ever been used for childhood games like hide-and-seek, to hide Jews from the Nazis during the Holocaust. Any other house would've been insufficient to hide so many individuals — it had to be the Beje, it had to be the ten Booms, and it had to be Corrie. Even a crooked house can be used by God, and in this case, especially a crooked house could be used by God! God specializes in supplying the needs of his people.

"Go to the sea, cast in a hook, and take the fish that comes up first. And when you have opened its mouth, you will find a piece of money; take that and give it to them for Me and you" (Matthew 17:27).

There are no limitations to the ways God can provide for those who are carrying out the work He's given them to do. Not only was the Beje a miracle, but so was the architect who was sent to Corrie's doorstep, offering to create the Angels' Den. This man, known only as "Mr. Smit," said of the ten Boom house, "What an extraordinary house! No two walls meet at right angles, no two rooms are on the same level. This is a wonderful opportunity. Here, I'll do my best work."[14] Only God can bring about such a timely provision, and seemingly out of nowhere. Just as Peter was given money from a fish's mouth, Corrie was given a hiding place by an architect.

Corrie's courage inspired people from all walks of life to join in and help the underground operation. People offered to deliver babies,

---

13. Ibid., p. 42.
14. Ibid., p. 65.

reconnect phone lines, forge documents, and of course an architect offered to build the Angel's Den. But the help Corrie received wasn't just the result of her own courage or bravery, as inspiring as those things were. The help Corrie received demonstrates God's kindness, His attentiveness, and His willingness to provide for those who are willing to join His work.

Application

The things that we may consider to be negatives in our lives — like an awkward house with uneven floors and strange-looking rooms — can be used by God in ways we could never imagine. A hundred years before the Holocaust, God knew the Beje would play a key role, and he planted the ten Boom family there "for such a time as this." Similarly, just as God provided money from the mouth of a fish for a disciple in need, He can reach into our situation and provide everything we need to do what He's given us to do. Just as Corrie chose to be obedient and courageous, it's up to us to choose how we respond to the opportunities God gives us.

Each of us has also been placed in our situations "for such a time as this." But it's important to realize that Corrie's story hinged on her relationship with God prior to her assignment from God. And while most of us will never be given the harrowing assignment of saving Jews from being murdered by hiding them in secret rooms in our homes, we will all be given assignments, nonetheless! If we have been established in a relationship with God, then we can be sure that He has work for us to do, and this work will require courage.

Persecuted, but not Forsaken

"But we have this treasure in earthen vessels, that the excellence of the power may be of God and not of us. We are hard-pressed on every side, yet not crushed; we are perplexed, but not in despair; persecuted, but not forsaken; struck down, but not destroyed" (2 Corinthians 4:7–9).

God didn't forget about Corrie while she was imprisoned in Scheveningen. In fact, He opened doors for her to preach the Gospel — which was alive and well inside of her — to anyone who would listen. Below are examples of how the light of God's Word was able to shine in that dark place:

♦ A kind prison worker gave Corrie four small books containing the Gospels; Corrie used these small blessings to hold Bible studies with her cellmates.

♦ Corrie was summoned by a German lieutenant who was hoping to extract critical information about her underground operation. Not surprisingly, Corrie turned her interrogation into a Gospel presentation. Corrie told this lieutenant that God loves all people great and small, and while the lieutenant initially mocked God, he continued to bring Corrie into his office because he wanted to hear more from the Bible.[15]

♦ Corrie earned favor with this lieutenant, and he even arranged a meeting between Corrie and her siblings so they could read their father's will. During the meeting, Corrie was given a Bible by her sister Nollie.

At Vught concentration camp:

♦ Corrie was reunited with her sister, Betsie, and the two used Nollie's Bible to lead Bible studies with the other female prisoners.

♦ Corrie and Betsie were constantly surrounded by other women, which provided many opportunities for the ten Boom sisters to share the Gospel.

♦ The prisoners that listened to Corrie and Betsie's Bible studies were from all over Europe, and they spoke many different languages. Thankfully, Casper ten Boom had the foresight to require Corrie and her siblings to learn multiple languages as

15. Ibid., p. 125.

children. This unique skillset allowed Corrie and Betsie to talk
with other prisoners, to listen to their stories, and to share the
Gospel with them in their native language.

At Ravensbruck death camp:

♦ The prisoners were stripped, showered, clothed, and searched
by the guards. If they found the Bible Corrie was hiding in her
clothes, it would've been confiscated. Corrie prayed, "God, we
can go through anything if we have this Bible with us. Please
send your angels to hide it from the guards."[16] The guards
searched every single prisoner and made their way toward
Corrie. As Corrie's turn arrived, the guards passed right by her,
as if she was invisible to them. Corrie walked through the line of
guards and was the only prisoner that wasn't searched; she was
able to keep her Bible.

Application ------------------------------

This part of Corrie's story demonstrates just how important it
is to have a love for and dependence on the Bible. It can be easy
to take the Bible for granted when things in life are going well,
but when a crisis hits and our life turns upside down, we need
the Word of God living inside us. When Corrie's life was turned
upside down, she had a lifetime of love for and dependence on
the Word of God to fall back on — it was priceless. Corrie's Bible
was a lifeline for her and Betsie; it maintained her grasp on hope
and gave hope to those around her as well.

As believers, we have this treasure, the light of the gospel, the
message of Jesus, in earthen vessels; and it's meant to be shared
with those who are hurting, hungry, and lost. Do we have this
message deep inside our hearts and on display in our own
lives? Are we ready to share it with a world in crisis? Christ has
commanded us to do just that and to share the Gospel, our
treasure, with the world.

16. Ibid., p. 156.

Spiritual conflict can be found all over the place — at work, at school, in families, among friends, and even in churches; we don't have to look very hard to find it. It came to the ten Boom's front door, into their house, and carried them away in chains. But Corrie didn't just suffer religious persecution, and she didn't just survive the Nazi concentration camps — she was working the whole time. Corrie was always about her Father's business, praying and preaching to all who would listen. That's a job precious few are willing to take, but it was a task for which Corrie stepped forward, raised her hand, and in essence said, "Here I am, Lord, send me."

Telling Others

After Corrie's discharge from Ravensbruck, she traveled back to Holland and spent nearly two weeks recovering in a hospital. She then reunited with Willem and his family, who were still running their elderly care facility. When she finally made her way back to the Beje, she found Nollie and her family living there. They all worked hard to clean up the Beje and get things back in working order, even the clock shop.

Things were never really the same after the war. Corrie went back to her job running the clock shop, but her mind was constantly being drawn elsewhere. One day, as she was working on clocks, the urgency of Betsie's last words came rushing back to her memory and she heard the whispers: "We must tell them, Corrie. We must tell them there is no pit so deep that God's love cannot reach it."

Suddenly, everything became clear. Corrie knew why her mind was being drawn away from the clock business: God was calling her to help the multitudes of broken and hurt people; she must share the message of God's love and forgiveness through Jesus Christ — she must tell them! Corrie felt that if she could encourage just one person to keep going, in the same way Betsie encouraged her to keep going in the concentration camps, then she must go on telling her story no matter how painful it may be.

Corrie gave her first speech in 1946 and she began speaking anywhere she could, mostly in churches, schools, and prisons; and everywhere she went, she found more and more people who were suffering from the trauma of the war. She met Jews who had lost their families, Dutch citizens who had lost their homes, and she met Germans who had worked alongside the Nazis during the war who were suffering from the shame and guilt of contributing to so many deaths.

Application

When God gets a hold of your life, everything changes, and your old life just won't do. Corrie's story shows that life doesn't end in the fiery furnace; and once you come through the other side, you'll have a story to tell that will change the lives of others — one that will point others to Jesus and open the door to forgiveness and healing in their lives. Corrie not only survived the Nazi concentration camps, but she thrived for decades after.

Corrie obeyed God's call on her life, but that didn't mean she instantly forgot about the horrors of the Holocaust, or no longer felt the effects of the trauma she experienced in the concentration camps. Instead, God gave Corrie the grace and the strength to use her traumatic experiences to connect with others in such a way that she could more effectively present them with the message of God's love and forgiveness. The point is, while you may have been battered and bruised in battle, know that God can cause your story to bring great help to others.

God's Amazing Love

Corrie traveled the world, sharing her experiences in the concentration camps, and telling people about God's love and forgiveness. After one speech, Corrie was approached by a wealthy woman named Mrs. Bierens de Haan. Mrs. de Haan had a special

message for Corrie: God had instructed this woman to donate her
56-room home to Corrie's ministry. And in obedience to God, Mrs.
de Haan gave the mansion to Corrie, who turned it into a place of
rest and healing for those who were suffering from the traumatic
experiences of WWII. Corrie counseled these individuals and
shared with them the message of God's love and forgiveness. "The
de Haan House" became a huge success, thanks in part to Corrie's
talent for running clubs and meeting people's needs — skills she
had developed earlier in life.

The de Haan house was so successful that Corrie was asked to help
set up a similar establishment in Germany. Believe it or not, many
Germans were suffering, too. However, as the world learned more
about the evils that took place during the Holocaust, there was
little sympathy for the Germans. Corrie knew the evils of Nazism
as well as anyone, and to her the thought of extending sympathy
and kindness to former Nazis seemed impossible. But God placed
a special burden on Corrie's heart specifically for the German
people. Corrie's attitude was that if Jesus Christ had died for even
the Nazis (and He did), then she shouldn't require anything more
from them. Corrie said this:

> "It is not on our forgiveness any more than on our goodness
> that the world's healing hinges, but on His. When He tells
> us to love our enemies, He gives, along with the command,
> the love itself."[17]

So, Corrie agreed to help set up a facility in Germany to counsel
Germans. And if working with the Germans wasn't difficult
enough for Corrie, this facility was set up inside a former
concentration camp, which meant Corrie would have to physically
go there and revisit her own traumatic experiences. While
Corrie understandably had mixed feelings about using a former
concentration camp as a place of rest and healing, she considered
how God — when saving us from our sin — moves us from death
to life. Corrie acted in kind and turned this place of death into a

17. ten Boom, Sherrill, and Sherrill, *The Hiding Place*, p. 248.

place of healing. She determined to provide kindness and beauty
to every person who came to her for help, showing the depths of
God's healing and forgiveness.

Application ---------------------------------

"The gifts and calling of God are without repentance"
(Romans 11:29; KJV). When God gives us gifts and callings,
He intends on using them. Corrie didn't instantly become an
evangelist one day after the war; she had been preparing and
practicing for that role since she was a young woman, telling
others about God everywhere she went. The gifts and calling
were already there. So, whether it's cleaning toilets in your
church, teaching a Sunday School class for toddlers, being an
advocate for the helpless, or preaching to a congregation of only
a few people, we should never discredit a work that is done out of
love for God and a desire to serve Him and others. No matter how
small or insignificant your role may seem to you, if God is in it,
it matters!

We're not meant to be isolated or shut off from those around
us; God brings people together to accomplish His work in this
world. He used Mrs. de Haan to bring a much-needed resource
to Corrie's ministry, so that others could have a place where they
could learn about God's forgiveness and receive His healing;
without Mrs. de Haan, Corrie would not have had such a place.
But this is how God works. Nobody has it all together and nobody
has all the pieces to do the job on their own. God brings people
together so they can work together as a community. So, whether
in giving or receiving, faithfulness and obedience are key.

No matter how dark or painful our past may be, God can turn it
around and give us a beautiful life — one that demonstrates His
power and love, not just for us, but for others as well. A perfect
example is what God did through Corrie when she turned a
former concentration camp into a place of counseling, healing,

and forgiveness. Try to imagine what Corrie must've experienced in the Nazi concentration camps. The embarrassment, the shame, the dehumanizing, and the torture. Think of the human emotions that would be attached to such a horrifying experience and the anger and bitterness there must've been toward the prison guards. Think of the losses Corrie suffered through the death of her father and her dear sister. Consider all these things and then consider the fact that God led Corrie right back to that place so that people could be healed. God wanted to heal Corrie as well.

You never know what someone else is going through or has gone through. That old cliché is true, and it applies in this section. The world is hurting and yearning for the love and power of Jesus, and Christians aren't exempt from that. You may have experienced, or are still experiencing, trauma in your life. Don't give up! Just as it was for so many people Corrie helped after the war, your healing may be just ahead. If that's the case, I believe there is an encouraging message in Corrie's story here that proves God can heal the most shattered heart and He can forgive even the vilest sinner.

God's Forgiveness

Like many others who lived through the horrors of the Holocaust, Corrie carried her own deep wounds and trauma, which were overwhelming at times. For years Corrie struggled to live her own message of forgiveness, and she often prayed asking God to give her the strength to forgive others. In June of 1945, Corrie wrote a letter to Jan Vogel, the man who likely betrayed her family to the Gestapo. Corrie explained how his betrayal had led to the death of her father, sister, and nephew; but despite all that, she was willing to forgive him for this terrible thing. Corrie concluded her letter by urging Jan to ask God for forgiveness as well.

But perhaps Corrie's most well-known story took place two years after she was released from Ravensbruck. By 1947, Corrie had begun speaking in other countries, and on this particular occasion, she traveled to Germany to speak at a church in Munich. After her speech, Corrie was approached by a tall, blond German man, whom she recognized immediately. This man was a former SS guard at Ravensbruck while Corrie and Betsie were imprisoned there. Corrie remembered seeing this man in the Nazi camp, along with the other guards, mocking the prisoners after they had been stripped naked and forced into the shower room. She was overwhelmed just at the sight of him.

Here stood Corrie, in a German church having just preached a message on God's love and forgiveness, yet in her own heart she felt only hatred toward this man. No matter how hard she tried or how calm her demeanor, Corrie could not find forgiveness in her heart for this man. And who could blame her? This was a man who committed unspeakable atrocities and acts of pure evil against her and thousands of other women, if not more. This was someone who, indirectly, contributed to the death of her beloved sister, Betsie.

The man approached Corrie after the conclusion of her speech. He looked at her, reached out to shake her hand, and spoke: "It is so wonderful to know God forgives all our sins, isn't it?" Corrie stood motionless, arms at her sides, frozen. She knew what this man had said was true — that God can forgive us all our sins — but despite that knowledge, she was unable to find forgiveness in her heart.

Like always, Corrie turned immediately to God and prayed silently, "Oh God, help me to live my message." And like a shock of electricity, the Holy Spirit moved within her, touching her heart and her body. Without thought, Corrie's hand immediately shot up to shake his, and she replied with all sincerity, "Yes, it is wonderful to know God forgives all our sins." Corrie could feel her hatred melt away as the love of God took its place.

"And though I bestow all my goods to feed the poor, and though I give my body to be burned, but have not love, it profits me nothing" (*1 Corinthians 13:3*).

Application -------------------------------

As Christians, we live in a broken world, and no one goes through life unscathed; eventually, we all get hurt and we hurt other people, too. Sometimes we're hurt by the very people that should've protected us, and sometimes we're hurt by another Christian we thought we could trust. There's always a temptation to fan the flames of anger and bitterness toward people who have hurt us, and it can be a battle to try to forgive and move past the hurt, anger, and disappointment. It leaves a wound.

Corrie's story is a light in the darkness, giving hope in the worst of circumstances. There are some wounds we cannot heal and some pain we cannot forgive, but Corrie's story lays out the path of forgiveness and healing that's found only with God. Only when the Holy Spirit comes in and empowers us can we forgive others and be healed. Isn't this the Gospel — forgiveness and healing through Jesus Christ? Without Him, we are utterly helpless in life.

To me, Corrie's interaction with the former SS guard is perhaps the most courageous and inspirational part of her whole story. Even though Corrie couldn't forgive the man on her own, she didn't reject him, as she may have been inclined to do. Instead, she decided to ask God for help, and God provided. When she faced the man who brought so much pain and trauma into her life, she was willing to allow God to change and heal her own heart first, so that she could forgive this man.

Corrie ten Boom

By 1953, all of Corrie's siblings had died and she especially missed her sister, Betsie. Corrie remembered that on the day Betsie died, she saw Betsie's blue sweater on a pile of clothes at the

Ravensbruck hospital. Corrie wanted to grab the sweater and keep it as her last connection to Betsie, but the sweater was infested with lice, and it had to be burned. Corrie left the sweater, realizing it wasn't her last connection to Betsie after all; her final connection to Betsie, and to the rest of the ten Booms, was the family reunion they would have in heaven one day.[18]

Corrie's ministry was profoundly shaped by two things: her father's willingness to share God's love with others and Betsie's determination to tell others about God's forgiveness. Corrie lived out the remainder of her life traveling the globe, telling her story, and sharing the message of God's love and forgiveness. Below is a summary of Corrie's journeys after WWII:

◆ As an evangelist for over 30 years, Corrie traveled the world preaching the Gospel in places such as Holland, Germany, the United States, Switzerland, Africa, Canada, England, France, Indonesia, Japan, Sweden, Taiwan, the Philippines, New Zealand, Australia, Israel, Spain, Cuba, Mexico, India, Korea, Russia, Vietnam, Argentina, Brazil, Poland, Finland, and Hungary.

◆ In addition to Corrie's traveling, preaching, and counseling, she authored over 40 books and created many teaching films.

◆ February 28, 1968: Corrie was honored at a Holocaust Memorial in Israel for the lives she and her family saved during WWII; she planted a tree in the Garden of the Righteous.

◆ 1973: Corrie spoke at the Billy Graham Crusade in Atlanta, Georgia.

◆ 1975: Corrie's childhood home, the Beje, was opened as a museum; it was closed two years later because of too many visitors.

---

18. Ibid., p. 230.

- September 29, 1975: a movie on Corrie's life (*The Hiding Place*) was set to premiere but was interrupted by suspected neo-Nazis who threw tear gas bombs into the theater. Instead, Corrie, along with Billy Graham and Pat Boone, held an impromptu street meeting which was televised internationally.

- 1977: Corrie spoke at the Billy Graham Crusade in Gothenburg, Sweden.

- August 23, 1978: Corrie suffered her first stroke and lost most of her ability to communicate. She suffered two more strokes over the next two years and became bedridden.[19]

- April 15, 1983: Corrie ten Boom died on her 91st birthday.

Even though Corrie became famous and was friends with people like Billy Graham and Queen Wilhelmina of the Netherlands, fame was never important to Corrie. She knew there were thousands of people all over Holland and throughout Europe who had suffered just as much as she had, and who were just as brave. But Corrie used whatever influence she had to spread God's message of love and forgiveness everywhere she went.

Corrie touched the world through her ministry, but she didn't do it alone — she had help along the way, especially from her own family. If her grandfather Willem didn't hold prayer meetings in the clock shop, would Casper have prayed for his customers or read from the Bible every day? If Willem hadn't prayed for peace in Jerusalem, would Casper, Corrie, and the ten Booms have felt compelled to help the Jews? If Corrie's parents hadn't set such a godly example, what would she and her siblings have believed about God? And if Betsie didn't encourage Corrie to tell others of God's forgiveness, or model how to pray for our enemies, would Corrie have gone on to be an evangelist? Those are just a few examples of how God brings people into our lives to help us, and how God uses us to help others as well.

---

19. Ibid., p. 266.

Corrie's story compels us to act on our godly convictions. But how? Here are three things to consider:

- Having a servant's heart. Corrie consistently stepped forward and raised her hand to serve wherever the need was greatest. This allowed God to use Corrie in ways she never thought possible.

- Demonstrating a godly love for others, especially when it's not convenient to do so. This love didn't come from Corrie, it came from God, but God moved through Corrie to show others the power of His love.

- Preparing for eternity. Corrie's life and ministry were all about rescuing souls from darkness, whether through serving others, hosting Bible studies, or preaching the Gospel.

Application

Sadly, many aspects of Corrie's story are not all that unique from the other millions of people who suffered before, during, and after WWII. But one thing that is unique about Corrie's story is her constant and consistent willingness to say "yes" to God's call, no matter how difficult, challenging, painful, traumatizing, or unpredictable. It's easy to look at her life after the war and admire who she was, but none of it would have happened if Corrie hadn't had the courage to stand before, during, and after the war. She never took the easy way out — in fact, she was usually forced to take the hardest way — but she still said "yes" to God every time. How can you begin to say "yes" to God more in each new day?

chapter nine

Esther

Esther's story took place nearly one thousand years after the Red Sea miracle, at a time when God's children had been chastised, conquered, and scattered among many nations. And, as we all have at one time or another, they had strayed from God. We will learn through Esther's story that no matter how far we have drifted or how far away God seems, He is always with us and ready to save — including in ways that we'd never expect. He is still moving in this world, and we have a part to play in reaching others with the Gospel.

In this story, Esther is depicted as an advocate, prepared by God for "such a time as this," who risked her own well-being to stand in the gap for her people. Just as Daniel was placed in a position to interpret Nebuchadnezzar's dream, Esther was placed in a position by God to intercede for His people, who were about to face a genocide.

The Book of Esther plays out like a suspenseful action film that's full of twists, turns, and thrills. Some might even say this dramatic story has everything. However, there is one (surprising) thing missing from this inspiring biblical account — God's name. It's true: the name of God is nowhere to be found in the Book of Esther. But even though He is not mentioned by name, we can see His hand moving on every page — in the timing of events, the divine placement of His people, and the provisions given to them.

One could argue that the absence of God's name in this story is even more encouraging than was His visual presence at the parting of the Red Sea. At the Red Sea, everyone saw God go before them in the pillar of cloud, and they could believe Him because they saw Him. But in this story, God's children didn't have the pillar of cloud or any other physical thing as indisputable evidence of God's presence — they didn't even hear the mention of His name. But God was just as present in the Book of Esther as He was at the Red Sea. God can move in any number of ways: He can give a great physical demonstration of His power, or He can remain unseen and move in a less obvious way through those who are willing to be used.

 The king in this story (Ahasuerus) ruled over his powerful and expansive kingdom made up of 127 provinces. His reach was wide and far, and he was very much aware that he was the richest and most powerful man on earth at the time. The Book of Esther begins with the king holding an elaborate party to showcase his immense wealth and riches — and this was no ordinary party. In fact, the Bible says the king's party lasted 180 days (Esther 1:4)! Suffice it to say this king could do whatever he desired, whenever he desired, and a lack of money was never an issue.

This also applied to his wife, Queen Vashti. During this incredibly lavish party, the king was "merry with wine" and called on Vashti to come and present herself before his guests. The king sought to impress his guests with Queen Vashti's great beauty (Esther 1:12). But Vashti had the audacity to go against the king's wishes — she "refused to come" at his command — which caused the king to be overcome with embarrassment and rage. Even though Vashti's actions were understandable, and even quite commendable, the king would not tolerate it. How dare she deny the king of his request? It was completely unacceptable! The king asked his wisest men for advice, and they stated Vashti's rebellion was more than just an insult to the king; but that it was also an insult and a threat to husbands everywhere.

"For the queen's behavior will become known to all women, so that they will despise their husbands" (Esther 1:17).

The king decided to act swiftly to show he would not tolerate any acts of rebellion. So, the king removed the queen's royal title, took her royal estate from her, and banished her from his kingdom. This harsh punishment sent the resounding message that anyone who refused to obey the king's wishes would face serious consequences (Esther 1:19).

As time passed, the king sought a new queen to replace Vashti (Esther 2:4). For the king, finding a new queen was a serious endeavor as he was looking for someone truly impressive, a woman above all other women, worthy to be in this powerful and esteemed position, and pleasing to himself. While the woman chosen as the new queen would be entitled to the queen's wealth, riches, and power, she would also be ruled — literally — with an iron fist and held to the same harsh standards as Vashti — one misstep and you're gone. The excitement of becoming the new queen was overshadowed by the cloud of Vashti's banishment; whoever became the new queen would instantly enter a great conflict.

"Let beautiful young virgins be sought for the king.... And let beauty preparations be given them. Then let the young woman who pleases the king be queen instead of Vashti" (Esther 2:2–4).

Essentially, the king's men organized an elaborate beauty pageant to see who could impress the king enough to win the title of Queen. It's important to notice that throughout this entire drama surrounding the king — his party, Vashti's banishment, and the search for the most beautiful and impressive woman in the land — the unseen hand of God was lovingly and meticulously working behind the scenes the whole time. The stage was set for Esther's debut.

Esther and Mordecai

Esther's family was among the group of Israelites taken captive by Nebuchadnezzar and brought into Babylon. And after her parents died, Esther was raised by her older cousin, Mordecai, who was a good man and had raised Esther as his own daughter. The Bible also tells us that Esther was very beautiful, so it's no surprise that she quickly became the leading candidate in the king's search to find a new queen. Mordecai, being Esther's only father-figure, made the careful decision to present Esther to the king (Esther 2:8–9).

One might think that Mordecai was not wise in presenting Esther for the king's consideration, given what had happened to Vashti. But God, though not mentioned here by name, was behind the scenes, orchestrating events, and giving Esther favor with the king's men. Mordecai made another wise decision — which is incredibly significant to this story — when he "charged" Esther not to reveal her Jewish heritage to the king (Esther 2:10).

For those who are not familiar with this story, it may seem odd that Mordecai would instruct Esther to keep their Jewish heritage from the king. But at this time, Jews were not held in favor and were seen as lowly servants in the kingdom. If the king's men knew Esther was Jewish, they most likely wouldn't have allowed her to move forward in the process. It would soon be revealed why Mordecai's instructions were so important — again drawing attention to fact that God was always preparing the way.

"The king loved Esther more than all the other women, and she obtained grace and favor in his sight more than all the virgins; so, he set the royal crown upon her head and made her queen instead of Vashti" (Esther 2:17).

Esther found great favor with the king and was chosen to be his new queen. Esther was no doubt well-aware that becoming the new queen to this king meant she was entering a potentially hostile environment, especially if her Jewish identity was revealed; so, while the position came with great power and influence, the timing of Esther's appointment gives an even greater testimony of God's hand in her story.

God would use Esther to thwart the incredibly evil plot of genocide against her people, and to bring deliverance to God's people, now and for generations to come. But before that happened, God had been working behind the scenes to bring Mordecai to a place of prominence. One day, Mordecai overheard a plot by the king's own officials to kill the king. Mordecai told Esther, who was now the queen, and she told the king, who then investigated the allegations and discovered they were true. The king's officers who were involved in the plot were hanged on the gallows.

Esther's reign as queen had begun with quite an impressive sequence of events which would prove to be crucial in the days to come. But was Mordecai simply in the right place at the right time, ready to do the right thing? Or did God have a hand in it? Would Mordecai have had the ability to warn the queen had the queen not been his cousin Esther? Here, the beauty of God's precision begins to shine through.

"For precept must be upon precept, precept upon precept; line upon line, line upon line; here a little, and there a little" (Isaiah 28:10).

Application -

Christians know full-well that today's culture is largely hostile toward the Bible and Christianity. Even so, God is still calling His people into those hostile environments to accomplish His purpose. Esther understood the dangers of her situation and, more than likely, fear and intimidation factored into her thinking. Similarly, God may be calling you into a situation that may become hostile if people learn you're a Christian who actually believes what God has said in His Word.

But it's important to remember that before Esther took a single step in the process to become queen, God had positioned Mordecai to raise Esther. Then Mordecai positioned Esther to be the queen, and God positioned them both to find unique favor with the king.

If we ever find ourselves in a hostile environment, it's good to remember that just as God went before Esther and Mordecai, He goes before us as well. He knows all about the environment He's placed us in. He also knows what the result will be when — after He's called us to do so — we obey His call and stand courageously for the truth of His Word.

God knows your situation and, if you're where He wants you to be, He will be with you when you face your conflict. But the real conflict is not with individuals or institutions; the real conflict is a spiritual one. The Bible says, *"The steps of a good man are ordered by the Lord, and He delights in his way" (Psalm 37:23).* So, just as the unseen hand of God was guiding Esther's steps through her conflict, God is ordering your steps as well.

Nebuchadnezzar

Since becoming the queen, Esther lived in her own type of spiritual Babylon. In this section, we will see her face her own type of spiritual Nebuchadnezzar. Esther's conflict would begin with the king's right-hand man, Haman, and his hatred for Mordecai, her closest family member. Haman and the king represent Nebuchadnezzar in Esther's story.

As mentioned, the king was likely the most powerful man in the entire world, and Haman was his second in command. Haman was accustomed to being highly revered and treated with ultimate deference and respect. In fact, the Bible says Haman expected people to bow before him wherever he walked; the king had commanded it. But Mordecai worshiped only one God — the true God — and he wouldn't bow to anyone else, including Haman. Mordecai had the courage to stand in his own spiritual conflict.

"And all the king's servants who were within the king's gate bowed and paid homage to Haman, for so the king had commanded concerning him. But Mordecai would not bow or pay homage. Then the king's servants who were within the king's gate said to Mordecai, 'Why do you transgress the king's command?' Now it happened, when they spoke to him daily and he would not listen to them, that they told it to Haman, to see whether Mordecai's words would stand; for Mordecai had told them that he was a Jew" (Esther 3:2–4).

Mordecai's stance suddenly brought attention on God's people, the Jews. If Mordecai would not bow because of his faith, that meant other Jews might do the same — just as the husbands at the king's party feared that their wives wouldn't listen to them if they heard about Queen Vashti.

"When Haman saw that Mordecai did not bow or pay him homage, Haman was filled with wrath. But he disdained to lay hands on Mordecai alone, for they had told him of the people of Mordecai. Instead, Haman sought to destroy all the Jews who were throughout the whole kingdom of Ahasuerus — the people of Mordecai" (Esther 3:5–6).

Haman was so enraged by Mordecai's refusal to bow that his desire to kill Mordecai spilled over onto every Jew in the kingdom. At this point, neither Haman nor the king were aware that Esther was also a Jew.

The King's Evil Decree

Haman — enraged by Mordecai's courage — reported to the king how the Jews were not conforming to the king's commands, saying *"their laws are different ... they do not keep the king's laws. Therefore, it is not fitting for the king to let them remain" (Esther 3:8–11).* Haman then suggested that the king make a decree that all Jews should be destroyed, and without a thought the king gave Haman permission to carry out his evil plot. A decree was issued *"to destroy, to kill, and to annihilate all the Jews, both young and old, little children and women" (Esther 3:13).* The king ordered a genocide.

After hearing the order of genocide, Mordecai sent another message to Esther, another charge. Mordecai pointed out to Esther God's divine timing in her becoming queen, indicating there was a divine call on her life. A plan had now come into focus and it was time for Esther to step into the role for which she was called.

"Do not think in your heart that you will escape in the king's palace any more than all the other Jews. For if you remain completely silent at this time, relief and deliverance will arise for the Jews from another place, but you and your father's house will perish. Yet who knows whether you have come to the kingdom for such a time as this?" (Esther 4:13–14).

Esther was perhaps the only person on the planet who could make an appeal to the king such that he would hear it — and that's precisely why she was put in this position of prominence and proximity to the king. If it wasn't clear to Esther before, it was clear now — she must get involved, she must act! But how? What could she do?

If Esther did nothing, then her people would be slaughtered in a genocide — but she might possibly remain safe. If she went to the king and made an appeal to save the Jews, she would have to reveal the fact that she herself was a Jew and risk being included in the genocide; she could become the first victim.

This is perhaps the moment where we start to understand why Mordecai previously instructed Esther to conceal the fact she was a Jew.

Esther's Response

How would Esther proceed? I think most people would be tempted to formulate a plan, craft a speech, or manipulate the situation in a way they felt would give them the best chance for success. But that's not what Esther did. When her life was on the line — the lives of every Jew were on the line — Esther called on her people to fast on her behalf. The act of fasting was an acknowledgment that God alone is the Giver and Sustainer of life, and that His presence and help were being sought. So, with Esther's request of the Jews to fast, they were making a powerful appeal to God to move on their behalf. Esther's response to this spiritual conflict was both a testament to her faith in a God who answers prayer and an inspiring act of restraint. When Esther was faced with death, she didn't react out of natural panic; instead, she compelled her community to seek God. Only after seeking God and hearing from Him did she step out and act on her faith.

The Bible doesn't say Esther received some miraculous revelation from heaven or divine reassurance that she would be successful. In fact, Esther had no idea what the result would be, but she chose courage anyway. It was time for her to go see the king.

"And so, I will go to the king, which is against the law; and if I perish, I perish!" (Esther 4:16).

Esther had other options. She could've waited for a "sign" telling her what to do, or she could've decided to sit back and wait for the king to summon her. Esther knew the very act of going to the king on her own — without being summoned — would be breaking the law. Esther hoped that since the king's heart was softened toward her, that he would allow her to come into his presence without first being summoned. But then again, the king had given no grace to Vashti — there was no telling what his response would be. I imagine a great conflict was wrought inside Esther, given her deep sense of obligation to go before the king and the uncertainty of what his response would be. Her determination to take this courageous stand and to endure the consequences can be summed up in the words, "if I perish, I perish." It's such an inspiring example of courage! It's almost as if Esther quoted the words of Jesus in the Garden: *"Nevertheless, not as I will, but as You will" (Matthew 26:39).*

Again, God was never mentioned by name, but these verses are saturated with His presence. Esther didn't elevate herself to be queen — God did. She didn't place Mordecai in his position —

God did. She didn't call herself to be an advocate for the Jews — God did. And through prayer and fasting, she trusted that God would give her the words to say when she approached the king. Esther knew that the only hope for her and her people was in God.

Application

Today's culture stands in opposition to God in countless ways, and as Christians, we may eventually be faced with a spiritual conflict if we refuse to conform to the culture surrounding us. And when our counter-cultural beliefs are made known, we may experience rejection, anger, threats, and some form of harassment. But when an immoral command is given — one that stands in opposition to God's Word — it is morally imperative to stand against it. Both Mordecai and Esther had the courage to take such a stand, no matter the cost.

If Mordecai had bowed to Haman, the Jews would not have been at risk of being murdered. However, because we know that we do not war against flesh and blood, we know that God has an enemy who undoubtedly orchestrated the plot against the Jews. Haman's arrogance and pride were used as instruments and weapons in that plot. If Mordecai had taken the path of personal safety and bowed down to Haman as he was expected to do, God's enemy certainly would've crafted a new way to accomplish the genocide of God's people. But God will always prevail and would not allow His people to utterly perish. As Mordecai told Esther: *"For if you remain completely silent at this time, relief and deliverance will arise for the Jews from another place, but you and your father's house will perish" (Esther 4:14).*

The point is: we get to choose if we want to be a part of what God is doing in our world. If we choose to take the easy road and avoid any personal risk, then we opt out of what God is doing and we forfeit our opportunity to be part of God's victories.

Your conflict might come in waves, with each new wave being more intimidating than the last. It may start with an uncomfortable conversation, then a contentious meeting, then hostility, threats, and accusations; and if you'd just give in and bow, then it would all go away. Things would be much easier, and you'd find comfort in Babylon, if you would just "bow to Haman."

In our most harrowing moments, we must remember Esther's example — how she was placed in a seemingly unwinnable position "for such a time as this." Also, we should remember that her resolve was to seek God's guidance and stand courageously, no matter the consequence. I hope this story inspires you to also act courageously as you face your spiritual conflicts.

FIERY FURNACE

After the period of fasting, Esther was determined to speak with the king on behalf of the Jews. But just because she fasted and committed her works unto the Lord, doesn't mean everything was going to be easy. In fact, as is often the case, things would get worse before they got better. Esther would eventually have to reveal the fact that she was also a Jew — a revelation that could cost her life. But we'll see God's wisdom shine in this section as Esther so delicately approaches the king.

"So it was, when the king saw Queen Esther standing in the court, that she found favor in his sight.... And the king said to her, 'What do you wish, Queen Esther? What is your request? It shall be given to you — up to half the kingdom!' So, Esther answered, 'If it pleases the king, let the king and Haman come today to the banquet that I have prepared for him.'" (Esther 5:2–4).

Esther's meeting with the king went so well that he offered to give her half of his kingdom. Esther could've accepted the kings' offer of half the kingdom and been on her merry way. But that personal and temporal gain for Esther would not have rescued the Jews

— her people — from death. Instead— at this banquet —Esther requested the king and Haman come to a second banquet the following day. Again, the king accepted Esther's invitation for the following day.

Esther's Banquet and Haman's Gallows

It's awesome to observe the depth of Esther's wisdom and understanding on how she was to approach the king. Now, the plan was falling into place, but only after Esther and all the Jews sought God with their whole hearts.

"So, Haman went out that day joyful and with a glad heart; but when Haman saw Mordecai in the king's gate, and that he did not stand or tremble before him, he was filled with indignation against Mordecai" *(Esther 5:9).*

Haman felt particularly special because, other than the king, he was the only person invited to Queen Esther's banquet. Haman left the queen's banquet in high spirits until he bumped into Mordecai at the gate. From that point on, all Haman could focus on was his hatred toward Mordecai and the fact that Mordecai still refused to bow to him. Haman no doubt felt he deserved to be honored alongside the king, as his arrogance and pride poured out in every area of his life. And because Haman was consumed by his pride, he was "filled with indignation" when Mordecai refused to bow before him.

So, even though Esther's plan was moving forward successfully, Haman's hatred was boiling against Mordecai; this made Esther's goal of saving the Jews even more challenging.

Once again, the timing of these two events (Esther's banquet and Mordecai's encounter with Haman at the gate) is divine intervention: Haman didn't know Esther and Mordecai were related, but Mordecai "just happened" to be at the king's gate as Haman passed by. As we'll see, God used Esther's invitation to

Haman as an occasion for Mordecai to once again show deference to Haman, this time with a dramatic result.

"Moreover, Haman said, 'Besides, Queen Esther invited no one but me to come in with the king to the banquet that she prepared; and tomorrow I am again invited by her, along with the king. Yet all this avails me nothing, so long as I see Mordecai the Jew sitting at the king's gate.' Then his wife Zeresh and all his friends said to him, 'Let a gallows be made, fifty cubits high, and in the morning suggest to the king that Mordecai be hanged on it; then go merrily with the king to the banquet.'" (Esther 5:12–14).

So, based on the encouragement of his wife and friends, Haman made gallows 75 feet high from which he intended to hang Mordecai, specifically. This seems especially cruel, given the fact that Mordecai was already sentenced to death along with the rest of the Jews, but Haman was obsessed with his hatred for Mordecai because Mordecai would not bow to him. So, why go through the trouble of building gallows just to send Mordecai to an early death? From every perspective, the fiery furnace was getting hotter and hotter for Esther, Mordecai, and the Jews — genocide had already been decreed.

If God was in control of Esther's situation, why would He allow things to proceed this way? Why would he allow His people to be subjected to such fear and persecution? The next section will address those questions.

Application -

This section shows how quickly and how easily an evil plot can gain momentum, simply when a group of people come together and are rooted in nothing more than arrogance and a desire to elevate themselves. As far as we know, Haman's wife and friends had never met or interacted with Mordecai; yet, instead of challenging Haman's self-righteousness, they were more than happy to fan the flames of his hatred toward Mordecai and to support his delusions. As their emotions became more and more energized, they came up with a radical "solution" to Haman's anger — the gallows. Though their plot was scandalous and hateful, Haman and his posse felt justified in their point of view because they perceived themselves to be superior to Mordecai.

This sort of "mob mentality" is perhaps a classic example of what often takes place in our society as well.

For many people, it's easier to follow the crowd and participate in bad behavior than to think about things from a biblical perspective and stand alone. And a crowd — like a tidal wave — has both the power and the capacity to inflict greater harm on others than a few individuals would inflict if standing alone. Crowds can become powerful in bringing about harm, especially crowds that don't care about what God thinks.

But the opposite is also true. As we've already discussed in this book, when one person is willing to take a stand for truth — apart from the crowd — it has the power and capacity to inspire others to stand against what they know is wrong.

Riley Gaines was an All-American swimmer on the University of Kentucky women's team. In 2022, Riley placed 5th in her event at the NCAA Championships, but her trophy was instead given to a male swimmer who was swimming on the women's team under the guise of being "transgender." Riley said: "When I started speaking out, I was terrified. I was so nervous that all the things they told me would happen would happen: I would never get a job, I would never get into grad school; I would lose my friends and my family and my scholarship and my playing time. NONE of those things happened. And know that courage begets courage. One person speaking out will lead to three more speaking out. And those three to bigger and bigger — it's like a wildfire! And there's strength in numbers."[1]

---

1. https://www.prageru.com/video/riley-gaines-i-stood-up-for-all-women-after-losing-to-a-man.

There definitely is strength in numbers, and when we're willing to stand for God's Word and apart from the crowd, we're likely to inspire others to stand with us.

 One of the key aspects of this story (and really, all the stories in this book) is how God was working behind the scenes, and He continued to work in Esther's favor. In fact, after the king's meeting with Esther, God moved upon the king through something as common as a little insomnia.

"That night the king could not sleep. So, one was commanded to bring the book of the records of the chronicles; and they were read before the king. And it was found written that Mordecai had told of Bigthana and Teresh, two of the king's eunuchs, the doorkeepers who had sought to lay hands on King Ahasuerus. Then the king said, 'What honor or dignity has been bestowed on Mordecai for this?'" (Esther 6:1–3).

God, through His divine intervention, reminded the king that Mordecai had once saved his life, but nothing had been done for Mordecai as a show of gratitude. The hand of God moved here in several ways: keeping the king from sleep, having records read to the king that "just happened" to concern Mordecai, and stirring a desire within the king's heart to honor Mordecai for saving his life.

Haman Ordered to Honor Mordecai

So, to help him bestow an honor upon Mordecai, the king summoned none other than his right-hand man, Haman. The king asked Haman's advice to a very generalized question: *"What shall be done for the man whom the king delights to honor?" (Esther 6:6).* Unsurprisingly, Haman, being as self-focused as he was, assumed the king was referring to him. So, Haman described the kind of honor he wanted for himself.

"And Haman answered the king, 'For the man whom the king delights to honor, let a royal robe be brought which the king has worn, and a horse on which the king has ridden, which has a royal crest placed on its head. Then let this robe and horse be delivered to the hand of one of the king's most noble princes, that he may array the man whom the king delights to honor. Then parade him on horseback through the city square, and proclaim before him: "Thus shall it be done to the man whom the king delights to honor!"'" (Esther 6:7–9).

As the saying goes, "Be careful what you wish for."

"Then the king said to Haman, 'Hurry, take the robe and the horse, as you have suggested, and do so for Mordecai the Jew who sits within the king's gate! Leave nothing undone of all that you have spoken'" *(Esther 6:10).*

To Haman's shock and horror, he was ordered by the king to publicly honor Mordecai, the man he hated more than anyone and anything. There is a great sense of poetic justice to this part of the story, and it's one of many prime examples how — even in the fire — God has a sense of humor.

Esther's Second Banquet

But the genocide was still looming, and Esther still intended to move forward with her second banquet for the king and Haman. This was her one chance to advocate for her people.

By delaying her request for the king to spare the Jews, Esther caused the king's curiosity to rise about what she might want from him. And by the end of the second banquet, after the king's heart had been warmed toward Esther, she was ready to make her appeal.

"If I have found favor in your sight, O king, and if it pleases the king, let my life be given me at my petition, and my people at my request. For we have been sold, my people and I, to be destroyed, to be killed, and to be annihilated" (Esther 7:3–4).

Esther explained the situation to the king with clarity and power, and she made a plea for her own life as much as for the lives of her people; and by doing so, she revealed to the king that she was a Jew.

The king was shocked! His next question required even more courage from Esther as it required her to reveal to the king that his right-hand man, his most trusted advisor — Haman — was the man who had plotted the genocide.

"So, King Ahasuerus answered and said to Queen Esther, 'Who is he, and where is he, who would dare presume in his heart to do such a thing?' And Esther said, 'The adversary and enemy is this wicked Haman!'" (Esther 7:5–6).

While Esther had previously presented herself as meek and mild, she now proved herself to be bold and courageous. She capitalized on the opportunity God had arranged and she was prepared to state her case with passion.

"So, Haman was terrified before the king and queen. Then the king arose in his wrath from the banquet of wine and went into the palace garden; but Haman stood before Queen Esther, pleading for his life, for he saw that evil was determined against him by the king" (Esther 7:6–7).

What a turn of events! The precision of God's timing and the power of His Word can bring clarity and understanding to any conflict. Here, it's as if the scales had fallen off the eyes of the king, who had unknowingly yielded himself as an instrument in God's hands. God worked in the king's heart and mind to achieve His purposes, and honored both Esther's and Mordecai's courage and obedience.

Haman Is Hanged

To this point, God had steadily and intentionally placed Esther and Mordecai in their positions, like pieces on a chess board, working in their lives both directly and behind the scenes. But now, because of her courage and obedience, circumstances turned quickly in favor of Esther, Mordecai, and the Jews. In fact, in another moment of poetic justice, the king decided that Haman, for his evil plot, should be hanged on the 75-foot gallows he created specifically to hang Mordecai.

"So they hanged Haman on the gallows that he had prepared for Mordecai. Then the king's wrath subsided" (Esther 7:10).

For his part, Mordecai went from a modest gatekeeper to wielding the full power and honor of the king while Haman lost all that he had and was hung on the very gallows he made for Mordecai.

"So, the king took off his signet ring, which he had taken from Haman, and gave it to Mordecai; and Esther appointed Mordecai over the house of Haman" (Esther 8:2).

For her part, Esther continued to advocate for her people, and asked for the king to revoke the death sentence decree for the Jews.

"How can I endure to see the evil that will come to my people? Or how can I endure to see the destruction of my countrymen?" (Esther 8:6).

Esther's advocacy paid off to the extent that the king empowered Esther and Mordecai to write the new decree as they saw fit, with the full power of the king and the seal on his ring (Esther 8:8). The result of this conflict moved God's people from a powerless position to a position of great strength.

"By these letters the king permitted the Jews who were in every city to gather together and protect their lives — to destroy, kill, and annihilate all the forces of any people or province that would assault them, both little children and women, and to plunder their possessions" (Esther 8:11).

Esther, Mordecai, and the Jewish people were not only under the umbrella of God's protection, but "many people" became Jews as a result of their strength.

"The Jews had light and gladness, joy, and honor. And in every province and city, wherever the king's command and decree came, the Jews had joy and gladness, a feast and a holiday. Then many of the people of the land became Jews, because fear of the Jews fell upon them" (Esther 8:16–17).

God's plan for His people wasn't going to be thwarted by Haman or anyone else for that matter. Though we're living in a spiritual Babylon, God will overcome those who seek to overthrow His kingdom in order to replace it with their own.

"The Jews gathered together in their cities throughout all the provinces of King Ahasuerus to lay hands on those who sought their harm. And no one could withstand them because fear of them fell upon all people" (Esther 9:2).

There is a limit to how strong and powerful man can become, but there's no limit to God's strength and power.

Application -

This story shows that God works ahead! He works through circumstances we can't possibly know will be important in our lives. Calling a Jewish girl to be queen, concealing the fact that Esther was a Jew, the king's sleepless night which led him to search the records and honor Mordecai — these were all seemingly small, disconnected, and unnoticeable details that were woven together and divinely arranged by God to carry out His purpose. God was constantly at work behind the scenes, even when the situation looked completely hopeless and terrifying. So, when wickedness seems to be in control, remember that God can (and does) work through situations and events that we often can't see until they're fully revealed.

This story also emphasizes the importance of trusting God's timing. God's timing is important because it's so easy for us to become impatient and impulsive in trying to change a situation.

We don't always see God's hand moving in the moment, and we may be tempted to work things out for ourselves. But we're able to look back at our own lives, and at stories like this, and see that God was there the entire time. That's the point of this story — to be encouraged in knowing that God's ways are above our ways; we can trust that even when we don't see Him, He's working! We don't always need to know how things will work out in order to trust God, but we can be inspired to stand courageously on God's Word and trust His character, reminding ourselves that we aren't alone in our story, just as Esther wasn't alone in hers.

As a result of their faith and courage, Esther and Mordecai were able to re-write the law in such a way that it saved the lives of their people. Similarly, God may be using you within your current situation to bring about a change for good; God's vision is always bigger than ours. And as was the case at the end of Esther's story, God can use you and your willingness to take on the opportunities He places before you to impact others. If our lives demonstrate what is good and right, and if our lives demonstrate God's character, then lives will be saved as people are drawn to Christ.

chapter ten

Takeaways

As a former teacher, I try to have at least one takeaway from every lesson. And as a former coach, I try to learn something, win or lose. I have learned a lot writing this book and want to share some of what I've learned.

Three major themes kept popping up, story after story. I didn't plan on including these themes when I started working on this book, they just kept coming up on their own. My takeaways, or themes, from this book are: (1) preparation, (2) seeking God, and (3) obedience. Every chapter in this book contains all of three of these themes to varying extents, but here are a few examples that stood out to me the most.

Preparation

Our lives often seem insignificant, but God can and does use our experiences — even the ones that seem the least important — to prepare us for our future, especially our conflicts of faith.

William Tyndale's knowledge of languages and dialects prepared him to translate the Bible from Greek, Hebrew, and Latin into English. He spent years and years in the mundane aspects of pure study, and it set him up to change the world.

Corrie ten Boom spent years creating popular social clubs as a young woman. She never could've imagined those skills would help her decades later to organize and coordinate complicated secret rescue operations during WWII. Another standout to me is the impact her father's faith had on her as an evangelist later in life. To him, it was just consistency in praying and reading the Bible with his family every day, but to her, it became the foundation on which she stood during the toughest times.

Esther was prepared by God for "such a time as this," meaning that by becoming queen, she was perhaps the only person who could influence the king to save the Jews from genocide. The aspects of her everyday life in the palace helped establish a trusting relationship between her and the king, which she relied on when she went to him with her request.

Seeking God

We can easily get caught up in the commotion of life, especially when we're in a spiritual conflict. But the urge to act can be dangerous if we act on our own accord — based on what we think is right, what we think sounds good, or what seems to make sense to us — instead of following God's plan. This was always a principle I knew and appreciated, but it's been reinforced and refreshed in virtually every chapter of this book. It's a principle that can change the course of our lives and our own stories.

Three Hebrew Children sought God on Daniel's behalf when Daniel was given the opportunity to interpret Nebuchadnezzar's dream. Without God's answer to their prayer, Daniel's interpretation would've failed, the three Hebrew children would've never been in their prominent position, and their story of refusing to bow to Nebuchadnezzar's golden idol never would've been told.

Jessica Tapia took three months off work to seek God before responding to her school district's directives. During that time,

Jessica received a divine phone call from a Christian couple that gave her the inspired message she was looking for. In fact, Jessica was leaning towards simply resigning — a completely fair and logical choice — but it wasn't what God had in mind for her. If Jessica hadn't taken the time to truly seek God, and she'd just gone her own way, her story would've looked very different.

Bonhoeffer left the safety of America to return to Germany at the beginning of WWII. He felt compelled to join the fight, but he wasn't sure exactly what to do — so he prayed to God for guidance. Soon, Bonhoeffer became a preacher/spy in a plot to kill Hitler. Again, seeking God's guidance proved to change his life forever.

Another thing that struck me about this theme is that it's not always possible to take days, weeks, or months to seek God. We don't always have the opportunity (or luxury) of slowing everything down like that. Sometimes we have no other option but to act in an instant. So, what do we do in those situations? Jesus told His disciples:

"But when they arrest you and deliver you up, do not worry beforehand, or premeditate what you will speak. But whatever is given you in that hour, speak that; for it is not you who speak, but the Holy Spirit" (Mark 13:11).

The Holy Spirit can, does, and will be with us in those (and all other) moments, speaking through us and guiding us as we go. This doesn't mean we shouldn't give a thoughtful or sound answer when we speak, but in this passage, Christ is assuring us that we are not alone. In these moments, of course, it's imperative that the Word of God be living and dwelling inside of us.

"Walk in the Spirit, and you shall not fulfill the lust of the flesh" (Galatians 5:16).

Obedience

It's one thing to know what to do, but it's another thing to actually do it. Every person in this book faced a conflict and was forced to decide whether they'd trust God and obey His Word — or rationalize their way out of it.

The Apostle Paul was begged by his fellow Christians to avoid the dangers awaiting him in Jerusalem, even though the Holy Spirit told him explicitly to go. He had every excuse and reason to rationalize his way out of following God here, and certainly no one there would've blamed him. But Paul chose to trust God and obey, and the result of his obedience was the spreading of the Gospel around the world. Not only that, but Paul entered into a new depth of relationship with God, which he ultimately found was more satisfying than all that he walked away from.

Joshua and Caleb faced extreme peer pressure — even death — to return to slavery in Egypt rather than believe God's promise about their future in an unknown land. But Joshua and Caleb chose to believe God's promise, regardless of how many obstacles there appeared to be, and they stood up to all their peers, loudly and affirmatively. In the end — because of their obedience — Joshua and Caleb were the only ones to inherit God's promise.

Josh Alexander was told by his school administrators that he must obey school policies that directly contradicted the Bible, but Josh's obedience to God's Word has opened the door to greater opportunities. Josh has been blessed with speaking opportunities — both nationally and internationally — to provide a biblical defense against gender confusion as well as lead a national movement to return to traditional values in Canada.

Summaries

I also learned a lot from each individual chapter, too, through researching and writing about each of them. Here are just a few

of the messages, or encouragements, I took away from each of the
profiles, and what has inspired me about each of them the most.

The Three Hebrew Children epitomize boldness, courage,
conviction, and faith; the strength and inspiration I want for my
life are found in their timeless story. My favorite part is when they
told Nebuchadnezzar they believe God can save them from the fire,
but even if God didn't save them, they weren't going to bow to the
golden idol. It shows how rooted they were in their faith; even if
they died all alone in the fire and there's no earthly gain for their
courage, they were still going to serve God.

Jessica Tapia was prepared for her conflict, even though she may
not have felt like it in the moment. She learned through experience
that God uses our past to prepare us for our future. She'd seen
Him come through before, so she knew He could come through
again. While Jessica was persecuted, accused, and forced to defend
her Christian beliefs, she never quit trusting God. And because of
Jessica's obedience, God was able to turn her situation around —
the more she was persecuted, the more she was given a platform to
preach the Gospel. In this way, I see her story much like the Apostle
Paul's story featured in this book from the Book of Acts.

Dietrich Bonhoeffer encourages us to live out our faith, to be doers
of the Word and not hearers only (James 1:22). His story shows
how dangerous it is to only know what the Bible says, but not
live what the Bible says. Bonhoeffer had all the worldly comforts
one could want — a nice home, great parents, loving siblings,
the best education, intelligence, talent — but Bonhoeffer's desire
was to have more of God. Even in his last moments of life, he was
so devoted to God that it left a significant impression on those
watching him.

The Apostle Paul demonstrates what it looks like to be brave,
courageous, and completely sold out to God. Paul wasn't willing to
face just a single fiery furnace, he was willing to face a fiery furnace
to get to an even hotter fiery furnace. He was willing to leave his

community and comforts to stand alone in constant physical and spiritual crisis. And no matter what kind of trial he endured (and there were many), he was always ready to give a defense for the hope that was in him (1 Peter 3:15).

William Tyndale shows us what it looks like to have a heart for others, and to have a godly burden so great that you're willing to die for it. Tyndale was incredibly brilliant and talented, yet he committed all these gifts to serving God. Tyndale reminds us that death is not the end of life but the beginning of eternity with the Lord. I was also struck by some key similarities between Tyndale and Bonhoeffer: they both believed in the importance of being able to communicate complex biblical doctrines in such a way that a child could understand; they both were killed for their beliefs; and they both went to their deaths fully submitted to God's will, seeing death as the beginning of eternity with God, not just the end of a life here on earth.

Joshua and Caleb remind us to have a simple, childlike faith, to take God at His word, and that becoming overwhelmed with fear and doubt can be catastrophic. We have a bad tendency to talk ourselves out of believing God or relying on God in general, but especially when we are confronted with worldly obstacles, even though we've seen Him come through for us time and again. Their story shows how God sees our hearts and honors our properly placed faith and obedience.

Josh Alexander encourages us to serve God above all else, to do what's right in His eyes, to find our contentment in Him, and to allow Him to open doors as we walk in obedience. Josh encourages us to waste no time and to do as much work for the Lord as we can, right now. Josh didn't wait until he was out of high school before he started serving God, neither did he look for someone else to do the work of defending and preaching God's Word. Much like David when he ran to slay Goliath, Josh boldly joined the battle even at such a young age.

Corrie ten Boom shows us that a strong person can have a soft heart — and that sometimes, courage can take the form of forgiveness. Corrie reminds us to have an urgency in telling others about Jesus and that there is no pit so deep that God's love cannot reach it. She teaches us that God heals and forgives, and He gives us the strength to forgive as well. Corrie often prayed for God to give her the strength to forgive others, but God didn't just grant her wish and give her strength. Instead, God put Corrie in uncomfortable positions where she could help people receive God's love — even people who some might've thought were too far gone — and in doing so, Corrie received grace and strength to forgive others; she lived her message.

Esther teaches us that God has a sense of humor, He is the divine orchestrator of our lives, and His love for us is beyond our comprehension. We might be placed in positions that are high, low, or in between for "such a time as this," but every person matters and, in God's perfect timing, He has something special for each of us to do on earth, if we will just trust and obey (Proverbs 3:5–6).

I hope this book has made clear how God can use anybody regardless of their background — rich or poor, old or young, strong or weak. What's inspiring about each person in this book is not his or her personal accomplishments, but how they yielded themselves to God, even (and especially) when it was hard and scary. And because of their willingness, God used them in huge ways — I'm sure in ways well beyond their wildest dreams. They all served, loved, and trusted the same God — the God of the Bible — that we serve today.

About the Author

Thank you so much for taking the time to read this book! I wanted to briefly introduce myself to those who may not know me. I grew up in a Christian home in rural Indiana. My dad was an ironworker, and my mom was a stay-at-home mom. In the early 1990s, my parents made the decision to homeschool my three older siblings and me so that we could receive an education rooted in God's Word. I was homeschooled for about half of my K-12 education. I didn't know it then, but my parents' decision to homeschool would have a profound impact on the rest of my life.

I spent 13 years as a teacher and a coach, in both public and private schools. Throughout my years as an educator, I taught many different subjects and taught students in every grade level K–12. My wife, Jenna, is an attorney, and we have been married since 2018. I like to brag that she was valedictorian of her class in law school!

In addition to being a brilliant attorney, she's also a gifted writer; as such, her fingerprints are all over this book. Jenna and I were blessed with our first child, a son, in early 2024, and we live in Illinois.

Outside of my salvation, being with Jenna has been the highlight of my life.

I never thought I would write a book, let alone multiple books. I always figured I would be a teacher and a coach until I retired. But, as I discussed in my first book, I made the difficult decision to leave my teaching career in 2021 after I experienced the radical indoctrination process taking place in my school and in public schools across the country. I did my best to sound an alarm about the destructive ideologies that were being implemented in classrooms, and I urged parents to homeschool their children. As a veteran teacher, I also wanted to warn my fellow teachers about the conflicts they may soon face in their schools if they were to stay.

Many parents have decided to homeschool their children in recent years, and homeschooling numbers are still on the rise. Similarly, many teachers have decided to leave the public schools or the teaching profession entirely. Some teachers have even been fired for not compromising their Christian beliefs. I'm thankful God has put me on this path, and even though I'm not in the classroom anymore, my goal is the same now as it was when I was teaching and coaching: to do the best I can with what God's given me and to encourage others to do the same.